MW01038502

DRINK, POWER, AND CULTURAL CHANGE

A SOCIAL HISTORY OF ALCOHOL IN GHANA, c. 1800 TO RECENT TIMES

Emmanuel Kwaku Akyeampong

HEINEMANN
Portsmouth, NH

JAMES CURREY
Oxford

Heinemann
A division of Reed Publishing (USA) Inc.
361 Hanover Street
Portsmouth, NH 03801-3912
Offices and agents throughout the world

James Currey Ltd.
73 Botley Road
Oxford 0X2 OBS

ISBN 0-435-08994-3 (Heinemann cloth)
ISBN 0-435-08996-X (Heinemann paper)
ISBN 0-85255-673-X (James Currey cloth)
ISBN 0-85255-623-3 (James Currey paper)

Library of Congress Cataloging-in-Publication Data
Akyeampong, Emmanuel Kwaku.
　　Drink, power, and cultural change : a social history of alcohol in Ghana,
　c. 1800 to recent times / Emmanuel Kwaku Akyeampong.
　　　　p.　cm. — (Social history of Africa)
　　Includes bibliographical references (p.　) and index.
　　ISBN 0-435-08994-3 (cloth : acid-free paper). —ISBN 0-435-08996-X (ppk. : acid-free paper)
　　1. Drinking of alcoholic beverages—Ghana—History. 2. Drinking of alcoholic beverages—Social aspects—Ghana. 3. Social change—Ghana.
　4. Ghana—Social conditions.　I. Title.　II. Series.
　HV5247.G4A49　1996
　394.1'3'09667—dc20　　　　　　　　　　　　　　96-32887
　　　　　　　　　　　　　　　　　　　　　　　　　　CIP

British Library Cataloguing in Publication Data
Akyeampong, Emmanuel Kwaku
　　Drink, power and cultural change : a social history of alcohol in Ghana, c1800 to
　recent times. — (Social history of Africa)
　　1. Drinking of alcoholic beverages — Ghana — History
　　2. Drinking of alcoholic beverages — Social aspects — Ghana
　I. Title
　394.1'3'09667
　ISBN 08255-623-3 (Paper)
　ISBN 0-8525-673-X (Cloth)

Cover design: Jenny Jensen Greenleaf
Manufacturing: Daamen

Cover photo: Statue of an elder pouring libation in Kumasi; photograph by Emmanuel Akyeampong.

Printed in the United States of America on acid-free paper.
Docutech OPI 2010

For Salome, Ruth, and Nana Pomaa

Social History of Africa

DRINK, POWER, AND CULTURAL CHANGE

Social History of Africa Series
Series Editors: Allen Isaacman and Jean Hay

Colonial Conscripts: *The Tirailleurs Sénégalais in French West Africa* MYRON ECHENBERG

Law in Colonial Africa KRISTIN MANN AND RICHARD ROBERTS (EDITORS)

Women of Phokeng: *Consciousness, Life Strategy, and Migrancy in South Africa, 1900–1983* BELINDA BOZZOLI

Burying SM: *The Politics of Knowledge and the Sociology of Power in Africa* DAVID COHEN AND ATIENO ODHIAMBO

Peasants, Traders, and Wives: Shona Women in the History of Zimbabwe, 1870–1939 ELIZABETH SCHMIDT

The Moon is Dead—Give Us Our Money! *The Cultural Origins of an African Work Ethic, Natal, 1843–1900* KELETSO ATKINS

"We Spend Our Years as a Tale that Is Told": *Oral Historical Narrative in a South African Chiefdom* ISABEL HOFMEYR

Work, Culture, and Identity: *Migrant Laborers in Mozambique and South Africa, c. 1860–1910* PATRICK HARRIES

Cutting Down Trees: *Gender, Nutrition and Agricultural Change in the Northern Province of Zambia, 1890–1990* HENRIETTA MOORE AND MEGAN VAUGHAN

Insiders and Outsiders: *The Indian Working Class in Natal* BILL FREUND

Feasts and Riot: *Revelry, Rebellion, and Popular Consciousness on the Swahili Coast* JONATHAN GLASSMAN

Money Matters: *Instability, Values, and Social Payments in the Modern History of West African Communities* JANE GUYER (EDITOR)

African Workers and Colonial Racism: *Mozambican Strategies and Struggles in Lourenço Marques, 1877–1962* JEANNE PENVENNE

The Realm of the Word: *Christianity, Conflict, and Meaning in a Southern African Kingdom* PAUL LANDAU

Cotton, Colonialism, and Social History in Africa ALLEN ISAACMAN AND RICHARD ROBERTS (EDITORS)

Are We Not Also Men? *The Samkange Family and African Politics in Zimbabwe* TERENCE RANGER

Cotton is the Mother of Poverty: *Peasants, Work, and Rural Struggle in Mozambique* ALLEN ISAACMAN

Gender, Ethnicity, and Social Change on the Upper Slave Coast: *A History of the Anlo Ewe* SANDRA GREENE

Drink, Power, and Cultural Change: *A Social History of Alcohol in Ghana* EMMANUEL AKYEAMPONG

In Pursuit of History: *Fieldwork in Africa* CAROLYN KEYES ADENAIKE AND JAN VANSINA (EDITORS)

Agriculture and Apartheid: *Agrarian Struggle and Transformation in Rural South Africa* JONATHAN CRUSH AND ALLAN JEEVES (EDITORS)

A Lion Amongst the Cattle: *Reconstruction and Resistance in the Northern Transvaal* PETER DELIUS

CONTENTS

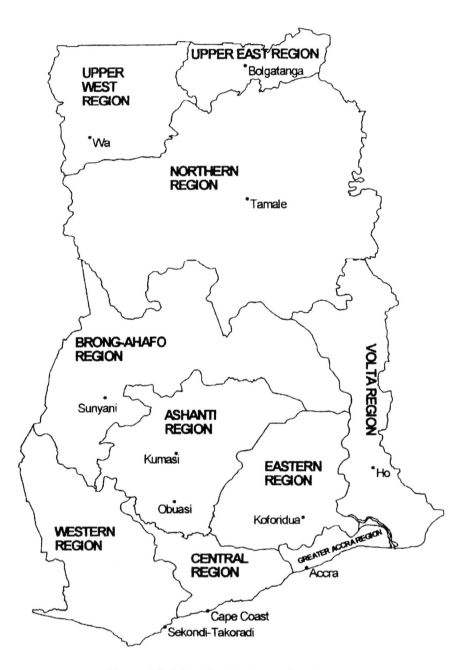

UPPER EAST REGION
• Bolgatanga

UPPER
WEST
REGION

• Wa

NORTHERN
REGION

• Tamale

BRONG-AHAFO
REGION

VOLTA REGION

• Sunyani

ASHANTI
REGION

Kumasi

EASTERN
REGION

• Ho

Obuasi

Koforidua •

WESTERN
REGION

GREATER ACCRA REGION

CENTRAL
REGION

• Accra

• Cape Coast
• Sekondi-Takoradi

Ghana: Administrative Regions and Major Towns

LIST OF PHOTOGRAPHS
IN THE TEXT

All photographs were taken by the author.

GLOSSARY

Most of the words in the glossary are Twi words with the Asante spelling. Twi is the language of the Akan. There are some Ewe, Ga, and Adangme words, and these are indicated in the translations. Unless otherwise stated, all the words below are in Twi.

abele (Ga; sing. and pl.): corn.
abirempon (sing., *obirempon*): big men.
abosom (sing., *obosom*): lesser deities.
abusua (pl., *mmusua*): matrilineage.
adae: day of rest; Akan festival in commemoration of the ancestors. Recurs every forty–third day. The major *adae* falls on a Sunday (*akwasidae*), and the minor *adae* on a Wednesday (*wukudae*).
adutofo (sing., *odutufo*): a sorcerer who deals in charms; poisoner.
ahen nsa: chief's drink.
ahenkwaa (pl., *nhenkwaa*): servant of a king.
ahomaso: exaltation of oneself; pride.
ahosi (Ewe): widow.
ahotsilele (Ewe): ceremonial washing of the widow.
akonkofo (sing., *akonkoni*) rich men; traders; new men.
akpeteshie (Ga): illicit gin; local gin.
akrakyefo (sing., *krakye*): educated people; clerks.
akwasidae: Sunday adae.
alhaji (fem., *alhajia*): title given to Muslims who have visited Mecca.
asafo (sing. and pl.): military companies or organizations.
asamando: the place of the dead.
asantehemaa: queen mother of Asante
asantehene: king of Asante
asase: earth.
asikafo (sing., *osikani*): the rich; the wealthy.
asomdwa (sing. and pl.): service stool.
asuman (sing. *suman*): charms; amulets.
aworonte (sing. and pl.): rum.
awowa (pl., *nwowa*): pawn; pledge; hostage.
awunnyadee: death duties.
awurabafo (sing., *awuraba*): ladies; liberated women
ayefere: adultery appeasement fine.

ayibuadie: inheritance duties.

bara or *bra*: life; to be born; to settle; to mature.

blemabii (Ga): ancestors

Bore bore: Creator of all things; appelation of the Supreme Being.

brafo: king's executioners.

bragoro: nubility or puberty rites.

dipo: puberty rites among the Krobo.

dondo: gong.

edwibisofo: indigenes of Kumasi.

(e)kyim: a dish made from sheep's blood and palm nuts; associated with fertility.

eto: a dish of mashed plantain or yam.

etiguafo: "prostitutes." Root of word unknown.

fufu: a dish of pounded plantain and cassava, eaten with soup.

fufuo: white.

gyuapae: a charm that bestows physical strength

homowo: "hooting at hunger." Ga festival to commemorate the dead.

huanim (Krobo): spouse in the ancestral world.

kabasrotu: a corruption of the English "cover–shoulder" dress.

kokoo: red.

kowensanyi: drunkard; alcoholic.

kpekpei (Ga): cooked dough kneaded with red palm oil; it is served with palm nut soup and fish, and constitutes the ritual food at *homowo*.

Kumasefo: people of Kumasi.

kyima: to menstruate.

madan (Ga): corn wine.

mantse (Ga; pl., *mantsemei*): chief.

mankralo (Ga): town guardian.

Mawu (Ewe): Supreme Being.

mmaa nsa: "women's drink"; sweet (weak) palm wine

mmerantee (sing., *abrantee*): young men.

mmomomme: female spiritual warfare.

mogya: blood.

Nai (Ga): sea; the principal Ga deity.

nkonguafieso: stool house.

nkwankwaa: young men

nsa: drink; wine.

nsamanfo (sing., *saman*): ancestors.

nsuo: water.

ntoro (sing. and pl.): patrilineal spirit groups.

ntwema: red earth.

Nyonmo (Ga): Supreme Being.

obaa panin: female head of an *abusua*.

obaabun: a virgin.

obirempon: sing. of *abirempon*.

obosom (pl., *abosom*): deity, god.

Odomankoma: Creator.

odunsini (pl., *adunsifo*): herbalist; healer.

Odwira: week-long ceremony held to honor and propitiate Asante's dead kings and to purify the whole nation.

omanhene: paramount chief.

Onyame: Supreme Being.

osikani: sing. of *asikafo*.

oyere akoda: child-marriage.

pato a yekye mu nsa: a place for the distribution of drinks.

peregwan: gold dust worth about £8

pintoa: bottle. The establishment of local breweries turned bottle redemption into a new trade.

sa fie se: a palm-wine house.

sasa: life force.

seprewa: Akan lute.

tiri aseda: thanks–offering at marriage.

tiri ka: debt paid by groom at marriage on behalf of bride's family. Husband then takes his wife as pawn (*awowa*).

tiri nsa: head–wine. Drinks offered to cement a marriage contract.

tiri sika: head–money; dowry.

togbewo (Ewe): ancestors.

trowo (Ewe): lesser deities.

tufuhen: commander of an *asafo* company.

tumi: the ability to produce change; power.

tuntum: black.

wirempefo: court functionaries in charge of ancestral stools.

wodzi (Ga): lesser deities.

wolomo (Ga; pl. *wulomei*): priest.

wukudae: Wednesday *adae*.

Introduction:
Drink, Power, and
Cultural Change

This book originated in my 1993 doctoral dissertation on "Alcohol, Social Conflict and the Struggle for Power in Ghana, 1919 to Recent Times."[1] The dissertation examined the use of alcohol as a metaphor for power among the Akan, Ga–Adangme, and Ewe peoples of southern Ghana. As a metaphor for power, struggles over the uses and meanings of alcohol informed intergenerational and gender conflicts in precolonial Ghana, as well as urban social formation and temperance agitation in early colonial Ghana. The importance of liquor revenues to the colonial administration in Ghana ascribed a parallel importance to alcohol in the political economy of British colonialism. Liquor policy became for chiefs and educated Africans, a sphere for negotiating relations of power. Protest against liquor policy and illicit distillation represented prominent aspects of popular politics. Not surprisingly, popular culture—and in particular drinking bars—became crucial to mass mobilization in the nationalist politics of the 1940s and the 1950s. With political authoritarianism and economic decline in independent Ghana, alcohol remained a symbol of protest while offering an "exit" option: it presented a medium of (physical and psychological) escape, a means of disconnecting from the political arena. The abuse of alcohol was closely tied to endangered autonomy and self–identity, an understandable paradox considering alcohol's cultural and historic ties to power.

These insights inform this book. However, the scope of this book has broadened considerably. The book has two objectives: to present a social history of alcohol in southern Ghana from 1800 to recent times; and to examine the culture of power in southern Ghana. Crucial to the framework of this book is my endeavor to conceptualize and incorporate gender as an important plank. I was troubled by the absence of women as actors in the struggle over alcohol in Ghana before the era of urbanization and migration.[2] Social history documents the daily

---

[1] Emmanuel Akyeampong, "Alcohol, Social Conflict and the Struggle for Power in Ghana, 1919 to Recent Times" (Ph.D. diss., University of Virginia, 1993).

[2] The literature on the social history of alcohol in Ghana is very sparse. There has been no monograph-length study outside Barbara Hagaman's unpublished "Beer and Matriliny: The Power of Women in a West African Society" (Ph.D. diss., Northeastern University, 1977), which examines the economic impor-

struggles of ordinary people to subsist and prosper, their leisure activities, relations between men and women, the political structures within which ordinary people operate, and how they relate to those in authority. The literature on alcohol in Africa often reveals a disinterest on the part of women in consuming alcohol.[3] Women sold alcohol in rural and urban settings, but featured less in the elaborate construction of the culture linking alcohol consumption to power. Were women not interested in power? Examining gender and power in the precolonial era led me into the history of ritual and, in particular, the ritual significance of water and blood.[4]

The Twi proverb: *ade'a ye de nsa ye no, yemmfa nsuo nye* ("what alcohol is used for, water cannot be a substitute") does not necessarily devalue the importance of water, for the reverse equally holds true—what water is used for, alcohol cannot be a substitute. Water traditionally has ties to the Supreme Being and spiritual equality among the peoples of southern Ghana. Alcohol represents a hot fluid: aggressive, flamboyant, domineering. It was essentially male. Water signifies coolness, purity, equality. It stood in ritual juxtaposition to alcohol: they were not interchangeable in spite of their uncanny similarity, especially water and gin or schnapps.[5] Blood is a hot fluid that symbolizes danger and fertility. It lay at the core of gender relations and conflicts, which often revolved around sexuality, biological reproduction, and production. The history of alcohol intertwines with these other fluids that lubricated social relations. Together, alcohol, water, and blood facilitate an examination of the culture of power in southern Ghana.

The image of the "big man" (Twi: *obirempon*; pl. *abirempon*) has been an enduring and alluring image for the peoples of southern Ghana. Originally restricted to the aristocracy, European trade expanded opportunities of accumulation and gave ordinary people access to *obirempon* status.[6] The lifestyle of the *obirempon* was distinguished by generosity, use of imported drinks, rich cloths, gold ornaments, and

---

tance of commercialized brewing among the agrarian Lobir of northern Ghana. On southern Ghana, see Raymond Dumett, "The Social Impact of the European Liquor Trade on the Akan of Ghana (Gold Coast and Asante), 1875–1910," *Journal of Interdisciplinary History* 5 (1974): 69–101; G. R. E. Swaniker, "Beer—The National Drink," *Ghana Medical Journal* (December 1975): 332–42; and C. C. Adomako, "Alcoholism: The African Scene," *Annals of the New York Academy of Sciences* 273 (1976): 39–46. My recent publications are discussed below in the context of the intellectual development of this book.

[3]   For a useful guide to this literature, see Jose C. Curto, "Alcohol in Africa: A Preliminary Compilation of the Post-1875 Literature," *A Current Bibliography on African Affairs* 21 (1989): 3–31.

[4]   My thoughts on the symbolism of water and power were first set out in Emmanuel Akyeampong, "Powerful Fluids: Alcohol and Water in the Struggle for Social Power in Urban Gold Coast, 1860–1919" (paper presented at Northwestern University, Evanston, 1994). For a detailed study of blood and power in the Asante context, see Emmanuel Akyeampong and Pashington Obeng, "Spirituality, Gender, and Power in Asante History," *International Journal of African Historical Studies* [hereafter *IJAHS*] 28, 3 (1995): 481–508.

[5]   Schnapps is Dutch gin distilled in a pot-still. It has a slightly harsher taste than gin and is the preferred drink for ritual in contemporary Ghana.

[6]   Ivor Wilks, "Founding the Political Kingdom: The Nature of the Akan State," Ch. 3 in Ivor Wilks, *Forests of Gold: Essays on the Akan and the Kingdom of Asante* (Athens, Ohio, 1993); Ivor Wilks, "The Golden Stool and the Elephant Tail: An Essay on Wealth in Asante," *Research in Economic Anthropology* 2 (1979): 1–36; T. C. McCaskie, "Accumulation, Wealth and Belief in Asante History: I To the Close of the Nineteenth Century," *Africa* 53, 1 (1983): 23–43; Kwame Arhin, "Rank and Class Among the Asante and Fante in the Nineteenth Century," *Africa* 53, 1 (1983): 2–22; and Ray A. Kea, *Settlements, Trade, and Polities in the Seventeenth-Century Gold Coast* (Baltimore, 1982), 85–94.

a large number of wives, children, and other dependents.[7] It was a lifestyle that meshed well with the male ideology that underpinned gerontocracy, patriarchy, and the state.[8] Women were for so long classified as wealth and subordinated to male control that historians of Ghana have, until recently, overlooked their active role in accumulation and their quest for autonomy. Women are beginning to emerge as actors in the recent literature exploring gender relations in the colonial era.[9]

The recent, and expanding, secondary literature on gender in colonial and independent Ghana, as well as the scattered evidence on women and gender relations in the precolonial era, facilitate the reconstruction of an historical outline of gender relations in Ghana.[10] This is extremely useful to the social history of alcohol. It enables us to understand when and how women inserted themselves into the struggles over alcohol. It also reveals how women's use(s) of alcohol have changed over time. Such an outline makes women "visible," even when their presence is not felt on the historical stage. But a comprehensive examination of gender history in all its permutations would require another book. It is redundant to argue—as if it demands proof—that women have desired financial security and autonomy throughout the history of Ghana. What have changed over time are the material conditions and opportunities for accumulation, and the cultural norms regulating gender relations.

Early European accounts of the Gold Coast contain abundant references to ordinary women, "whores," and "prostitutes." They deserve to be read carefully and reinterpreted.[11] Pieter de Marees (1602) commented on enterprising coastal female

---

[7]   See, for examples, T. C. McCaskie, "Accumulation, Wealth and Belief in Asante History: II The Twentieth Century," *Africa* 56, 1 (1986): 2–23; and Kwame Arhin, "A Note on the Asante Akonkofo: A Non-Literate Sub-Elite, 1900–1930," *Africa* 56, 1 (1986): 25–31. In contemporary Ghana, the lifestyle of successful businessmen evokes that of the traditional *abirempon*. For an insight into the life of a successful Ghanaian businessman, see Michelle Gilbert, "The Sudden Death of a Millionaire: Conversion and Consensus in a Ghanaian Kingdom," *Africa* 58, 3 (1988): 291–313.

[8]   For the position of women in the male dominated, precolonial Asante society, see T. C. McCaskie, "State and Society, Marriage and Adultery: Some Considerations Towards a Social History of Precolonial Asante," *Journal of African History* [hereafter *JAH*] 22, 3 (1981): 477–94.

[9]   See, for examples, Emmanuel Akyeampong, "What's in a Drink? Class Struggle, Popular Culture and the Politics of *Akpeteshie* (Local Gin) in Ghana, 1930–1967," *JAH* 37, 2 (1996); Penelope A. Roberts, "The State and the Regulation of Marriage: Sefwi Wiawso (Ghana), 1900–1940," in *Women, State and Ideology: Studies from Africa and Asia*, ed. Haleh Afshar (London, 1987), 48–69; Gareth Austin, "Human Pawning in Asante, 1800–1950: Markets and Coercion, Gender and Cocoa," in *Pawnship in Africa: Debt Bondage in Historical Perspective*, ed. Toyin Falola and Paul E. Lovejoy (Boulder, 1994), 119–59; Beverly Grier, "Pawns, Porters, and Petty Traders: Women in the Transition to Cash Crop Agriculture in Colonial Ghana," *Signs* 17, 2 (1992): 304–28; Jean Allman, "Of 'Spinsters,' 'Concubines' and 'Wicked Women': Reflections on Gender and Social Change in Colonial Asante," *Gender and History* 30, 2 (1991): 176–89; Jean Allman, "Round ing Up Spinsters: Unmarried Women, Moral Crisis and Gender Chaos in Colonial Asante" (paper presented at the Annual Meeting of the African Studies Association, 1993); and Jean Allman, "Making Mothers: Missionaries, Medical Officers and Women's Work in Colonial Asante, 1924–1945," *History Workshop* 38 (Autumn 1994): 23–47.

[10]   For excellent longue durée studies of women in Accra and Kumasi, see Claire C. Robertson, *Sharing the Same Bowl: A Socioeconomic Study of Women and Class in Accra, Ghana* (Ann Arbor, 1990); and Gracia Clark, *Onions Are My Husband: Survival and Accumulation by West African Market Women* (Chicago, 1994).

[11]   This is not to argue that prostitutes did not exist in the Gold Coast. For a sensitive and insightful essay on sexuality and gender relations in precolonial Gold Coast, see Adam Jones, "Prostitution, Polyandrie oder Vergewaltigung? Zur Mehrdeutigkeit Europäischer Quellen über die Küste Westafrikas zwischen 1660 und 1860," in *Aussereuropaische Frauengeschichte: Probleme der Forschung*, ed. Adam Jones (Pfaffenweiler, 1990), 123–58.

traders who carried fish well over a hundred miles to interior markets, and interior women who brought farm produce daily to coastal markets.[12] De Marees also believed Fante women to be prone to "whoredom," and especially promiscuous where Dutchmen were concerned.[13] Jean Barbot (1688) described *etiguafou* ("prostitutes"), "distinguished from the others [ordinary women] by their fine appearance and their clothing."[14] Unfortunately, we lack biographical data on these women, but their descriptions and their activities raise interesting parallels with the *signares* of precolonial Senegal.

The *signares* were women of slave and creole descent along the Senegambian and upper Guinea coast, who struck opportunistic alliances (marital and concubinage) with Portuguese and French traders. Several emerged as wealthy traders, acquiring autonomy and a social status denied them by birth.[15] European men and African women strongly appreciated the mutual advantages of economic collaboration and cohabitation.[16] On the Gold Coast in 1702, the Dutch administration found it necessary to decree that:

> From now onwards all servants of the company will have to desist from taking any goods from the store houses or let them sell by their boys [personal servants] or by their whores. Goods will only be sold to black merchants coming to the fortresses of the company straight from the interior, and servants of the company shall no longer be allowed to defraud the Noble Company through the refinements of their black whores and boys.[17]

Dutch officials were perturbed by the improper accumulation of wealth by company employees in conjunction with their African mistresses. Europeans contracted marriages with African women, which were undoubtedly subjected to different cultural interpretations concerning marital obligations. Resident Danes referred to these "marriage" arrangements as *cassare*. Occasionally, Danish chaplains would stress the legality of these unions and insist that "these concubines were lawful wives, who should accompany their husbands when they left for Europe."[18] Sensitive to these mixed marriages, and the welfare of the resulting mulatto children, the Dutch administration in the Gold Coast resolved in 1700 that:

---

[12]   Pieter de Marees, *Description and Historical Account of the Gold Kingdom of Guinea*, trans. and ed. Albert van Dantzig and Adam Jones (Oxford, 1987), 64.

[13]   De Marees, *Gold Kingdom of Guinea*, Ch. 7.

[14]   P. E. H. Hair, Adam Jones, and Robin Law, eds., *Barbot on Guinea: The Writings of Jean Barbot on West Africa 1678–1712* II (London, 1992), 495.

[15]   George E. Brooks, "The *Signares* of Saint-Louis and Goree: Women Entrepreneurs in Eighteenth-Century Senegal," in *Women in Africa: Studies in Social and Economic Change*, ed. Nancy J. Hafkin and Edna G. Bay (Stanford, 1976), 19–44. Euro-African marital alliances were documented by European sources where the African women were wealthy or from royal or aristocratic families. Such alliances were economically and politically vital. On the Euro-African society on the Gold Coast, see Margaret Priestley, *West African Trade and Coastal Society* (London, 1969).

[16]   Brooks, "Signares of Saint-Louis and Goree," 22.

[17]   West Indian Company (WIC) 228: Instructions Book 1664-1702. Draft circular by W. De la Palma (n.d.). A. van Dantzig, *The Dutch and the Guinea Coast 1674-1742: A Collection of Documents from the General State Archives at the Hague* (Accra, 1978), 89.

[18]   Georg Nörregård, *Danish Settlements in West Africa 1658–1850*, trans. Sigurd Mammen (Boston, 1966), 166.

anybody who . . . has bred or is breeding children in whoredom, shall be obliged to take them on their departure with them to our fatherland on their expense, or, in case he happens to die here, to reserve, each for himself, according to his position, a proper sum for honest maintenance and Christian education of such products.[19]

In spite of the difficulties involved in what were often temporary relationships, such mixed marriages were attractive for African women not only for their economic benefits, but also because European political influence offered them an opportunity to escape the control of elder kinsmen. Women who were fortunate could acquire enough wealth to remain independent after the departure of their European partners.

In 1679, Jean Barbot's presence at an elaborate feast at Fort Frederickburgh, hosted by the Danish General Witt, afforded him a rare opportunity to comment on the Gold Coast version of successful *signares*.

> Afterwards the General's concubines arrived, followed by those of other white men at the fort and by several other black women from Manfrou itself, all dressed in the finest attire, and radiant more on account of the many gold ornaments with which they decorated many parts of their bodies . . . They arranged themselves around us and were served sweet oranges, French wine, Palm wine, mum [beer], and brandy.[20]

In precolonial Akan society, noted for its exclusion of women from strong drink, the lifestyle of these women was a testament to their empowerment.[21]

What is historically striking is that women have been compelled to pursue accumulation and independence within the context of their relationship with men—including European men. It was in the early colonial period (from c. 1874 to the 1930s), that political, economic, and social change—engendered by the fluidity of early colonial rule, the dual judicial structure of British common law courts and customary law courts, an expanding cash (export) economy, and missionary activity—provided women with the first opportunity to define their autonomy outside their relationship with men. The irony is that the colonial policy of indirect rule through chiefs, capitalist operations, and missionary ideology all aimed at subordinating women in the domestic realm.[22] However, the convergence of these developments had unintended benefits for women. In urban and rural areas, retailing beer and liquor, other types of petty trade, prostitution, cocoa and food farming broadened the economic horizons of women. By the late 1920s and 1930s, some rural women in cocoa-producing areas had concluded that even marriage was an unnecessary constraint. In Sefwi Wiawso and parts of Asante in 1929 and the 1930s, traditional authorities ordered the arrest of spinsters. They were to be released if they agreed to marry, named a suitor, and paid a "release fee."[23] In Akan and Ga–

[19] (Resolution concerning morals and religion) 10th March 1700. Van Dantzig, *The Dutch and the Guinea Coast*, 60.

[20] Hair et al., *Barbot on Guinea* II, 565.

[21] Dumett, "Social Impact of the European Liquor Trade," 80.

[22] Allman, "Making Mothers." For an excellent discussion of the genderized experience of class formation and the colonial state, see Margot Lovett, "Gender Relations, Class Formation, and the Colonial State in Africa," in *Women and the State in Africa*, ed. Jane L. Parpart and Kathleen A. Staudt (London, 1989), 23–46.

[23] Allman, "Of 'Spinsters,' 'Concubines' and 'Wicked Women'"; Allman, "Rounding up Spinsters"; and Roberts, "The State and the Regulation of Marriage."

Adangme societies where children were seldom considered illegitimate, being single did not exclude the privileges of motherhood.[24] In southern Ghana, parents considered children an investment for their old age.[25] Increasingly, women were taking accumulation and childbirth out of the context of marriage or concubinage.

It is unfortunate that the socioeconomic conditions of women have deteriorated in the late colonial period and during Ghana's independence (achieved in 1957). The multiple causes include unequal access to higher education, adverse developments in trading conditions, and hostile governments.[26] Ghanaian women have been forced to retreat to their traditional place of survival and accumulation: the marketplace.[27] The other option is the old one of forging opportunistic relations with men.[28] The increasing fragility of marriage has saddled women with more responsibilities just when their finances have become most tenuous. Ghanaian governments have passed intestate laws to protect wives and children, but these are often ignored by the kin groups of deceased men.[29] Economic difficulties have affected Ghanaian perceptions of adulthood. A popular saying in contemporary Ghana states that: "poverty has turned men into women, and women into children." In Asante society, for example, nothing is more crushing for a woman than barrenness or more emasculating for a man than impotency or the inability to provide for his family.[30]

Parental contests over children, the inability of working men to provide for their families, the harsh realities of single parenting, and deferred marriages by young men because of financial insolvency have changed the face of gender conflict, especially in cities. Whereas gender conflict in the precolonial and colonial era revolved around male elders and women (often younger), contemporary gender conflicts are fought within the same generation. I lived in Kumasi during the 1979 and 1981 military coups by Jerry John Rawlings and the lower ranks of the army. The anger of young male soldiers against women in general was astounding. The Rawlings coups provided just the political immunity for young men to vent their individual frustrations over marriage difficulties and impoverishment on women. In 1979 and 1981, there was widespread support, especially male, for the destruction of the Makola (Nos. 1 and 2) markets in Accra, and other markets in Sekondi, Koforidua, and Kumasi. The government blamed market women for Ghana's economic difficulties. "How and why do people believe the government propaganda?"

[24] T. C. McCaskie, "*Konnurokusem*: Kinship and Family in the History of the Oyoko Kokoo Dynasty of Kumase," *JAH* 36, 3 (1995): 377; and Claire C. Robertson, "Post-Proclamation Slavery in Accra: A Female Affair?" in *Women and Slavery in Africa*, ed. Claire C. Robertson and Martin A. Klein (Madison, 1983), 236.

[25] See, for example, Claire Robertson, "Ga Women and Socioeconomic Change in Accra, Ghana," in *Women in Africa*, ed. Hafkin and Bay, 128.

[26] Robertson, *Sharing the Same Bowl*.

[27] Ibid.; Clark, *Onions Are My Husband*.

[28] See Emmanuel Akyeampong, "Constructing and Contesting Sexuality: 'Prostitution' in the Gold Coast, c. 1650 to 1950" (paper presented at the Annual Meeting of the African Studies Association, 1995); and Carmel Dinan, "Sugar Daddies and Gold-Diggers: The White Collar Single Women in Accra," in *Female and Male in West Africa*, ed. Christine Oppong (London, 1983), 344–66.

[29] See Gwendolyn Mikell, "The State, the Courts, and 'Value': Caught Between Matrilineages in Ghana," in *Money Matters: Instability, Values and Social Payments in the Modern History of West African Communities*, ed. Jane Guyer (Portsmouth, 1995), 225–44.

[30] Victoria B. Tashjian, "'You Marry to Beget': Menopause and Non-Marriage in Asante" (paper presented at the African Studies Association Annual Meeting, 1993).

queried a disturbed Claire Robertson.[31] Because the government's propaganda on ordinary market women converged with the financial frustrations of ordinary men who found their manhood threatened.

In the socioeconomic conditions of contemporary Ghana, an alcoholic may be a man or a woman.[32] This is a radical departure from the precolonial and colonial era, when male elders accused young men of alcohol abuse. But economic decline, gender conflict, and the paradox of independent and impoverished women, have made the (dis)empowering metaphor of alcohol appealing to women. As one young female alcoholic explained to me: "Nsa (drink) is not sweet. Why should I make it my food?" In the words of obaa panin Afua Pokua, "when you are sad or grieving, that is when you drink."[33] Alcohol has been an ideal metaphor for power because it encapsulates the spectrum of power relations—from empowerment to disempowerment.[34] It is a valuable prism for the reconstruction of social history and the history of power.

A Note on Structure, Method, and Sources

The rest of this book is divided into eight thematic and chronological chapters. Chapter 1 raises a question fundamental to the social history of alcohol: why do people drink? It is so basic that several recent studies on alcohol do not address it. I examine important insights provided by the social science literature. I then present an anthropology of three fluids: alcohol, blood, and water. The chapter ends with an overview of the social history of alcohol in Ghana. Chapter 2 discusses the ritual significance of alcohol, blood, and water in the precolonial histories and cultures of the Akan, Ga–Adangme, and Ewe.

Chapter 3 shifts the social context more to the colonial towns, and I examine the role of alcohol in social formation among new migrants between c. 1890 and 1919. This period was also an era of significant socioeconomic gains for women, and I discuss important transformations in gender relations. Data is drawn largely from the cities of Accra, Sekondi–Takoradi, Kumasi, and Obuasi. Chapter 4 analyzes the importance of liquor legislation in relations of power between the colonizer and the colonized. Temperance agitation intrudes into this vital political domain and reduces the importance of liquor legislation as a sphere for negotiating relations of power. Official cuts in liquor imports from 1930 opened up a pandora's

---

[31]   Claire Robertson, "The Death of Makola and other Tragedies," Canadian Journal of African Studies [hereafter CJAS] 17, 3 (1983): 472.

[32]   It is significant that three B. A. theses in the sociology department, University of Ghana, were produced in the late 1970s, when it was generally acknowledged that Ghanaians might have a drinking problem. Joyce Robertson, "The Beer Drinking Phenomena: A Study of Beer Drinkers in Legon" (B. A. thesis, University of Ghana, 1978); B. K. Bayor, "The Social Relevance of Pito Drinking Among the Dagaaba" (B. A. thesis, University of Ghana, 1978); and Yaw Agyemang Beniako, "The Social Significance of Palm Wine Drinking—A Case Study at Bechem" (B. A. thesis, University of Ghana, 1979).

[33]   Akyeampong Field Notes [AFN]: Interview with Afua Pokua, obaa panin, Kumasi, August 18, 1994.

[34]   The complex connections between alcohol's (dis)empowering effect and the relevance of liquor revenues for the Ghanaian state are explored in Emmanuel Akyeampong, "The State and Alcohol Revenues: Promoting 'Economic Development' in Gold Coast/Ghana, 1919 to the Present," Histoire Sociale/Social History 27 (November 1994): 393–411.

box. Illicit distillation proliferated overnight, and Chapter 5 explores the connections between *akpeteshie* (illicit gin), popular culture, and class formation in the
pre–World War II era.

Chapter 6 focuses on alcohol, popular culture, and nationalist politics from
1945 to independence. The spiritual power of fluids informed the epic struggle for
political independence. It was a struggle that harnessed the powers unique to
women and men. Chapter 7 analyzes Ghana's political, economic, and social decline, the impact on gender relations and drinking patterns, and new nuances in
alcoholism as a tool in the definition of social identity. Chapter 8 concludes this
book and offers reflections on the culture and history of power.

Tracking permutations in the uses and meanings of alcohol, water, and blood
encouraged me to adopt an interdisciplinary approach and to explore multiple
sources. The quest has taken me outside history into cultural anthropology, Christian theology, sociology, political science, and social medicine. Cultural anthropology and Christian theology provided invaluable tools for conceptualizing a study
of alcohol, water, and blood. The realm of belief and ritual has for too long remained the terrain of anthropologists. Belief motivates the actions that preoccupy
historians. And belief can be historicized.[35] The cognitive world needs to be brought
within the purview of historical interpretation. Studies of power in sociology and
political science served as sharpening tools in my reflections on power in the Ghanaian context. They were instructive in my examination of how power has been
exercised; but they often omitted belief as a source of, and a legitimation for, power.
I found recent works in anthropology that grounded studies of power in culture
especially pertinent. Social medicine helped me wrestle with my desire to historicize
alcoholism. The phenomenon and physiological consequences of alcoholism are
universal, but its manifestation and causation are influenced by specific cultural
and historical factors.[36]

The sources utilized in this book range from early European accounts of the
Gold Coast; available ethnographies on the Akan, Ga–Adangme, and Ewe; colonial
and missionary archives in England and Ghana; the huge secondary literature on
Ghana; highlife music[37] housed at archives in England and Ghana; popular fiction,
particularly "chap book" literature;[38] comic opera; photography; and oral interviews
in Ghana in 1992 and 1994.[39] Some of these sources, such as highlife music and
comic opera, are essentially twentieth-century sources. The relative strengths of
these sources are evident in the separate chapters, depending on the chronology
and the relevant themes. Social history encourages creativity when it comes to
sources because of the gaps in archival material. My sources, together, forge a more
complete picture of the history of alcohol and power.

---

[35]   For an excellent example, see T. C. McCaskie, *State and Society in Pre-Colonial Asante* (Cambridge,
1995).

[36]   Colleagues at the Harvard Medical School encouraged me to present a paper in their social medicine
series in April 1994. A revised version appeared as "Alcoholism in Ghana—A Socio-Cultural Exploration," *Culture, Medicine and Psychiatry* 19, 2 (1995): 261–80. I am grateful for their gentle prodding.

[37]   The genre of highlife music represents a unique synthesis of Akan lyrics and rhythms with Western
instrumentation. It is essentially a twentieth-century creation.

[38]   For background, see Richard K. Priebe, ed., *Ghanaian Literatures* (New York, 1988).

[39]   The taped interviews will be deposited at the Institute of African Studies, University of Ghana, in the
summer of 1996.

I have been asked several times by my colleagues outside Africa what it feels like to write history from an insider's perspective. My response: challenging, frustrating, exciting, and rewarding. Two specific examples may be illuminating. When I read early missionary accounts of Ghana in general and Asante in particular, I go through interesting processes of dissonance and assonance. These accounts are often racist, patronizing, and propagandist. I flit between my identities as an Asante, a Christian, and an historian. I am grateful to Joseph Miller for his encouragement to think as an Asante in my struggles to resolve these tensions. The year 1992 was a fascinating time to conduct fieldwork in Ghana because it coincided with political elections. In towns and villages, people strove to ascertain whether I was a political figure, and which party I represented. I had stimulating conversations with the elders and people of Binsere, a village just outside Obuasi. Each time I departed, they insisted on giving me messages for Rawlings, the head of state. To such interviewees I owe the textured accounts of culture, history, and the life portraits used in this book.

The reality of social formation and urbanization as precolonial and multiethnic phenomena where Ghana is concerned, encouraged me to push beyond ethnic specialization and a narrow timeframe. The result is a book that transcends the regional, ethnic, and chronological (precolonial, colonial, and postcolonial) divides that have characterized studies of Ghana. It strives for an indigenous perspective of the same momentous events and developments that feature prominently in Ghanaian historiography. It places at center stage intergenerational and class struggles over alcohol, gender relations, and popular culture.

Acknowledgements

Funding for this book was made possible by grants from the African Development Foundation (1991–1992), and the Milton Foundation at Harvard University (Summer 1994). I am grateful to the librarians at Alderman Library (University of Virginia), the School of Oriental and African Studies (University of London), Balme Library (University of Ghana); and archival staff at the Public Records Office (London), Rhodes House (Oxford), the National Sound Archives (London), National Archives of Ghana (Accra, Cape Coast, Sekondi, and Kumasi), Ghana Broadcasting Corporation (Accra), and Bokoor Music Archives (Accra) for their invaluable assistance.

I am deeply indebted to Joseph C. Miller for my intellectual nurturing and guidance. I also acknowledge my scholarly debt and gratitude to Jeanne Toungara, William B. Taylor, Robert Fatton, Mary–Alice Kraehe, Richard Rathbone, Charles Ambler, Jean Allman, Jean Hay, Allen Isaacman, Caroline Fox, David Owusu Ansah, Larry Yarak, Leroy Vail, Pashington Obeng, Isaac Tufuoh, Albert Mawere Poku, Nana Kobina Nketsia, Isaac Newman, J. B. Asare, Rev. Kofi Asare, Ko Nimo, Ruhi Grover, Kenda Mutongi, Pauline Page, John Haysel, and many others I cannot list for want of space. I thank my numerous informants who were kind enough to share their knowledge and their lives. To my large family and friends, I am overwhelmed by their moral and material support. This book is dedicated to three special people, who have made great sacrifices for my academic career and scholarly pursuits: Salome (my mother), Ruth (my wife), and Nana Pomaa (my daughter).

1

Order Over Unorder: Alcohol, Autonomy, and Power in Ghana

Obosom a oye nnam na odi aboade

The god that is sharp is the one that has offerings promised to it

Twi proverb

Why do people drink? This basic question is fundamental to the social history of alcohol because it raises the issue of meaning: the meaning(s) people attach to drink. Beginning as studies of the "other," the social science literature on the use of alcoholic drinks, nevertheless, has contributed valuable insights on how social structures, social relations, stress, and cultural change impinge on drinking patterns in different societies.[1] Recent studies on drinking behavior have indicated that these factors have universal relevance to understanding societal use of alcoholic drinks.

Anthropologists, in their preoccupation with food and drink, have pioneered studies from the late nineteenth century of why and how people use and abuse alcoholic drinks. In all societies, the uses of alcoholic drinks have been defined by cultural parameters. Unfortunately, many of the nineteenth- and early twentieth-century works produced on drink in non–Western societies exhibit an Eurocentric assumption that the use of alcoholic drinks was always destructive in non–Western societies. In this approach was reflected the increasing influence of medical findings that alcohol was addictive,[2] and the hold of diffusionism on anthropolo-

---

[1] For a detailed review of drinking theories, see Juha Partanen, *Sociability and Intoxication: Alcohol and Drinking in Kenya, Africa, and the Modern World* (Helsinki, 1991), 199–250.

[2] The late eighteenth-century writings of the Englishman, Thomas Trotter, and the American, Benjamin Rush, portrayed habitual drunkenness as an illness with physiological and mental consequences. In the mid–nineteenth century, a Swedish doctor, Magnus Huss, coined the word "alcoholism," establishing it as a new disease. It was, however, up to the American, E. M. Jellinek, to popularize the disease concept of alcoholism. Jean–Charles Sournia, *A History of Alcoholism*, trans. Nick Handley and Gareth Stanton (Oxford, 1990).

1

gists between 1910 and 1930.[3] Products of European imperial expansion, early anthropologists argued that "civilization" spread through cultural diffusion. But to
save "primitive" peoples from degeneration through acculturation, they must be
protected from certain aspects of European civilization—especially European alcoholic drinks. Early anthropologists were so convinced of the disastrous effects of
drink on the uncivilized, that they ignored evidence of culturally sanctioned, integrative uses of drink in the non–Western societies they studied. The reports of the
Human Relations Area Files (HRAF), compiled by Yale University, highlight this
bias.

The growth of functionalism in anthropology from the 1930s accounts for a
new thrust in works dating from this period that drink had to fulfill some functional role in relieving tensions in primitive societies. The classic work in this vein
is Donald Horton's 1943 study.[4] Horton argued that primitive societies used drink
to reduce "anxiety" or "fear" and that the level of drunkenness in a society was a
reflection of the degree of such stress. This anxiety or fear may be caused by insecure food supply or tensions resulting from Western acculturation. The release of
aggressive impulses during drinking alleviates the feeling of anxiety.

Horton ignored the cultural uses of drink in an integrative manner, and the
fact that drinking does not represent the only medium for reducing stress. His
awareness that some societies had rules governing drinking, and even punished
drunken aggression, made Horton qualify his thesis by arguing that the act of drinking itself may then elicit new anxiety.[5] Horton's desire to frame general social laws
governing drinking behavior obscured the reality that each culture defines its own
drinking patterns. That he drew his data from the HRAF, compiled from earlier
ethnographic reports with a different ideological bent, posed further problems for
Horton's thesis.

However, Horton made a valid observation in linking drinking to fear or anxiety; an observation that has been substantiated by subsequent research in non–
Western and Western societies. Boris Serebro has analyzed the connection between
drinking and anxiety among urbanized Africans in response to economic insecurity.[6] Parallel studies of economic insecurity, anxiety, and drinking in Western societies and ethnic drinking in the United States are offered by Robin Room and Raul
Caetano.[7]

The first coherent rebuttal of Horton's thesis was offered by Peter Field.[8] Pursuing a comparative analysis of circumstances that encourage drinking, Field found
a positive correlation between the level of drunkenness in a society, and the rigid-

---

[3]   Henrika Kuklick, *The Savage Within: The Social History of British Anthropology* (Cambridge, 1991).

[4]   Donald Horton, "The Functions of Alcohol in Primitive Societies: A Cross–Cultural Study," *Quarterly Journal of Studies on Alcohol* 4, 2 (1943): 199–320.

[5]   Ibid.

[6]   Boris Serebro, "Total Alcohol Consumption as an Index of Anxiety Among Urbanised Africans," *British Journal of Psychiatry* 67 (1972): 251–54.

[7]   Robin Room, "Alcohol Problems and the City," *British Journal of Addiction* 85 (1990): 1395–1402; and Raul Caetano, "Hispanic Drinking in the US: Thinking in New Directions," *British Journal of Addiction* 85 (1990): 1231–36.

[8]   Peter B. Field, "A New Cross–Cultural Study of Drunkenness," in *Society, Culture and Drinking Patterns*, ed. D. Pitman and C. Snyder (New York, 1962), 48–74.

ity of its social organization. Drawing on the HRAF, Field observed that tight, hierarchical, formal societies tended to drink less, while loose, informal, bilateral societies tended to exhibit extreme drunkenness. Field found no evidence tying fear to drunkenness, and concluded that Horton's features of insecure food supply and acculturation indicated a loose social organization rather than fear.[9]

Field apparently viewed social structures and social relations as static, with societies existing in isolation and hence shielded from external influences. Societies change, and so do drinking patterns. His theory also failed to take account of tight, hierarchical societies which saw drunkenness as a desirable social end. Among the hierarchical Chagga society of Tanzania, drunkenness was enjoyed by male elders, who often ended up beating their wives—a reality enshrined in the rain songs of Chagga children.[10] And likewise there are loose societies where drinking is enjoyed but controlled.[11]

Scholars like David Mandelbaum recognized the limitations of data abstracted from the HRAF, and encouraged culture–informed studies of the uses of drink in specific societies instead of broad generalizations derived from statistical analysis.[12] Mandelbaum's significant contribution was his assertion that culture influenced drinking patterns, and that as a whole culture changed, so did the drinking mores of its people.[13] Moreover, different drinking patterns may coexist within a single society, reflecting social relations between different groups.

But in his endeavor to emphasize the importance of culture to studies of drink, Mandelbaum reified culture, arguing that culture even influenced the physiological effects attributed to chronic drunkenness. He advocated that in some societies where drink was positively viewed, chronic drunkenness did not result in hangovers or addiction.[14] Although tolerance levels vary for individuals, and rates of metabolism may differ for men and women, the physiological and mental effects of alcohol addiction appear to be universal.[15]

A similarly deterministic utilization of culture, culture being defined as learned attitudes and habits, was applied in a sophisticated theory explaining drunken comportment among Amerindians by Craig MacAndrew and Robert Edgerton.[16] They

---

[9]   Ibid., 72.

[10]   Chandler Washburne, *Primitive Drinking: A Study of the Uses and Functions of Alcohol in Preliterate Societies* (New York, 1961), 26.

[11]   Robert Netting, "Beer as a Locus of Value Among the West African Kofyar," *American Anthropologist* 66 (1964): 375–84.

[12]   David G. Mandelbaum, "Alcohol and Culture," *Current Anthropology* 6, 3 (1965): 281–93.

[13]   Ibid , 283.

[14]   Ibid., 282.

[15]   Ethanol, the toxic quality in alcohol, is destroyed by the enzyme aldehyde dehydrogenase. It appears many southeast Asians are unable to tolerate alcohol because they have only low levels of this enzyme. Sournia, *History of Alcoholism*, 165. But genetic studies are far from precise to enable us to make absolute statements about cultural differences in alcohol tolerance. T. Y. Lin and D. T. C. Lin, "Alcoholism Among the Chinese: Further Observations of a Low–Risk Population," *Culture, Medicine and Psychiatry* 6 (1982): 109–16, have examined the arguments advanced to explain the low incidence of alcoholism among the Chinese.

[16]   Craig MacAndrew and Robert B. Edgerton, *Drunken Comportment: A Social Explanation* (Chicago, 1969). For a historical account of Indians and alcohol in early America, see Peter C. Mancall, *Deadly Medicine: Indians and Alcohol in Early America* (Ithaca, 1995).

argued that drunken comportment is a learned process that is culturally defined, it is not inherent or universal. The limits of disinhibition when drunk are thus culturally defined; almost a theory of "inhibition within disinhibition." Certain behavior becomes acceptable when drunk, but there are also rigid cultural limits to drunken behavior. MacAndrew and Edgerton see drunkenness as "time–out," a state in which "drunk" people get away with certain conduct that is "within–limits." In essence, drink is used to release internal social tensions.

The new centrality of culture to studies of drink is reflected in the culture–specific studies of anthropologists like Robert Netting, Walter Sangree, and Ivan Karp.[17] These anthropologists emphasized drink's role in facilitating community building and in reinforcing social hierarchy. Karp points out in his study of the Iteso of Kenya and Uganda, that the incorporation of beer into rituals—which re-enact and reinforce the beliefs and practices of the people—makes beer a gateway into understanding the philosophy and religion of the Iteso.

By the 1970s two distinct interpretations had emerged in the studies of drink, emphasizing either its functional or dysfunctional effects. An attempt to bridge the gap between these two schools, raising critical questions in the process, was the collection of essays on constructive drinking edited by Mary Douglas.[18] In the introduction to the collection, Douglas commented on the problems raised by the extension of one culture's attitudes towards drink to another. Do we redefine our concepts of "problem–drinking," "alcoholism," "alcohol–related problems," to accommodate another society's drinking mores?

But that the functionalist approach to drink had ignored the concomitant dysfunctional uses of drink was also apparent. As Douglas points out, drinks act as markers of personal identity and markers of inclusion and exclusion. The more drink is used for signifying selection and exclusion, the more might we expect its abuse to appear among the ranks of the excluded. The functional and dysfunctional uses of drink represent two sides of the same coin.[19]

In highlighting the use of drink as a social marker, Douglas brings us closer to the fact that drink—as a ritual object, social good, economic commodity—has meaning(s), and that these meanings differ from society to society. Jonathan Crush and Charles Ambler take up this challenge to explore the meaning of drink in southern Africa's politics of labor, race, class, gender, and age.[20] Their emphasis on the very meaning of drink itself—and the recognition that these meanings differ for various protagonists and may change over time—gives a rich dynamism to how individuals and groups use drink to construct meaningful social identities and to oppose imposed identities. In southern Ghana, the meanings of alcohol, forged within a changing culturo–historical context, were closely linked to conceptions of power—and by extension disempowerment.

---

[17]   Netting, "Beer as a Locus of Value"; Walter Sangree, "The Social Functions of Beer Drinking among the Bantu Tiriki," in Pitman and Snyder, 6–21; and Ivan Karp, "Beer Drinking and Social Experience in an African Society: An Essay in Formal Sociology," in *Explorations in African Systems of Thought*, ed. I. Karp and C. Bird (Bloomington, 1980).

[18]   Mary Douglas, ed., *Constructive Drinking: Perspectives on Drink from Anthropology* (Cambridge, 1987).

[19]   A fact underscored by a recent study of the uses of alcoholic drinks among the Tonga of Gwembe District in Zambia. Elizabeth Colson and Thayer Scudder, *For Prayer and Profit: The Ritual, Economic, and Social Importance of Beer in the Gwembe District, Zambia, 1950–1982* (Stanford, 1988).

[20]   Jonathan Crush and Charles Ambler, eds., *Liquor and Labor in Southern Africa* (Athens, Ohio, 1992).

On April 8, 1992, this author posed the question of how people become alcoholics to several junior staff at the hospital of the Ashanti Goldfields Corporation in Obuasi.[21] I expected informed opinions on the addictive nature of alcohol; this was a hospital. Rather, I received detailed social explanations of why people drink. Mr. Donkoh opined that a bad wife could lead a man to drink. But Mr. Donkoh denied the author's suggestion that a bad husband could lead a woman to drink. He also saw a link between poverty and habitual drinking. Nurse Comfort Marfo believed that nagging wives often drove their husbands to drink. She recalled the example of a female friend of hers who was a flirt. Her husband always came home drunk. But Comfort Marfo also pointed out that grief, especially the loss of a loved one, could lead a person to drink and alcoholism. Mr. Andoh recalled a time when he drank a lot. It was because his wife, who trades in the market, often came home late. He took to drinking, while waiting for his wife to come home and prepare the evening meal. At this juncture, one of the women in the room asked Mr. Andoh why he did not cook something for himself? Andoh exclaimed: "Me! In a compound house with witnesses around?" The sexual division of labor ruled out the option of Mr. Andoh preparing his own meals while he had a wife. A common theme running through these responses was that of balance or control. An individual drank when his or her world was out of balance: poverty, a death, an unhappy marriage. Somehow, both male and female respondents did not see drink as providing the same avenue of escape for women. The culture of alcohol is not only linked to power or control, it is also very male oriented.

The worldviews of the Akan, Ga–Adangme, and Ewe peoples of southern Ghana encompassed the living, the dead, and the unborn in a religious structure in which interaction with the Supreme Being (Twi: *Onyame*), the ancestors (Twi: *nsamanfo)*, and the gods (Twi: *abosom*) occupied a central place in day to day existence. Communication with the spiritual world was essential in the pursuit of social goals, and drink (Twi: *nsa*)[22] facilitated communication between the spiritual and physical worlds.[23] Male elders in precolonial southern Ghana viewed alcohol as possessing potent spiritual power; without alcoholic drinks, one could not communicate through libation (Twi: *nsa guo* or *mpae yi*) with the ancestors and the gods.[24] Human subsistence and prosperity was predicated on a harmonious balance between the physical and spiritual realms. The ritual use of alcohol was thus crucial to the very pursuit of life. But alcohol shared its quality to bridge the physical and spiritual worlds with two other fluids, water and blood. To examine alcohol's meaning within the context of these other fluids lends a nuanced texture to the appeal

---

[21]   An alcoholic is defined in this book as an individual whose habitual drinking has interfered with his or her family, community and/or work life.

[22]   *Nsa* originally referred to palm wine (*nsa fufuo*, tapped from the oil palm and raffia palm trees), but its usage has been extended to all types of drink, including European beer, wine, and spirits. Other indigenous alcoholic drinks included *pito*, brewed from millet or guinea corn, and *akpeteshie*, a potent liquor distilled from palm wine or sugar cane especially from the 1930s.

[23]   See also David J. Parkin, *Palms, Wine, and Witnesses: Public Spirit and Private Gain in an African Farming Community* (Prospect Heights, Ill., 1994).

[24]   Libation is prayer accompanied and punctuated by the pouring of *nsa*. Libation essentially involves three processes: invoking the presence of the Supreme Being, the gods and the ancestors; explaining to these supernatural beings the occasion for the human gathering; and supplicating these spirits to grant the human assembly success in their endeavors. See Marion Kilson, "Libation in Ga Ritual," *Journal of Religion in Africa* 2, 3 (1969): 161–78.

of, and the struggle over, alcohol. It also incorporates different notions of spirituality that sometimes competed with alcohol's ritual use. An anthropological examination of these fluids in the cultures of southern Ghana will enhance our understanding on how they intersect with power.

Powerful Fluids

Alcohol

Thomas Bowdich, an English visitor to the Asante capital of Kumase in 1817, intro-
duces us to the world of alcohol and power in his description of the Asantehene's
odwira.[25] On the fourth day of the festival (September 7), *odwira nwonakwasie*, the
Asantehene, or king of Asante, supplied free rum to the populace of Kumase, precipitating what seemed to Bowdich a disorderly drunken orgy.[26]

> The . . . King ordered a large quantity of rum to be poured into brass
> pans, in various parts of the town; the crowd pressing around, and drink-
> ing like hogs; *freemen and slaves, women and children,* striking, kicking, and
> trampling each other underfoot, pushed head foremost into the pans, and
> *spilling more than they drank.* In less than an hour, *excepting the principal
> men,* not a sober person was to be seen, parties of four reeling and rolling
> under the weight of another, *whom they affected to be carrying home;* strings
> of women covered with red paint, hand in hand, falling down like rows
> of cards; *the commonest mechanics and slaves furiously declaiming on state pa-
> lavers;* the most discordant music, the most obscene songs, *children of both
> sexes prostrate in insensibility.* All wore their handsomest cloths, *which they
> trailed after them to a great length, in a drunken emulation of extravagance and
> dirtiness* [emphasis added].

> Towards the evening the populace grew sober again, . . . the kings and the
> dignitaries were carried in their hammocks. . . .[27]

The above represented a choreographed scene in the relations of power in Asante,
in which alcohol symbolized royal power, patronage, generosity, accessibility, and
uneasiness.

Asante expansion in the eighteenth and nineteenth centuries had resulted in a
stratified society rife with tension: a huge class of slaves, commoners subjugated
under a military aristocracy, juniors subordinated to elders, and men elevated over
women. The fourth day of the Asantehene's *odwira* offered the opportunity to de-
fuse these tensions under the guise of drunkenness. As David Birmingham has
argued in his study of carnival in Luanda, carnivals, at one political level, "exor-
cise the fear of authority among the powerless."[28] As such, carnival has the ability

---

[25] The *Odwira* was a week–long ceremony held to honor and propitiate Asante's dead kings and to
purify the whole nation. For detailed descriptions of this ceremony and its significance, see R. S. Rattray,
Religion and Art in Ashanti (Oxford, 1927), 27–131; and McCaskie, *State and Society*, Ch. 4. Akyeampong,
Alcohol, Social Conflict," 94–96, explored the relevance of alcohol to the *odwira* festival.

[26] Bowdich ascribed this scene to Sunday, the third day of the *odwira*, but Thomas McCaskie argues
convincingly that this was an error in Bowdich's diary. McCaskie, *State and Society*, 218 and 423.

[27] Thomas Edward Bowdich, *Mission from Cape Coast Castle to Ashantee*, 3rd ed. (London, 1966), 278–79.

[28] David Birmingham, "Carnival at Luanda," *JAH* 29, 3 (1988): 103. On carnival as a context for political
contestation, see also Emmanuel LeRoy Ladurie, *Carnival at Romans*, trans. Mary Feeney (New York, 1979).

to "service" social inequities, and to prevent social inequities from immobilizing the social system. In precolonial Asante, the *odwira* carnival entailed an inversion of the *status quo* and, more importantly, a subsequent reversion to the *status quo*. It reflected social formation and political process.

Although carnival served as a medium for political and social catharsis, it was fraught with unpredictability. Thomas McCaskie has examined the *odwira* festival as the site of the state's ideological structuration of belief and knowledge in precolonial Asante. The annual enactment of *odwira* reinforced state ideology and the hegemony of Asante's ruling class.[29] But carnival or public ritual was never an uncontested site. As Jonathon Glassman emphasizes in his study of feasts and riot on the Swahili coast, public ritual has long been an important forum for reproducing relations of power as well as the contestation of power.

> The hegemonic version of these rituals disadvantaged certain categories of persons such as women, slaves, and newcomers of non–Muslim background: ritual defined their position as distinctly inferior, or excluded them from the community altogether. But although women, slaves and newcomers generally accepted the patriarchal and Islamic idioms that gave shape to public rituals, they did not necessarily share the dominant interpretation of them.[30]

McCaskie and Glassman both draw on Gramscian thought for their studies of state and society with strikingly different emphases. McCaskie highlights the state's ability to structure belief and knowledge in the service of its hegemony; Glassman underscores the independent strains in popular consciousness. Both perspectives reflect the contested nature of public ritual, and the *odwira* was no exception.

"Freemen and slaves, women and children," those who were normally politically quiescent, dominated this "drunken" scene at the *odwira*. They spilled more than they drank, yet in less than one hour they affected drunkenness. The "principal men" (guardians of "order"?), however, remained sober. Their presence ensured that the celebration by the lower orders stayed within the confines defined by the state. The "commonest mechanics and slaves furiously declaiming on state palavers"; an opportunity they seldom exercised in public. But commoners and slaves were keenly interested in politics in Asante and other Akan states. Indeed their survival sometimes depended on it. Accounts abound of how slaves fled their homes on the occasion of an aristocratic or royal death. The danger of being sacrificed to accompany the dead was a real one.[31] "Children of both sexes lay postrate in insensibility," but it is apparent from the literature on Asante that this was an aberration of the norm.[32] Only those with political power and wealth, trailed their handsome cloths behind them in the dirt, displaying an indifference to material possessions that came with wealth and power. Towards evening, all was normal again, and "the king and the dignitaries were carried in their hammocks." Frustra-

---

[29] McCaskie, *State and Society*.

[30] Jonathon Glassman, *Feasts and Riot: Revelry, Rebellion and Popular Consciousness on the Swahili Coast, 1856–1888* (Portsmouth, 1995), 23.

[31] See de Marees, *Gold Kingdom of Guinea*, 184; Hair *et al.*, *Barbot on Guinea II*, 595; and F. A. Ramseyer and J. Kühne, *Four Years in Ashantee* (London, 1875), 234–36.

[32] Dumett, "Social Impact of the European Liquor Trade," 79–80.

tions had been expended, order had been reestablished and reaffirmed, the *status quo* remained inviolate.

These inversions of the social order during the *odwira*, however, enabled commoners and slaves to rehearse the roles of the powerful and the wealthy. Playing at being wealthy and powerful once a year did not necessarily douse unexpressed ambitions among the lower orders. Once the political checks were removed, slaves and commoners would usurp the very roles they had rehearsed during carnival.

> In 1898 residents of Dar es Salaam complained that slaves had become more "mischievous" under German rule. Slaves now mimic their masters in everything, they said: male slaves wear turbans and shoes and carry umbrellas; female slaves veil themselves and wear even the *shiraa* [an elaborate costume].[33]

With the imposition of British rule in Asante in 1896, and the exile of the Asantehene and his leading chiefs, commoners would usurp the sumptuary practices of the aristocracy.[34] Carnival defused political and social tensions, but "carnival also dealt with social sins or ills, on which the community unfortunately could reach no consensus."[35] Carnival was a context pregnant with danger, and the choice of alcohol as the catalyst of inversion in the *odwira* is instructive.

Alcohol facilitated the inversion of the social order because of its intoxicating quality, strong scent and associated pattern of drunken comportment—garrulousness, slurred speech, unsteady gait.[36] It was easy to affect intoxication by simulating the accepted drunken behavior, especially since "drunkenness" was socially sanctioned on the fourth day of the *odwira*. The free distribution of valuable imported rum underscored the king's generosity, but the choice of alcohol as the fluid in this setting embodied a subtle caution. Alcohol was seen as a "hot" fluid, hence a potentially dangerous one.[37] It contained spiritual power vital in communicating with the spiritual realm but could also dethrone reason. Asante ethics of temperance continuously stressed alcohol's ambiguous qualities.[38] In the *odwira* carnival, alcohol was a mnemonic device that paradoxically created "inhibition within disinhibition."[39]

Water

The ritual use of water possibly preceded alcohol's ritual use among the peoples of southern Ghana. Part of an Asante drum language runs: "The stream crosses the

---

[33]   Glassman, *Feasts and Riot*, 264.

[34]   See Chapter 3.

[35]   Ladurie, *Carnival in Romans*, xvi.

[36]   MacAndrew and Edgerton, *Drunken Comportment*.

[37]   AFN: Interview with Nana Ewua Duku, Paramount Chief of Dutch Sekondi, March 3, 1992; AFN: Interview with Albert Mawere Poku, Accra, August 30, 1994.

[38]   R. S. Rattray, *Ashanti* (Oxford, 1923), 135. Rattray points out that: "No people in the world is more cognizant of the evils of alcoholic excess than the Ashanti."

[39]   Recognized limits to drunken comportment in Asante society are best captured in the proverb: *awudie wo wo tiri mu a, na wo boro nsa a wo bobo afe* ("when murder is in your head, and you become drunk with wine, you strike to wound"). R. S. Rattray, *Ashanti Law and Constitution* (Oxford, 1929), 302–303.

path, the path crosses the stream; which of them is the elder?"[40] The Asante believe God created the stream, alcohol—like the path that crosses the stream—was acquired by human endeavor. Both fluids, sometimes, were combined in a single ritual like libation. Water was esteemed for its clearness—"white" objects are considered pure—coolness and cleansing qualities.[41] Water, more importantly, represented the spirit of the Supreme Being and its use reflected one's dependence on God.[42] Water's spiritual connections to the Supreme Being were very evident in the activities of Ga *wulomei* (Ga: "priests," sing. *wolomo*).

> Our *wulomei* are purely priests, and all they do is . . . pray. They have a shrine. In the shrine is a pot and the pot contains only water, which is supposed to be holy water. There is no idol at all in the Ga *wolomo's* shrine. He only goes there to pray. When you see our *wulomei*, they always go barefoot, they never put on sandals. The philosophy or the doctrine is that every spot on the world [earth] is a holy ground, where God can manifest himself to the priest. . . . They must always go in white. This white is to remind them that their lives must be pure as white. In other words, they must be examples of virtue.[43]

There are three major priests among the Ga Mashi, and they are all associated with bodies of water: the priest of Sakumo lagoon, that of Korle lagoon, and the priest of *Nai* (the sea), who is also the head priest. To distinguish these priests from the priests and priestesses of the lesser gods, the *Sakumo, Korle,* and *Nai Wulomei* are never possessed by spirits.[44]

Since bodies of water were seen as abodes of deities, they also served as custodians of morality. The Ewe–speaking people of Anlo explicitly harness the sacred power of the sea, lagoon, or creek in the ritual ablutions that separate a widow or widower from the deceased spouse. Anlo widows observe a period of mourning that lasts sixteen months.

> At the end of this period, there is *ahotsilele*, the ceremonial washing of the widow. In the evening the *ahosi* [widow] is taken to the shores of the lagoon or creek or to the beach to see whether she has been seduced since the death of her husband. This is known as *zameyiyi*. As they reach the beach she steps into the water. It is said that she will be drowned if she has slept with any man, unless she confesses.[45]

Pure, sacred water stood in opposition to impure human acts.

---

[40] For a full transcription of this drum segment, see Rattray, *Ashanti*, 11.

[41] The Asante color spectrum, for example, encompassed three major colors: red (*kokoo*), black (*tuntum*), and white (*fufuo*). Red was associated with danger and hotness, and red fluids like blood and palm oil were central in rituals that rescinded misfortune, expelled ill–luck, and appeased angry spirits. Black symbolized darkness, gloom, and death. White was associated with coolness and purity. On color symbolism in Akan society, see Malcolm D. Mcleod, *Asante* (London, 1981), 173; and Paul S. Breidenbach, "Colour Symbolism and Ideology in a Ghanaian Healing Movement," *Africa* 46, 2 (1976): 137–45. On the importance of "coolness" in Akan society, see J. G. Platvoet, "Cool Shade, Peace and Power," *Journal of Religion in Africa* 15, 3 (1985): 174–99.

[42] On water's spiritual power, see Akyeampong, "Powerful Fluids."

[43] AFN: Interview with Nii Amarkai II, Asere Jaasetse, Bubuashie, August 31, 1994.

[44] Ibid.

[45] G. K. Nukunya, *Kinship and Marriage Among the Anlo Ewe* (London, 1969), 207.

Blood

In 1820, when another Englishman Joseph Dupuis visited the Kumase court, the Asantehene had experienced a recent palace coup engineered by the queen mother (Asantehemaa) and royal wives. The ubiquitous presence of blood—human blood sacrificed to the gods and ancestors, and the harnessing of menstrual blood—in Dupuis's account thrusts us into the symbolic realm of blood, the protracted struggles of gender politics, and the spiritual underpinnings of power.[46]

The context was Asante's war with the northern state of Gyaman in 1818–19. Adinkra, king of the vassal state of Gyaman, had made a golden stool for himself. As *the* golden stool was the symbol of Asante unity and the power of the Asantehene, Adinkra's act was seen as a direct challenge. Asante prepared for war, and the Asantehene made the necessary spiritual preparations to guarantee victory. Indigenous priests performed their various rituals. Although they sacrificed thirty–two male and eighteen female victims as an expiatory offering to the gods, the gods' response was still unfavorable. More human lives were sacrificed as an appeal to the royal ancestors to intercede on behalf of Asante. The gods relented. The priests prepared a special medicine for the Asantehene, and he was instructed to keep it burning in a consecrated fire pot during the entire period of the campaign. Victory depended on safely carrying out this assignment.

As the king planned to take the field himself, he entrusted this sacred ritual to the queen mother, Adoma Akosua. But in the king's absence, a conspiracy developed at the court to overthrow him. The chief architects were the Asantehemaa and seventeen of the king's wives. The main instrument was to destroy the sacred pot and doom the king to defeat and death on the battlefield. Asante troops now suffered a reverse in the field, and the king's divination revealed the cause. He sent a contingent home to suppress the rebellion. When the king returned to Kumasi, his council deliberated on the matter and sentenced the royal wives and other accomplices to death. The queen mother, Adoma Akosua, was exiled to the Nkwantanan ward of Kumasi, and her descendants barred from the offices of Asantehene and Asantehemaa in perpetuity.[47]

Events reached a climax.

While these butcheries were transacting, the king prepared to enter the palace, and in the act of crossing the threshold of the outer gate, was met by several of his wives, whose anxiety to embrace their sovereign lord impelled them thus to overstep the boundary of female decorum in Ashantee; for it happened that the king was accompanied by a number of his captains, who accordingly were compelled to cover their faces with both hands, and fly from the spot. This is said to have angered the monarch, although his resentment proceeded no farther than words, and he returned the embraces of his wives. But being afterwards told by some of the superintendents that these women were more or less indisposed from a natural female cause [menstruation], he was inflamed to the highest pitch of indignation, and in a paroxysm of anger caused these unhappy beings

[46] Joseph Dupuis, *Journal of a Residence in Ashantee*, 2nd ed. (London, 1966), 114–16.

[47] A biography of Adoma Akosua (ACPB/54) is provided in *Asantesem: The Asante Collective Bibliography Project Bulletin* 11 (1979): 14–17.

to be cut in pieces before his face; giving orders at the time to cast the fragments into the forest, to be devoured by birds and beasts of prey.[48]

The two types of blood featured in the account encapsulated different gender versions of power. The war against Kwadwo Adinkra of Gyaman was preceded by much spiritual preparation, as the king sacrificed human blood to the gods and ancestors to secure a favorable sign.[49] A distinction needs to be drawn between human sacrifices to the gods and human sacrifices to the ancestors. Blood was sacrificed to some gods because they were avaricious beings brought home from the bush by hunters or conjured down from the skies. These were known as *abosom brafo*—the *brafo* being the king's executioners—implying that these gods craved blood.[50] The ancestors did not crave blood: humans sacrificed to the ancestors were supposed to go and serve the ancestors in the spiritual world, a world believed to be an exact replica of the physical one.[51] Human sacrifices thus commonly took place at the funerals of the ruling aristocracy. Sacrificial victims were seldom selected at random, and most were prisoners of war or criminals who had been condemned to death by due process of the law but their execution postponed until occasions like royal funerals.[52] The king's actions in Dupuis' account expressed his supreme power as only he had the right to execute anyone in Asante.

The belief that authority was spiritually supported is evidenced in the fact that the 1818–19 coup mainly consisted of undoing the Asantehene's spiritual preparations—like breaking the fire pot—and utilizing unique forms of female power, such as menstrual blood. Biological reproduction was cherished in Asante society as people constituted wealth and status. Regulating childbirth was thus a potential weapon for women in gender politics, and the literature suggests the knowledge of abortive techniques in precolonial Ghana.[53] Menstrual blood was spiritually powerful because it was considered a fertility fluid.[54] But its presence combined the ambiguous message of reproductive capacity and failed fertilization, generating ambivalence among men. The image of menstrual flow became associated with draining power and filth, hence the numerous taboos circumscribing menstruating women in their contact with men and shrines. The 1818–19 palace coup presents just a page in the history of gender conflict in Asante, but the symbolic and spiritual power of blood is greatly visible in this clash.[55]

An important convergence in the history of southern Ghana, and for the culture of power, was that alcohol, water, and blood were also valued as spiritual

[48]   Dupuis, *Journal*, 116.

[49]   For some thoughts on human sacrifice in Asante, see Clifford Williams, "Asante: Human Sacrifice or Capital Punishment? An Assessment of the Period 1807–1874," *IJAHS* 21, 2 (1988): 433–41; and Ivor Wilks, "Asante: Human Sacrifice or Capital Punishment? A Rejoinder," *IJAHS* 21, 3 (1988): 443–52.

[50]   AFN: Interview with Kofi Akyerem, diviner and herbalist, Sekondi, August 16, 1994.

[51]   Arhin, "Rank and Class," 9; Bowdich, *Mission*, 262.

[52]   Rattray, *Religion and Art*, 106.

[53]   See, for example, Wolf Bleek, "Did the Akan Resort to Abortion in Pre–Colonial Ghana," *Africa*, 60, 1 (1990): 121–31.

[54]   On the anthropology of menstruation, see Thomas Buckley and Alma Gottlieb, eds., *Blood Magic: The Anthropology of Menstruation* (Berkeley, 1988); and Mary Douglas, *Purity and Danger: An Analysis of the Concepts of Pollution and Taboo* (London, 1966).

[55]   For a detailed study of these issues, see Akyeampong and Obeng, "Spirituality, Gender, and Power."

fluids in Christianity.[56] In the Christian sacrament of the communion, wine represents the blood of Christ in the rite enacted to remember his crucifixion. Wine (alcohol) and spiritual communion were thus linked. Water held a similar importance in indigenous religions in southern Ghana and in Christianity. It was used for purification and it embodied the Creator's spirit. In 1914, when Africans in the Ivory and Gold Coasts trooped to be baptized by the Liberian prophet, William Wade Harris, they could relate to this Christian ritual in a very African way. As Sheila Walker points out:

> In the traditional religious system water had been used for purifying baths and to prevent and cure illness and misfortunes. It was within this framework that the prophet's baptism was understood by his converts.[57]

The imagery of sacrifice is the cornerstone of Christian theology. Christ sacrificed his life, so that those who believed in him could have eternal life. His blood was the price of redemption. In indigenous religions and in Christianity, blood is a life–force.[58] These commonalities provided valuable bridges for African converts to Christianity, but it left intact the power of fluids.

To examine the history of alcohol within the context of these two other fluids has great merit for the cultural study of power. It has its frustrations also. It prevents a straight narrative revolving around alcohol. These fluids are like threads in the tapestry of power in southern Ghana. They emerge and submerge in the historical narrative of power, but that conforms to the historical reality. A distinction between power and authority emphasizes the complexity of power in southern Ghana, and its spiritual underpinning.

Power and Authority

Power is a historical product that manifests itself differently in time and place. Thus, the changing nature of power relations may reveal its wielders as individuals, classes, or institutions.[59] Definitions of power in social science highlight conflict and the ability of power holders to realize their will in spite of opposition from others.[60] Bertrand Russell's definition of power as "the production of intended

---

[56] See Samuel Z. Klausner, "Sacred and Profane Meanings of Blood and Alcohol," *Journal of Social Psychology* 64 (1964): 27–43.

[57] Sheila S. Walker, "The Message as the Medium: The Harrist Churches of the Ivory Coast and Ghana," in *African Christianity: Patterns of Religious Continuity*, ed. George Bond, Walton Johnson, and Sheila S. Walker (London and New York, 1979), 13. The prophet Ade Aina, of the Church of Aladura in Nigeria, wrote an exposition on the theology of water. He summed its healing qualities: "Water, the primeval element of Genesis 1:2, retains its primal purity, comes direct from heaven, and serves as the vehicle for the power of God to those who have faith in him alone." Harold W. Turner, *Religious Innovation in Africa: Collected Essays on New Religious Movements* (Boston, 1979), 229.

[58] The Musama Disco Christo Church in Ghana has wrestled with the indigenous and Christian meanings of blood in its religious practice. Kofi Asare Opoku, "Changes Within Christianity: The Case of the Musama Disco Christo Church," in *Christianity in Independent Africa*, ed. Edward Fashole–Luke *et al.* (Bloomington, 1978), 113.

[59] See the essays in Steven Lukes, ed., *Power* (New York, 1986).

[60] Max Weber defines power as "the probability that one actor within a social relationship will be in a position to carry out his will despite resistance, regardless of the basis on which this probability rests." S. N. Eisenstadt, ed., *Max Weber on Charisma and Institution Building* (Chicago, 1968), 15.

effects" subdues the necessity of coercion while emphasizing change as an important aspect of the exercise of power.[61] Indeed, social scientists examine the origins, distribution, and exercise of power partly in a search for the sources of social change:

> for the access points, the winning coalitions, the pivots, the levers, the bastions, the weak links . . . by means of which desired social changes may be brought about, or prevented.[62]

Although the perception of power as the locus of change in social relations is an important insight, the definitions of power in social science are limited because they assume that all protagonists in relations of power are human.

Michael Mann and Max Weber acknowledge the mobilizing power of religion. Mann argues that societies "are constituted of multiple overlapping and intersecting sociospatial networks of power."[63] He identifies four major sources of social power: ideology (often religion–based), economics, military, and politics. Mann asserts that in "various times and places each has offered enhanced capacity for organization that has enabled the form of its organization to dictate for a time the forms of society at large."[64] Weber has examined the role of protestantism in the emergence of capitalism, and the charismatic appeal of religious leaders in times of societal crises.[65] But the focus of both Mann and Weber is organized religion (that is the "human dimension"), and both view religion as just one of the sources of power, treating it as if it were secularly based.

The Akan, Ga–Adangme, and Ewe cosmos was permeated with power. Power is defined here as "the ability to produce change" (Twi: *tumi*). To gain a nuanced understanding of power in southern Ghana, it is necessary to distinguish between religion and spirituality, and between power and authority. The Akan, Ga–Adangme, and Ewe believe the Supreme Being created a universe impregnated with his power.[66] This universe contained numerous participants—spirits, humans, animals, and plants. Spirituality acknowledged the reality of a nonmaterial world, as the material world was seen as incapable of explaining the totality of human experience. It was a universe of experience in which some of the participants were invisible. Although some animals and plants had a potent life–force (Twi: *sasa*), it did not necessarily make them objects of worship (the realm of religion). Religion represented a distinct activity among the Akan, Ga–Adangme, and Ewe that revolved around beliefs, cultus, and ethics.

Since power was rooted in the cosmos, access to it was theoretically unlimited. What limited access to power in reality was knowledge. As Eugenia Herbert perceptively observed in her study of iron, gender, and power in African societies, "Power therefore involves an understanding of cosmology, the forces that effect

[61] Bertrand Russell, "The Forms of Power," in Lukes, *Power*, 19.

[62] Lukes, "Introduction," in Lukes, *Power*, 15.

[63] Michael Mann, *The Sources of Social Power. Volume 1: A History of Power from the Beginning to A.D. 1760* (Cambridge, 1986), 1.

[64] Ibid., 3.

[65] Max Weber, *The Protestant Ethic and the Spirit of Capitalism*, trans. Talcott Parsons (New York, 1958); and Eisenstadt, *Max Weber*.

[66] See, for examples, Kwame Gyekye, *An Essay on African Philosophical Thought: The Akan Conceptual Scheme* (New York, 1987), 75; and Madeline Manoukian, *The Ewe–Speaking of Togoland and the Gold Coast* (London, 1952), 50.

outcomes in the world, and with it a knowledge of how to influence them."[67] This
knowledge that could facilitate transformation in the spiritual or physical realm
was an acquired or an innate quality for some individuals. And alcohol, water, and
blood were central to the processes of transformation. The manifestation of power
spanned the range of aiding a barren woman to conceive through one's learned
knowledge of herbs to taking a rival's life through witchcraft, a power believed to
be often inherited. Some wielders of power went unnoticed for they chose to keep
their transformative powers secret.

In a universe suffused with different forms of power—beneficent and malefi-
cent—circumspection was required in the pursuit of life, health, and prosperity.
Unlike Christianity, indigenous religions in southern Ghana did not posit a battle
between the opposing forces of good and evil. As the Anlo elder, Togbuivi
Kumassah, emphasized: "It is worthwhile to stress here that the good and the evil
are just the two sides of the same coin."[68] Indeed, the most powerful gods were
also the most avaricious. Hence the Twi proverb: *obosom a oye nnam na odi aboade*
("the god that is sharp is the one that has offerings vowed to it"). Courting the
gods was crucial to a successful life, and in this respect knowledge was power.

It is authority, defined here as "the enforceable right to command others,"[69]
that became the preserve of those who controlled social institutions. The history of
societal power involved the attempts of authority holders to root their power effectively in the spiritual realm on one hand, and on the other a parallel struggle to co-
opt, subordinate, or neutralize other forms of power deemed useful or harmful to
the social order by those in authority. The interaction between the natural, social,
and supernatural worlds provided access to the sources of power as well as legitimacy for the exercise of political influence.[70]

Alcohol and Power Struggles in Ghana[71]

Alcohol has maintained its historical connections to power in southern Ghana for
more than three centuries. This feat is linked to alcohol's value as a cultural artifact, a ritual object, an economic good, and a social marker. Arjun Appadurai makes
a number of pertinent observations about commodities and the politics of value
that are relevant to understanding the politics of alcohol in the Gold Coast.[72] First,
that "*Politics* (in the broad sense of relations, assumptions, and contests pertaining
to power) is what links value and exchange in the social life of commodities."[73]

[67] Eugenia W. Herbert, *Iron, Gender, and Power: Rituals of Transformations in African Societies* (Bloomington, 1993), 2.
[68] Personal correspondence, May 12, 1995.
[69] Gerhard Lenski, "Power and Privilege," in Lukes, *Power*, 250.
[70] W. Arens and Ivan Karp, "Introduction," in *Creativity of Power: Cosmology and Action in African Societ-ies*, ed. W. Arens and Ivan Karp (Washington, D. C., 1989), xvii.
[71] This section draws more directly on the historiography on alcohol in sub–Saharan Africa for its conceptualization. A good bibliography is provided by Curto, "Alcohol in Africa."
[72] Arjun Appadurai, "Introduction: Commodities and the Politics of Value," in *The Social Life of Things: Commodities in Cultural Perspective*, ed. A. Appadurai (New York, 1986), 3–63.
[73] Ibid., 57. See also Eric Wolf, *Europe and the People Without History* (Berkeley, 1982), 85.

Second, that commodities have biographies or life histories, and these can be charted by examining the paths and diversions of these goods in exchange.[74] Third, that there is a "perennial and universal tug–of–war between the tendency of all economies to expand the jurisdiction of commoditization and of all cultures to restrict it."[75] This tension is most evident in the relations between political elites and merchants. A tendency in rural, precolonial Gold Coast, was for male elders to "de–commoditize" alcoholic drinks once they had been purchased from the exchange system. It was an uneasy resolution of alcohol's economic and ritual qualities. Fourth, and last, the "diversion of commodities from specified paths is always a sign of creativity or crisis, whether aesthetic or economic"—for example the emergence of *noveaux riches*.[76]

For chiefs and male elders in precolonial Akan, Ga–Adangme, and Ewe societies, who were the living representatives of the ancestors, their ritual use of palm wine in communication with the gods and ancestors reinforced their secular power. Male elders incorporated the ritual use of palm wine into all important social contracts and occasions—like rites of passage and community festivals. In these societies, where material differentiation had not become a significant avenue for maintaining social control, control over palm wine presented a badge that enhanced the social superiority and identity of male elders.[77] Male elders fastidiously excluded women and young men from using alcohol.[78] An indigenous ethic of temperance was forged by male elders to strengthen their monopoly over alcohol use and to codify their own temperate use of alcohol. For alcohol to contribute to the power of male elders, its sacred links had to be preserved through moderation in its use.

The male elders' monopoly over palm wine was facilitated by their control over land, the major means of subsistence and the source of palm wine. Control over land subordinated women and young men to the power of male elders. Gradually an ideology of wealth and power emerged, which stressed the conspicuous consumption of women and palm wine, and the amassing of followers and gold dust.[79] Challenges to the authority of chiefs and male elders from young men were often framed in the context of access to alcohol use. This was particularly so in the case of European liquor from the coastal trade, for such externally derived goods were visible mechanisms marking social differentiation—hence the reverence for *apo so nsa* (Twi: "overseas drink"). Social mobility for young men had come to be controlled by male elders, who at their convenience granted the young men parcels of land: the means of male elderdom, the economic ability to maintain wives, and the source of palm wine.

---

[74] Appadurai, "Commodities and the Politics," 17 and 21.

[75] Ibid., 17.

[76] Ibid., 26.

[77] See also Sangree, "Social Functions"; and Karp, "Beer Drinking."

[78] The "young men" were not necessarily youthful—even men in their thirties and forties fell within this amorphous category—and the term "young men" served more as a political classification for commoners of any age. On defining the "young men" (also referred to as *mmerante* or *nkwankwaa*), see Dennis Austin, *Politics in Ghana, 1946–1960* (London, 1964), 21–24; Jean Marie Allman, "The Youngmen and the Porcupine: Class, Nationalism and the Asante's Struggle for Self–Determination, 1954–57," *JAH* 31, 2 (1990): 263–79; and Richard Rathbone and Jean Marie Allman, "Discussion: The Youngmen and the Porcupine," *JAH* 32, 3 (1991): 333–38.

[79] See, for examples, McCaskie, *State and Society*; McCaskie, "Asante History 1."

A general expansion in coastal trading activities from the mid–nineteenth century, the development of railways and mines under colonial rule in the late nineteenth century, and the emergence of wage labor offered young men novel opportunities to circumvent the economic control of male elders. Migration to the coastal
towns, the foci of European economic activity, increased from the late nineteenth
century. But migration was conceived as a temporary expedient. The most desired
social goal was to return to the rural areas as an elder, a local "big man," once
financial gains had been secured in the city. At this early phase, migration was
mainly a male phenomenon, and it would not be until the 1920s and 1930s that
female migration became common. The few female migrants in the emerging towns
before 1920 often came from Liberia and Nigeria. Women were already present in
precolonial towns like Cape Coast, Accra, and Kumasi.

Town life was lonesome for these immigrant men, and the mental image of
rural social life, centered around the palm–wine bar, provided a model for young
rural migrants in their construction of social life. Drinking clubs were formed in
towns like Winnebah, and the number of rum shops increased from the late–nineteenth century. For male migrants, the ability to earn cash and their control over
these earnings was exhilarating. As one of the early highlife songs put it: *sika fata
merantee* (Twi: "money befits young men").[80] Young men expressed their new sense
of power and independence in a rather unrestrained consumption of European liquor—the fluid of the elders, that symbol of social ostentation. Women were also
active in accumulation in the early–twentieth century, and they increasingly as-
serted their autonomy over their sexuality, and the terms on which they associated
with men. Native court records from the late nineteenth century show evidence of
women contracting marriages and setting dowries without the support of male
kin.

Chiefs and male elders in the burgeoning coastal towns were alarmed at this
challenge from these young stranger–migrants. Youthful indigenes in coastal towns
like Sekondi did not dare touch liquor; and they even had to sneak away to consume palm wine.[81] But Western education, wage labor, and new lifestyles were even
altering that deference. Lynn Pan mentions unsuccessful attempts by coastal chiefs
in the Gold Coast to curtail excessive drinking in the early twentieth century.[82]

In the period before 1930, chiefs and elders sometimes collaborated actively
with the colonial government and European missionaries in their endeavor to curtail the access of young men to liquor. The small class of African intellectuals, many
of whom came from royal lineages, sided with the chiefs. But the importance of
liquor revenues for the colonial government made the colonial government an unreliable ally where the issue of prohibition was involved.[83] The government's con-

---

[80]   Kwame Boakye and his Band, "Sika fata merantee," Zonophone JVA 206. The author's use of highlife
songs from the colonial era owes much to the music collection at the National Sound Archives (NSA) in
Kensington (London). Several of these highlife songs were produced under the label of His Master's
Voice (HMV).

[81]   AFN: Interview with Opanin Kofi Twi, Opanin Kweku Mukuronka, and Opanin Nketsia, Sekondi,
May 26, 1992.

[82]   Lynn Pan, *Alcohol in Colonial Africa* (Uppsala, 1975), 72.

[83]   A large market for European liquor in Nigeria turned liquor revenues into a significant contributor to
colonial finances in that colony also. See A. Olorunfemi, "The Liquor Traffic in British West Africa: The

tinued efforts to balance the concerns of liquor revenue against social control transformed the formulation of liquor policy into a sphere for negotiating power between the colonial government on one hand and chiefs and educated Africans on the other. But prohibition was an option successive governors denied. The different interests of chiefs, African intellectuals, and missionaries notwithstanding, the temperance movement promised a better avenue for securing the political interests of chiefs and male elders.

Paradoxically, chiefs, who by virtue of their traditional political office had to use alcoholic drinks in rituals connected with their stools, often joined hands with Christian missionaries who were utilizing Victorian temperance strategies as part of their endeavor to convert Africans. It was an alliance of mutual benefit. The chiefs hoped to use the missionaries in their attempt to control troublesome young men, especially the increasing ranks of mission educated young men. The missionaries touted the "conversion" of chiefs as a lure to commoners who still feared the wrath of local chiefs if they converted to Christianity. Temperance held multiple meanings for members of the temperance movement, just as multiple meanings were attached to drink.[84]

Between 1928 and 1930, the temperance alliance succeeded in securing restrictive liquor laws, including the gradual proscription of schnapps, gin, and rum—the only drinks urban laborers could afford. The pre–World War II era had witnessed the emergence of a vibrant popular culture among urban dwellers.[85] This culture encompassed bars, dances, highlife music, film, and comic opera,[86] with social drinking as an important prop to leisure activities. The liquor laws between 1928 and 1930 threatened the existence of this popular culture as it put imported liquor beyond the income of commoners. *Akpeteshie* (illicit gin) distillation prolifer-

Southern Nigerian Example, 1896–1918," *IJAHS* 17, 2 (1984): 220–42; and Ayodeji Olukoju, "Prohibition and Paternalism: The State and the Clandestine Liquor Traffic in Northern Nigeria, c.1889–1918," *IJAHS* 24, 2 (1991): 349–68. West Africa had no significant European settler population, thus colonial liquor policy was not dominated by the concerns of race and class apparent in east and southern Africa. See Charles Ambler, "Drunks, Brewers and Chiefs: Alcohol Regulation in Colonial Kenya, 1900–1939," in *Drinking: Behavior and Belief in Modern History*, ed. Susanna Barrows and Robin Room (Berkeley, 1991), 165–83; Charles van Onselen, "Randlords and Rotgut, 1886–1903," *History Workshop* 2 (1976): 32–89; and Paul La Hausse, *Brewers, Beerhalls and Boycotts: A History of Liquor in South Africa* (Johannesburg, 1988).

[84] Several studies highlight the different, and sometimes conflicting, interests of temperance advocates. See, for examples, James Annorbah Sarpei, "A Note on Coastal Elite Contact with Rural Discontent Before the First World War: The 'Good Templars' in Akyem Abuakwa," in Communications from the Basel African Society, *Akyem Abuakwa and the Politics of the Inter–War Period in Ghana* (Basel, 1975); Wallace G. Mills, "The Roots of African Nationalism in the Cape Colony· Temperance, 1866–1898," *IJAHS* 13, 2 (1980): 197–213; Brian Harrison, *Drink and the Victorians: The Temperance Question in England, 1815–1872* (Pittsburgh, 1971); and Joseph R. Gusfield, *Symbolic Crusade: Status Politics and the American Temperance Movement* (Urbana, 1972).

[85] Urban populations expanded as the rapid growth of the indigenous cocoa industry, characterized by extensive land purchases by migrant farmers from the 1900s, put undue pressure on land and compelled more rural young men to migrate into the towns. The depression of the 1930s, which made urban jobs scarce and labor abundant, further promoted proletarianization as migrants faced great difficulty in meeting their economic goals. Migrants extended their residence in towns, and many went home to marry or had relatives marry for them and send the wives to join them in the towns.

[86] Drama troupes staged plays or "concerts" that theatricalized urban life. These plays were punctuated by music, with the actors as singers; the lyrics underscored the themes in the play. This genre has been dubbed "comic opera" by scholars, but ordinary Ghanaians prefer the term "concert."

ated to meet the large demand for cheap liquor. *Akpeteshie* became associated with popular culture, class formation, and social protest. *Akpeteshie* had an adverse effect on the government's revenue from liquor imports, but colonial attempts to stamp it out proved ineffective. The drink rather became associated with protest against the colonial state, paving the way for its symbolic role in nationalist politics after World War II.

World War II and the expectations it raised among Ghanaians encouraged virulent African nationalism when the cessation of the war brought no substantial socioeconomic benefits to those who had sacrificed for the war effort. Political parties were formed to champion the cause of Gold Coast nationalism, and by the close of the 1940s, two rival parties had emerged: the United Gold Coast Convention (UGCC), and the Convention People's Party (CPP). The Gold Coast Constitution of 1951 introduced universal adult suffrage and endorsed mass politics. Overnight, popular culture gained saliency as a means of gauging and shaping popular opinion.

The general elections between 1951 and 1956 gave political value to urban drinking bars: they became institutions for mobilizing popular support. Legalizing *akpeteshie* became an emotional political issue as it was associated with African grievances under colonial rule. Supporting popular culture endeared a political party to the masses; this was the era of "political dances" and "political concerts." Highlife songs were composed for parties and politicians. Popular culture had become respectable, and all parties irrespective of ideology patronized it. But old ways of tapping power continued to inform the nationalist struggle. As Jean Allman points out, the National Liberation Movement (NLM), in particular, highlighted the pouring of libations, sacrifices of sheep, and auspicious sacred sites—its inauguration was beside the sacred river Subin—in its campaign strategies. The party of "young men," the CPP, was not to be outdone. Political dances and the new popularity of cocktails accompanied libations, blood sacrifices, and rituals at the seaside. The CPP's domination of the elections of the 1950s was definitely aided by its image as the common person's party, and it ushered in the independent country of Ghana in 1957.[87]

Popular expectations were high with the onset of independence as Ghanaians looked forward to political democracy, economic prosperity and social progress. The move to legalize *akpeteshie* confirmed the CPP's image as the commoner's party. But disappointment soon set in, as a decline in the world price of the country's major export, cocoa, wiped out government funding for its planned development projects. Political power also induced aloofness on the part of CPP leadership, and rumors of extreme corruption seemed to be substantiated by the ostentatious lifestyles of some party leaders. A growing distance separated party elite from the party rank–and–file. Political dissent invited draconian measures of repression from the CPP government in its determination to exterminate opposition. The Trades

---

[87] Allman, "The Youngmen and the Porcupine." For studies on the political relevance of drinking bars and drink in nationalist politics in Africa, see Charles Ambler, "Alcohol, Racial Segregation and Popular Politics in Northern Rhodesia," *JAH* 31, 2 (1990): 295–313; and Michael O. West, "'Equal Rights for All Civilized Men': Elite Africans and the Quest for 'European' Liquor in Colonial Zimbabwe, 1924–1961," *International Review of Social History* 37, 3 (1992): 376–97.

Union Congress was effectively subordinated to the CPP in 1958, and channels for expressing grievances were closed to the urban workers.[88] A one–party state was declared in 1964.

The cohesion of classes and social inequity in independent Ghana was manifested in new drinking patterns. The new political elite and their affiliates patronized plush hotels and nightclubs, while urban and rural workers settled for their palm wine and *akpeteshie* bars. As Johnny Walker and Haig whiskies signified the superior status of the new political elite, and lager beer the comfortable position of the middle class, *akpeteshie* became the symbol of working-class poverty and discontent. Rapid change in governments between 1966 and 1981 and acute economic decline undermined the lot of workers. Medical doctors began to highlight evidence of the rising incidence of alcoholism.[89]

As disillusioned workers sought escape in drink, alcoholism came to play a paradoxical role in redefining social identity. For many poor workers, alcohol's links to spiritual power and conceptions of alcoholism as a spiritual illness exempted them from individual blame if they fell victim to drink. Men who faced difficulties supporting their families or other socioeconomic disabilities sometimes drifted into chronic drinking, redefining their social status from being "healthy" and socially irresponsible to being "unwell" and socially incapable. Since ordinary Ghanaians do not perceive alcoholism as a disease, it is unproblematic for "alcoholics" to effect remarkable cures once they acquire jobs or are able to resume their social responsibilities. Even alcoholism could not be disassociated from the quest for control and autonomy.

Conclusion

Alcohol and power are closely linked in Ghanaian history. Alcohol has been an indispensable fluid that opened doors socially and spiritually. Alcohol's connections to power have been maintained in spite of the increasing influence of Christianity. In fact, the three powerful fluids examined in this book—alcohol, water, and blood—were tied to spiritual power in Christian theology. In contemporary Ghana, to be able to afford expensive drinks is an expression of wealth and power. Not even the morally upright lead character in Ayi Kwei Armah's *The Beautyful Ones are Not Yet Born* could resist the thrill of wealth and power that suffuses the buyer of expensive drinks.[90] Yet he knew he could not afford it on his paltry wages. Alcohol's ritual use today also emphasizes spiritual connectedness. While libation is still central in rites of passage, it now also informs state protocol, especially in the conception of a pan–African family. Three incidents portrayed on Ghana television in early 1992 dramatized this latter use of alcohol. On January 27, the national football team, the Black Stars, returned home from an outstanding performance in

---

[88] See Rolf Gerritsen, "The Evolution of the Ghana Trades Union Congress under the Convention Peoples Party: Towards a Reinterpretation," *Transactions of the Historical Society of Ghana* [hereafter THSG] 13, 2 (1972): 229–44.

[89] Swaniker, "Beer—The National Drink"; and Adomako, "Alcoholism: The African Scene."

[90] Ayi Kwei Armah, *The Beautyful Ones Are Not Yet Born* (London, 1969), 114–15.

the African Cup Finals. The State *okyeame* (spokesperson), Akuffo, poured libation with the usual J. H. Henkes schnapps at the airport to welcome them. On January 31, the Ghana government sent a delegation to Zimbabwe to present the customary drinks to the bereaved President Mugabe. His late wife, Sally Mugabe, was a Ghanaian. And on February 3, a representative of the Ga *Mantse* was at hand to pour the welcoming libation for President Sam Nujoma of Namibia. Alcohol remains firmly embedded in spiritual and temporal power. Its early use in ritual is examined in the next chapter.

2

Alcohol, Ritual, and Power among the Akan, Ga–Adangme, and Ewe in Precolonial Southern Gold Coast

Ade'a ye de nsa ye no, yemmfa nsuo nye.

What *nsa* is used for, water cannot be a substitute[1]

Twi proverb

Among the peoples of the southern Gold Coast, alcoholic drinks were treasured fluids for they bridged the gap between the physical and spiritual worlds. And a harmonious balance between the two worlds was crucial to human existence and prosperity. Through libation, alcohol permeated religious ritual, and its use was carefully monitored by elders. Religious ritual represented a major site for the reproduction of relations of power, and for the subordination of women and young men. A major obstacle in the elders' control of alcohol was that liquor was an important trade item for Europeans. The value of alcohol as an economic good and a social marker threatened its more sacred functions. An indigenous temperance ethic emerged to protect alcohol's sacredness from abuse. Alcohol's use was restricted to social units and lineage heads. But the transformative powers of commerce and (mission) education proved powerful. From the nineteenth century, commercialism and individualism seemed to penetrate every aspect of social life, including ritual. These processes would become more prominent in the colonial and postcolonial periods.

---

[1] *Nsa* originally referred to palm wine in Twi, but its meaning has been extended to all types of alcoholic drinks. "Alcohol" will be used throughout the book to refer to all alcoholic drinks, except where the context demands specification.

The Historical Setting

Between c.1500 and c.1800 most of the peoples of the southern Gold Coast were migrating into the geographical niches they occupy today.[2] By 1500 the Akan matriclans had begun migrating in spiral waves away from their cradle between the Pra and Ofin river basin (the Adansie–Amansie district of present day Ashanti region). The Akan migrations accelerated in the seventeenth and eighteenth centuries due to incessant warfare generated by state formation and competition over the northern Mande–Hausa trade and the coastal European trade.[3] The Akan would eventually settle along the western coastline and in the interior forest region of modern Ghana (and the Ivory Coast). Ga–Adangme oral traditions trace their origins to the "east," perhaps from the present Republic of Benin or Nigeria. By the fifteenth century, they had settled around the Lolovor hills in the Accra plains, just behind the eastern coastline. From 1500 the Ga moved to settle along the coastline around Accra, and the Adangme moved to the east and north of the Ga. Ewe oral traditions point to Ketu in modern Benin as their ancestral home. Ewe traditions mention the Ga–Adangme as neighbors in Ketu.[4] Sometime in the fourteenth century, the Ewe began their westward migration from Ketu, and they subsequently established themselves in Notsie (Togo) by the early sixteenth century. By the mid–seventeenth century, some Ewe had begun migrating from Notsie to their homes in the Gold Coast.

Although the cosmologies of the Akan, Ga–Adangme, and Ewe were not identical, they shared important similarities. They all believed in a Supreme Being (Akan: *Onyame*; Ga: *Nyonmo*; Ewe: *Mawu*), lesser deities created by the Supreme Being (Akan: *abosom*; Ga: *wodzi*; Ewe: *trowo*), and a cult of ancestors (Akan: *nsamanfo*; Ga: *blemabii* ; Ewe: *togbewo*). There was also the common belief in the existence of mystical forces in the universe that could be tapped by humans with knowledge (magic, sorcery, witchcraft). More importantly, for our purposes, the Akan, Ga–Adangme, and Ewe shared a belief in the spiritual potency of water, blood, and alcohol. Their uses of these fluids varied in some respects due to different ecologies, unique migrational experiences, modes of livelihood, and specific political histories.

Again, though the social organization of the matrilineal (descent) and virilocal (marriage) Akan, the patrilineal and virilocal Ewe, and the patrilineal and bilocal Ga differed, common historical developments in which war–gods eclipsed nature gods, and chiefs displaced priests are discernible in the eighteenth and nineteenth centuries. Key to these developments was the social upheaval generated by Akan state formation from the sixteenth century, a period made more insecure by the Atlantic slave trade and large imports of firearms from c.1650.[5] Between c.1650 and

---

[2]   See Ivor Wilks, "The Mossi and Akan States 1500–1800," in *History of West Africa* 1, ed. J. F. Ade Ajayi and Michael Crowder (London, 1976), 413–55; and A. A. Boahen, "The State and Cultures of the Lower Guinean Coast," in *General History of Africa* 5, ed. B. A. Ogot (Berkeley, 1992), 399–433.

[3]   See the special issue on the Akan of Ghana in *Ghana Notes and Queries* 9 (1966); Kea, *Settlements, Trade and Polities*; and Wilks, *Forests of Gold*, Chs. 1–3.

[4]   D. E. K. Amenumey, *The Ewe in Pre–Colonial Times* (Accra, 1986), 2.

[5]   See Walter Rodney, "Gold and Slaves on the Gold Coast," *THSG* 10 (1969): 13–28; and S. Tenkorang, "The Importance of Firearms in the Struggle Between Ashanti and the Coastal States," *THSG* 9 (1968): 1–16. For a rather vivid portrayal of the intense insecurity generated in the southern Gold Coast by the slave trade, see Brodie Cruickshank, *Eighteen Years on the Gold Coast of Africa* 1 (London, 1853), Ch. 12.

c.1750, three Akan states quickly rose to prominence in the southern Gold Coast:
Denkyira, Akwamu, and Asante. Asante's power endured from c.1701 to 1874, and
Asante's conquests by 1811 exceeded the size of modern Ghana.[6] The success of
Akan military organization promoted among the Ga–Adangme and the Ewe a per-
ception of chieftaincy as a "war–medicine," and *abosom–brafo* (Akan gods that of-
ten originated as "hunting–medicines") as "war–gods."[7]

These historical developments were crucial to the changing uses of alcohol,
blood, and water. Warfare, chieftaincy, and state formation were connected, and
their spiritual dimension emphasized blood offerings and the ritual use of alcohol.
Chieftaincy, government headed by a ruler elected from a specific "royal" lineage,
superseded gerontocracy—the general rule of male elders. But warfare privileged
masculine strength, and young men and commoners in *asafo* (military organizations) became a force to reckon with.[8] As instruments of war, *asafo* companies acquired their specific "war–medicines" and their own religious shrines, which required rituals involving the use of alcohol.[9] Moreover, liquor was an important
logistic of war and a valued social lubricant in *asafo* social activities, which featured prominently music, dance, and sports. Chieftaincy and *asafo* organization,
both part and parcel of the baggage of warfare, had given new institutional form
to the age–old generational struggle—as the following chapters will reveal. Significant to this conflict was the fact that among the Akan, succession and inheritance
were matrilineal while *asafo* organization was based on patriliny.[10] But inter–*asafo*
conflict also existed, and can be dated among the coastal states to at least the mid-
seventeenth century.[11]

State formation and the ascendancy of war–gods and war *asuman* (protective
talismans) elevated masculine strength. Even among the less bellicose Krobo, women
acknowledged that "God has endowed man with excellence. If a war breaks out,
the men are summoned to battle, but a woman is not called."[12] But male ascendancy heightened the strong ambivalence in gender relations concerning menstrual
blood. What should be the relationship of women to new sources of power, such as
the shrine of a war–god? It is important to remember, in the transforming gender
relations, that women, as biological reproducers, represented another important
source of wealth and power for men. Among the Akan, blood (*mogya*) encapsulated concepts of matriliny (*abusua*), inheritance, and succession. What would hap-

[6]   For excellent studies on precolonial Asante, see Ivor Wilks, *Asante in the Nineteenth Century* (Cambridge, 1975); Larry Yarak, *Asante and the Dutch, 1744–1873* (Oxford, 1990); McCaskie, *State and Society.*

[7]   See Louis E. Wilson, *The Krobo People of Ghana to 1892: A Political and Social History* (Athens, 1991),
especially Ch. 4; Margaret J. Field, *Religion and Medicine of the Ga People* (London, 1937), 3 and 88; Margaret J. Field, *Social Organization of the Ga People* (London, 1940), 71–80; Amenumey, *Ewe in Pre–Colonial
Times*, 34–5; and D. J. E. Maier, *Priests and Power: The Case of the Dente Shrine in Nineteenth Century Ghana*
(Bloomington, 1983).

[8]   On the *asafo* institution, see Ansu Datta, "The Fante Asafo: A Re–examination," *Africa* 42, 4 (1972):
305–15; and I. Chukwukere, "Perspectives on the *Asafo* Institution in Southern Ghana," *Journal of African
Studies* 7, 1 (1980): 39–47.

[9]   See C. C. Reindorf, *History of the Gold Coast and Asante* (Basel, 1895), 122–24.

[10]   Chukwukere, "Perspectives on the *Asafo*."

[11]   Datta, "Fante Asafo," 310–13.

[12]   Hugo Huber, *The Krobo: Traditional Social and Religious Life of a West African People* (St. Augustin, 1963),
111–12.

An *asafo* shrine in Anomabo

pen if one form of power, a menstruating woman, came into contact with another form of power, the shrine of a war god? To forestall potential cosmological disequilibrium, taboos prevented menstruating women from coming into contact with the new sources of male power.[13]

But just as the complementarity of male and female was vital to a community's survival, so was power conceived as both male and female. Even in Asante, a federation that came into being as a military union, women could not be excluded from the business of war. If *Onyame* had granted women the capacity to bear life, the same gift made them the best defenders of life. And this was probably the origins of *mmomomme*, that distinctly female form of spiritual warfare.[14] When Asante troops were at war, Asante women in the villages would perform daily ritual chants until the troops returned, processing in partial nudity from one end of the village to the other. This ritual protected the soldiers at war, and sometimes involved women pounding empty mortars with pestles as a form of spiritual torture of Asante's enemies.[15] And when the Asante troops returned home victorious with their prisoners–of–war, Asante women had the singular privilege of "greeting" these prisoners—in actuality, taunting the vanquished.[16]

---

[13] See Akyeampong and Obeng, "Spirituality, Gender."

[14] Adam Jones, "'My Arse for Akou': A Wartime Ritual of Women on the Nineteenth–Century Gold Coast," *Cahiers d'Etudes Africaines* 132, 33–4 (1993): 545–66; A. B. Ellis, *The Tshi–Speaking Peoples of the Gold Coast of West Africa* (Oosterhout, 1887), 226–27; Ernest E. Obeng, *Ancient Ashanti Chieftaincy* (Tema, 1986), 20; and McLeod, *Asante*, 28.

[15] AFN: Interview with Albert Mawere Poku, Accra, August 6, 1994.

[16] See, for examples, Ramseyer and Kühne, *Four Years In Ashantee*, 52–54.

However, state formation and extensive trading engendered social hierarchies—chiefs, military aristocracies, *asikafo* (the wealthy), commoners, slaves—and encouraged elite lifestyles that demarcated social hierarchy. Where distinctions of wealth and power exhibited themselves in the southern Gold Coast, alcoholic drinks, particularly imported types, served as social markers. Raymond Dumett commented on Akan and Ga–Adangme societies between 1875 and 1910 that:

> In Ghana, drinking by young men, even those in their twenties, was frowned upon by the elders in Akan and Ga–Adangbe society; and since public bars had not yet come into existence, there was less opportunity than today for young men to join their confreres in group drinking.[17]

Dumett further pointed out that in Akan traditional society it was not considered proper for women to drink. Access to alcohol became a badge that marked the superior status of influential male elders. Even in the less centralized Ga society, women drank very little, for alcohol was linked to power and power was "thought of as a male prerogative."[18]

As alcoholic drinks become cultural markers of personal identity and cultural markers of inclusion and exclusion, they gain a social life of their own.[19] To flesh out the social life of alcohol, to understand the meanings the Gold Coast/ Ghanaian protagonists attached to alcohol in their struggles over power, and to be able to assess continuity and change in the uses of alcohol and the meanings attached to these uses, it is pertinent that we capture the symbolic significance of alcohol in the contexts within which people were familiar, that they took for granted.

Oral traditions about the origins of palm wine are instructive in this sense. They seek to reenact and sustain beliefs about the cosmos and the proper ritual and social uses of alcohol. The ritual and social uses of alcohol in the "traditional" context are best captured in the celebration of rites of passage and festivals. The availability of scattered information on alcohol use from Pieter de Marees (1602), Jean Barbot (1678–1712), W. Bosman (1705), T. Bowdich (1819), J. Dupuis (1824), T. B. Freeman (1844), B. Cruickshank (1853), F. A. Ramseyer and J. Kühne (1875), A. B. Ellis (1887), C. C. Reindorf (1895), J. Mensah Sarbah (1897); and the more detailed, twentieth–century ethnographic studies of R. S. Rattray (Asante), M. J. Field (Ga–Adangme), Hugo Huber (Krobo–Adangme), and G. K. Nukunya (Anlo–Ewe), enable us to chart historical change in the uses of alcohol.

Oral Traditions on the Origins of Palm Wine

The origin of the use of palm wine in the Gold Coast is shrouded in myth and mystery, but an examination of these myths sheds light on the perception of alcohol as the locus of sacred power and early concerns about the potential profaning

---

[17] Dumett, "European Liquor Trade," 79–80.

[18] M. E. Kropp Dakubu, "Creating Unity: The Context of Speaking Prose and Poetry in Ga," *Anthropos* 82 (1987): 519.

[19] For this dynamic cultural construction of meanings, see Mary Douglas and Baron Isherwood, *The World of Goods* (New York, 1981); and Appadurai, *Social Life of Things*.

of this fluid through substantive abuse. Reindorf recorded two oral traditions on the origin of palm wine.

> When the Fantes were on their way from Takiman to the coast, their king had a celebrated hunter called Ansa, who used to go hunting for him. . . . Ansa had a dog which accompanied him in hunting and scouting excursions.
>   It happened that in one of his hunting excursions, he found a palm–tree which had been thrown down by an elephant, and a hole made in the trunk of the tree by his foot. It seems that the sagacious animal had long known the secret of tapping the palm–tree, and had long enjoyed the delicious though intoxicating sap that it yielded. The hunter, perceiving some sap oozing freely from the orifice made by the elephant, was half inclined to taste, but fearing it might be poisonous gave some to his dog, who seemed to relish it greatly. Finding that his dog took a liking to this new liquor, he in the morning drank so freely of the sap of the palm–tree, that he got fairly intoxicated.[20]

Ansa soon found the best way of tapping the tree and took a pot to the king. The king liked the taste so much that he overindulged, got drunk, and fell into a deep sleep. The king's people, failing to arouse him, concluded that he had been poisoned by Ansa. Ansa was apprehended and beheaded; and "[e]ver since, the sap of the palm tree received the name of Ansa which is corrupted [in]to *nsa*."[21]

Reindorf records another tradition of the origin of palm wine. Wirempong Ampong, a hunter of chief Akoro Firampong of Abadwirem, with his dog discovered split palm trees thrown on the ground. Again the juice was offered to the dog first and the liquid found to be harmless. The hunter gave some of the palm wine to chief Firampong, who in turn initiated his friend Anti Kyei of Akrokyere into drinking palm wine. Anti Kyei overimbibed and died as a consequence. To prevent bloodshed, as a result of the desire of Anti Kyei's friends to take revenge, Firampong committed suicide.[22]

Mythical explanations of the origin of indigenous alcohol, as Luc de Heusch has illustrated in his Central African study,[23] can, sometimes, shed light on a people's worldview. The Akan myths may implicitly shed light on how palm wine, and later European liquor, came to occupy such central roles in the religious life of Akans and other ethnic groups of the southern Gold Coast. The early Akan users of palm wine were baffled by its intoxicating quality. In two of the myths on the origin of palm wine, the king and the high priest fell into drunken sleep assumed to be death. Their recovery amazed their followers: almost "a return from the dead."

Alcohol, in the Akan context, was often used in rituals involving the ancestors—for example, when new members were added to the family or when ancestral lands were leased. It is possible that in alcohol's intoxicating quality, enacted

---

[20] Reindorf, *Gold Coast and Asante*, 265–66. Ellis, *Tshi–Speaking Peoples*, 337–38, records the same tradition. See also, John Mensah Sarbah, *Fanti National Constitution*, 3rd ed. (London, 1968), 52–53.

[21] Reindorf, *Gold Coast and Asante*, 266.

[22] Ibid., 266–67. The author collected some oral traditions on the origins of palm wine, and they were very similar in structure to the ones transcribed by Reindorf, Sarbah, and Ellis. AFN: Interview with the Management Committee of the Western Region Distillers Cooperative, Takoradi, August 16, 1994.

[23] Luc de Heusch, *The Drunken King or the Origin of the State* trans. and annot. by Roy Willis (Bloomington, 1982).

in the myths on palm wine in an almost miraculous "return from the dead," lay its choice as a medium of communication between the living and the dead. In response to the author's query about the use of alcoholic drinks in libation, Nana Kobina Nketsia IV remarked: "*Nsa* is a definite link between man and his ancestor because it is spiritual. The ancestors are spiritual, and this [*nsa*] is a spirit."[24] The "spirit" in alcohol was its intoxicating ability. It is worth noting that in the articulation of male power, male elders were seen as the appropriate persons to handle hard liquor (spiritually potent) and that drinks with a low alcohol content (low spiritual power) were referred to as *mmaa nsa* ("women's drink").[25]

That palm wine was discovered by a hunter underscored its spiritual connection. Within Akan society, hunters, in their intimacy with nature, were seen as maintaining close connections with the supernatural world.[26] An early desire to guard palm wine against abuse is discernible in the myths. In both Reindorf's first tradition and Sarbah's version, the king and the high priest, respectively, overimbibed and fell into drunken sleep. In both versions, it is not mentioned if the king or the high priest drank with anybody, so it may be safely concluded that they drank alone. Also, in all the traditions of the origin of palm wine, tragedy (death) resulted. Ansa, the hunter, was beheaded in Reindorf's first tradition; Etum Eduansa was beheaded, and his father died of grief in Sarbah's version. In Reindorf's second tradition, Anti Kyei died of overindulgence, and Firampong committed suicide to prevent bloodshed. Akans frowned on solitary drinking. It was seen as a sign of a troubled person. Communal drinking was the norm, and solitary drinking was perceived as an antisocial act.[27] In the several Akan traditions about the origin of palm wine, excessive solitary drinking resulted in tragedy. The emphasis on tragedy in the Akan traditions was reflected in a real–life ambivalence towards alcohol. Although alcohol was central to all important ceremonies like rites of passage and festivals, its use was always public and communal and was circumscribed by rules and regulations.

It is impossible to pinpoint when the ritual use of alcohol commenced among the Akan, Ga–Adangme, and Ewe. Raymond Dumett points out that by the seventeenth century, rum (Twi: *aworonte*) had been incorporated into ritual in the southern Gold Coast societies, indicating a much earlier ritual use of palm wine.[28] Although the myths of the origin of palm wine among the Fante are woven into Fante migration myths, it is striking that written transcriptions of these myths were first compiled by Reindorf, Ellis, and Sarbah in the late–nineteenth–century period. This was a period characterized by social tensions between elders and commoners, and by the rise of individualism among the coastal Fante due to success in commerce. In the contest over alcohol use that accompanied power struggles, it is

---

[24] AFN: Interview with Nana Kobina Nketsia IV (Paramount Chief of English Sekondi), Essikadu, March 6, 1992. Among the Ewe the name given to a child, seen as a "reincarnated ancestor," was referred to as its "drink–name." Manoukian, *Ewe–Speaking People*, 42.

[25] De Marees, *Gold Kingdom of Guinea*, 79.

[26] K. A. Busia, "Ashanti," in *African Worlds*, ed. Daryll Forde (London, 1954), 196.

[27] Dumett, "European Liquor Trade," emphasizes communal drinking among the Akan between 1875 and 1910. De Heusch reached a similar observation in his analysis of Lunda and Kuba mythology on the origin of palm wine, *Drunken King*, 178–79.

[28] Dumett, "European Liquor Trade," 81.

possible that tragic consequences of individual/substantive use of alcohol were incorporated into the migration myths by male elders to give antiquity and legitimacy to sanctions over alcohol abuse. It is not unusual for myths of migration to be elaborated to take account of new historical developments.[29]

Two important observations need to be made on the assimilation of imported European rum, and later gin and schnapps, into the religio–cultural framework of the southern Gold Coast societies. First, elderly Asante informants highlighted the relevance of rum in offerings to the gods. *Obaa panin* (female head of *abusua*) Afua Pokuaa of Amoaman emphasized that the gods liked the golden color of "Bucaneer Rum," a color she described as *kokoo* (red).[30] Afua Pokuaa's family holds custodianship of an Asante war–god, *Abotirimu*, and the preference of *abosom brafo* (war-gods) for rum—"reddish" in color—is noteworthy. As McCaskie points out, the color of "redness" for the Asante "embraced that part of the spectrum ranging from red itself, through purple and orange, to violet and pink."[31] The connection between war–gods, blood, and rum was explicitly expressed by one of Huber's Krobo informants:

> In ancient time . . . if a warrior brought home an enemy's head, he was given rum, mixed with some drops of the enemy's blood, to drink. This, they say, not only protected him against the avenging ghost of the beheaded, but also made him braver.[32]

Warfare and the ascendancy of war–gods became more pronounced in the Gold Coast from the seventeenth century. Dumett's observation that rum had been incorporated into ritual in the southern Gold Coast by the seventeenth century is significant in this light. *Abosom* such as Kubi, Tano, and Apomesu preferred rum. In the absence of rum, brandy could be used for some of the gods for it "has the scent and color the *abosom* like."[33] In contrast to *abosom brafo*, gods associated with water were seen as pure. Some detested blood and alcohol. To aid humans, such gods demanded purity, a difficult requirement.[34] In the Guan town of Larteh, it was believed that the god *Brofo*, associated with rainfall and good harvests, "does not like to be contaminated by blood," and thus took no part in revenge or death.[35] Second, the quality common to palm wine, gin, and schnapps is their colorlessness ("white"), and in association with the perceived ritual power of white objects— white eggs, white fowls, and white calico—it is argued here that the quality of colorlessness helps to explain the ritual significance that people attributed to palm wine, gin, and schnapps.[36]

[29] See, for example, Janet M. Chernela, "Rethinking History in the Northwest Amazon: Myth, Narrative, Structure, and History in an Arapaco Narrative," in *Rethinking History and Myth: Indigenous South American Perspectives on the Past*, ed. Jonathan D. Hill (Chicago, 1989), 35–49.
[30] AFN: Interview with Afua Pokuaa, August 18, 1994.
[31] McCaskie, *State and Society in Pre–Colonial Asante*, 203.
[32] Huber, *Krobo*, 268.
[33] AFN: Interview with Afua Pokuaa, August 18, 1994.
[34] AFN: Interview with Kofi Akyerem, healer, Sekondi, August 16, 1994.
[35] David Brokensha, *Social Change at Larteh, Ghana* (Oxford, 1966), 160.
[36] On the symbolism of color in the sacred realm, see, Breidenbach, "Colour Symbolism and Ideology."

These drinks shared the quality of colorlessness with water, and evidence suggests an earlier ritual prominence of water over alcohol. This may have coincided with the migratory phase, when concerns about secure water supply and adjusting to different ecological environments were uppermost. These concerns prioritized the worship of nature gods. The Akan example is a good case in point. The spiritual power of water and its ties to the sacred realm are borne out by the Akan conception of the Supreme Being and access to him; the close links between the lesser gods (*abosom*) and bodies of water; and the association of the patrilineal "spirit groups" (*ntoro*) with streams, rivers, lakes, or the sea.

The Akan Supreme Being was seen as the Eternal One (*Odomankoma*) and the Creator of all things (*Bore–bore*). In the Akan conception of man, man is made of three elements: blood (*mogya*) from the mother; spirit–personality (*ntoro*) from the father; and soul (*kra*) from the Supreme Being. The *kra* represented the life-force in man, "the small bit of the Creator that lives in every person's body."[37] The presence of the *kra* made knowledge of the Supreme Being innate in man, a belief endorsed in Twi proverbs like: *obi nkyere abofra Onyame* ("no one shows a child the Supreme Being") and *wo pese wo kasa kyere Onyame, kasa kyere mframma* ("if you want to speak to the Supreme Being, speak to the wind"). The Supreme Being was omnipresent, and everyone had direct access to him, a fact expressed in an Asante proverb: *obi kwan nsi obi kwan mu* ("no man's path crosses another's"). Water was used in pouring libations to the Supreme Being, and the availability of water to all underscored man's equal access to the Supreme Being.[38]

The sacred use of water as a channel to the supernatural was further strengthened by the association of the major gods with bodies of water.

> Of these deities, the most powerful are those that are the spirits of rivers. An Ashanti myth has it that all the rivers, the Tano, the Bea, the Bosomtwe Lake near Kumasi, and the mighty sea, were children of the Supreme Being.[39]

The Asante regard many gods as the children of rivers. The sacred power of the Supreme Being and the lesser gods, who derived their power from the Supreme Being, was represented by water and its ritual use.

The *ntoro* groups, based on the spirit–personality inherited from fathers and distinguished from the tangible *mogya* (blood) derived from mothers, were seen as drawing their spiritual powers from rivers, lakes, or the sea. J. B. Danquah gave the number of *ntoro* groups among the Akan as twelve, Busia's informants enumerated seven, and R. S. Rattray cited nine.[40] All of Danquah's twelve *ntoro* groups—Bosompra, Bosomtwi, Bosommuru, Bosompo, Bosom–Dwerebe, Bosom–Akom, Bosomafi, Bosomayesu, Bosom–Konsi, Bosom–Sika, Bosomafram, and Bosomkrete—were affiliated to bodies of water. The very language that described membership of

---

37   Busia, "Ashanti," 197.

38   AFN: Interview with Okyeame Asonade, linguist of *obosom* (god) Nyano, Ayigya, June 7, 1992.

39   Busia, "Ashanti," 193.

40   J. B. Danquah, "Akan Society," cited in Busia, "Ashanti," 198; Busia, "Ashanti," 196; and Rattray, *Ashanti*, Ch. 2.

the *ntoro* was borrowed from the imagery of water. People who shared the same *ntoro* were seen as "washing the same spirit."
Warfare diminished the ritual importance of water vis-a-vis alcohol. Two students of Akan history noted this shift. Margaret Field commented on the relatively recent ascendancy of the ancestral cult in her study of the Akan state of Akyem Kotoku.

> The stool cult is recent compared with the land and river cults, but as warfare was for several centuries the main preoccupation of the people, the stool cult almost obliterated the earlier cults in so far as these were organized cults bound up with government and social organization.[41]

That the ritual use of alcohol was more related to the ancestral cults than to the Supreme Being was pointed out by S. G. Williamson:

> Although it is true that in Akan religious practice libation is offered, with the mention of the Supreme Being, the gods, the ancestors, and the earth, but it was at no time specifically related to the worship of the Supreme Being alone.[42]

And Akan proverbs rationalized the demotion of water: *nsu–hunu ye ome a, anka aka mfa darewa* ("if plain water was satisfying enough, then the fish would not take the hook").

Rites of Passage

Rites of passage illustrated the conception of life as a progression from the spiritual world, through the living world, and back into the spiritual world. Naming, puberty, marriage, and funeral ceremonies represented different epochal stages in life's journey. The human perception of the relative intimacy of the spiritual and living worlds associated with each phase was reflected in a minimal or profuse use of alcohol.

Male elders played key roles in all rites of passage because of the need for them to offer libations to secure the blessings of the ancestors on these occasions. The permeation of the ritual use of alcohol into rites of passage represented one of the earliest mechanisms for establishing control over women and young men utilized by Gold Coast male elders in their face–to–face communities. Infants were often named after living male elders or important ancestors, reinforcing the social prestige of elders. Male elders intruded into purely female dominated, nubility rites to pour libation to "ensure" its success. But in reality, this also enabled men to keep abreast on available young women eligible for marriage. Marriages often cemented alliances between male elders, and male elders were vital to funeral rites that ensured that the deceased entered the world

---

[41]   M. J. Field, *Akim–Kotoku* (Westport, 1970), 171.
[42]   S. G. Williamson, *Akan Religion and the Christian Faith*, ed. Kwesi Dickson (Accra, 1974), 132.

of the ancestors. All individuals underwent rites of passage; all were under the social control of male elders.

Ceremonies of Birth and Naming

It was usual for an Akan wife to leave her husband's home and return to her mother's house just before childbirth. This was because it was assumed that she would need the instruction and assistance of the females in her mother's house. It is also possible that in the matrilineal system of the Akans, the matrilineal family was seen as having an important stake in successful childbirth, hence the retreat to the matrilineal home. Among the patrilineal Tallensi in the northern Gold Coast, Meyer Fortes commented that: "It is a strict rule that a child must be born under the father's roof."[43] This rule was tied to the question of legitimacy and the rights of the legitimate child. Such rigid conceptions of legitimacy and rights did not apply to the Ga and Ewe, and mothers normally retreated to their maternal home for childbirth.

On childbirth, the "infant's throat is moistened with the juice of a lime or sometimes with a little rum, with which the finger is wetted and the back of the throat touched."[44] Rattray, the source of this information, does not explain the meaning of this act. Every Akan child was believed to have two mothers: an earthly mother through whom natural birth took place; and a "ghost mother" in the spirit world (*asamando*).[45] Just as a dying man was offered a last drink to help him in the tortuous journey towards *asamando*, it appeared necessary to wet the newborn's throat; a throat parched from the long journey from the spirit world.[46] The gesture was an expression of welcome, an entreaty to the newborn baby to stay with its earthly family.

Nonetheless, no one could be certain if the "ghost mother" would not reclaim her child in the first few days of childbirth. The Krobo–Adangme and the Ewe believe each newborn infant had a spouse in the ancestral world (Krobo: *huanim*). These spirit–spouses sought to effect a return of their partners, especially if they left for the living world without the permission of their spirit–spouses.[47] Thus, although the child was given a day–name at childbirth, it was not given a personal name among the Akan and Ga–Adangme till the eighth day. By the eighth day, it was believed the child would have disconnected itself from the "ghost mother" or spirit–spouse. The giving of a personal name on the eighth day transformed the child into a social person and a being of this world. According to Ellis, on the eighth day, the father of the newborn, his relatives and friends proceeded to the house where the mother was. They seated themselves at the entrance of the house.

---

43 Meyer Fortes, "Ritual and Office," in *Essays in the Ritual of Social Relations*, ed. Max Gluckman (Manchester, 1962), 84.
44 Rattray, *Religion and Art in Ashanti*, 57.
45 Ibid., 59.
46 Among the Akan, Ewe, and Ga–Adangme, a welcome drink of water was offered to visitors to refresh them from their walk.
47 Huber, *Krobo*, 137; and D. Westermann, *Worterbuch der Ewe–Sprache* (1905), 175, cited in Huber, *Krobo*, 137.

The child is then brought out and handed to the father,who returns thanks to the tutelary deity, and then gives it its second name, squirting at the same time a little rum from his mouth into the child's face. This second name, which is always used after the first, is generally that of a particular friend or a deceased relative.[48]

After the second name had been given, rum was used in libation to the ancestors, and the day ended with festivities.

Although Ellis did not explain the significance of the rum–spitting ritual he described, Rattray's account of naming among the Asante suggests that this was to transfer to the child the personality of the elder or ancestor after whom the child was being named. If a child was named after a living relative, for example, the maternal grandfather, this grandparent placed the child on his knees, spat saliva into the infant's mouth and named him after himself. The connection of spittle (white or colorless) with the *ntoro* (personality spirit) is very evident here. Rattray stated that: "The spittle has given to the infant some of the grandfather's spirit."[49] The Akan named children only after elders whose characters they found worth emulating.

But Rattray does not mention the use of rum or any other liquor in this naming ritual among the living. It is only when the relative after whom the infant was to be named was dead that the child's father poured out wine with the following words:

Receive this wine and partake, I place your grandchild [or whatever the relationship] before your face and give him your name, see that he does not lack food.[50]

Not only was the blessing of this particular deceased ancestor being solicited, all the ancestors of the family were informed in the libation of the new addition to the family; a family which incorporated the living and the dead.

A more elaborate version of the naming ceremony is mentioned in later accounts, in which dialectical meanings attached to the ritual use of water and alcohol may reflect concerns by male elders about the social abuse of alcohol. With slight variations, this version came to be adopted by the Akans and non–Akan groups of the southern Gold Coast.[51] The celebrant held the child in his arms, and two glasses were placed before him, one filled with water, the other with rum. The celebrant dipped his right forefinger into the glass of water and wet the child's tongue with it, at the same time counselling the baby to always tell the truth: "when you say it is water, let it be water." The same routine was done with the rum and a similar admonition expressed.[52]

---

[48]   Ellis, *Tshi–Speaking Peoples*, 233.

[49]   Rattray, *Religion and Art in Ashanti*, 64.

[50]   Ibid. Rattray appears to use "wine" to translate *nsa*, which is the correct Asante translation, but obscures the fact that *nsa* could be rum or gin. Field points out that naming ceremonies (*kpodziemo* or "going out" ceremony) among the Ga involved rum in the pouring of libation, and the gathering also drank rum and corn wine. Field, *Religion and Medicine*, 171–73.

[51]   For a Ga version of this, see AFN: Interview with Ayaa Tettey (Odantow family head), Accra, July 28, 1992.

[52]   See, for example, "When an Akan Names His Child," *Ashanti Times*, August 20, 1957.

Why the choice of water and liquor to demonstrate difference? Was it because both water and rum (or gin which was sometimes used) tasted so different
that they could symbolize truth as opposed to falsehood? It is certain that the
infant was being introduced to the two most powerful fluids in the life of the
Akan: water, indispensable for life here on earth and with sacred ties to the Supreme Being; and liquor, necessary for communion with the ancestors, but a wrong-
ful use of which could end in personal degradation—a living death. At a deeper
level, *nsa* was not representing falsehood in the naming ritual; it emphasized the
wisdom to distinguish between what was wrong and what was right, a distinction captured in the socially approved uses of *nsa* among adult Akans. The Ga
used only corn wine (*madan*) in their naming rite. Three drops of corn wine was
put on the child's tongue and it was advised: "When you come, come and eat
abele (corn), that is what we eat and nothing more."[53] The author asked Nii Amarkai
II, the informant, the significance of telling the child to come and eat corn. His
response: "Well, it means we don't drink anything but this corn wine. In other
words, don't take to spirits." It has been argued that the concern of male elders
about the youth abusing the use of alcohol became more evident from the late
nineteenth century.

Puberty Rites

The attainment of puberty introduced the individual into the adult living world; it
was a half–way stop through life, requiring a complex use of alcohol, water, and
animal blood. The individual had become an adult, declaring his/her "independence." The major social transition in initiation was that it qualified the individual
for marriage, to set up an independent household. Nukunya comments on how
Anlo–Ewe fathers were unwilling to concede responsibility and authority to their
sons: "One may speak of an institutionalized inequality and even antagonism between father and son."[54] Indeed initiation and marriage may be seen as a gratuity
granted by elders for years of faithful service. Among the Krobo:

> All the males are . . . entitled to have the circumcision and marriage
> rites performed for them by their paternal family; *they enjoy, subject*
> *though to the authority and sanctity of their ancestors* [emphasis added],
> formal corporate and inheritance rights, and are potential heads of their
> kin group. The females, in turn, can by right expect from their father's
> family the performance of their puberty rituals (*dipo*), and, in the case
> of their marriage, the customary arbitrations with their bridegrooms'
> families.[55]

It is pertinent that the rites of initiation, which conferred the essence of "Krobo–
ness" (circumcision and *dipo*), and marriage rites which affirmed adulthood, were
mediated by elders of a kin group. They interpreted the "authority and sanctity of
their ancestors." Thus, one can appreciate the clout of elder kinsmen in denying an
individual social mobility.

---

53   AFN: Interview with Nii Amarkai II, Bubuashie, August 31, 1994.
54   Nukunya, *Kinship and Marriage Among the Anlo Ewe*, 40.
55   Huber, *Krobo*, 24.

In Asante only females underwent nubility (puberty) rites.[56] Today they are seldom observed. The Christian confirmation has gradually assumed the place of nubility rites. One of the main functions of nubility rites was to inform the community that a female had attained marriageable age. In Asante, girls did not look for husbands, so it was necessary to publicize their availability when they reached maturity. The state of puberty could be described as *Wa bo no bara* ("the *bara* state has stricken her"). *Bara* also means "life" (the initiant was seen as having gained an understanding of what life was about), and *wa bo no bara* also means to "come of age," a phase symbolized by the onset of menstruation (*kyima*).

As soon as the daughter notified the mother that she had experienced her first menses, the mother informed the whole village. Old women came out to sing *bara* songs. The organization of puberty rites as a feminine affair may have reduced the presence of alcohol in this social event. The only occasion on which alcohol was used, according to Rattray, was when the girl's mother poured libation with *nsa*, saying:

Nyankopon Tweaduampon 'Nyame, gye nsa nom.
Asaase Ya, gye nsa nom.
Nsamanfo, munye nsa nom.
Oba yi a Nyankopon de ama me yi,
nne na wa bo no bara.
Oni a owo samandow,
ommefa no onnye bara nwu.[57]

Supreme sky god who is alone great, upon whom men lean and do not fall, receive this wine and drink.
Earth Goddess, whose day of worship is Thursday, receive this wine and drink.
Spirit of our ancestors, receive this wine and drink.
This girl child whom God has given to me,
today the *Bara* state has stricken her.
O mother who dwells in the land of ghosts, do not come and take her away and do not have permitted her to menstruate only to die.

If the woman belonged to a ruling lineage, the male head of the lineage poured the libation.[58] The prayer invoked the protection and blessings of the Supreme Being, the creator; Asase Yaa, the female earth goddess who provided day-to-day sustenance; and the ancestors, guardians of the social moral order. The structure of libation thus reveals the belief structure and the perceived intimacy between the physical and spiritual worlds. The prayer also shows the continued fear of the living mother of her daughter's ghost mother in spite of the eighth–day naming ceremony.

However, puberty rites may represent one social ceremony in which women retained control and did use alcohol in the social sense, though not reported by

[56] For an excellent study of nubility rites in Asante, see Peter Sarpong, *Girls' Nubility Rites in Ashanti* (Tema, 1977).

[57] Rattray, *Religion and Art in Ashanti*, 69.

[58] Sarpong, *Girls' Nubility Rites*, 26.

Rattray. It was an occasion for women to protest their exploited position by censuring, through songs, the conduct of mean husbands.

For the occasion is seized upon by the women to sing the praises of any men who, in their view, are good husbands, and to scold, not to say insult, the bad inconsiderate husband, who behaves as if women were married to be made slaves of, or drinks too much, or is too lazy to work.[59]

Obaa panin Afua Pokuaa recalled her *bragoro* (puberty rites), probably in the 1910s. It was performed at Nsuase, close to the center of Kumase.

There were no men. Women played the *dondo* [gong], only women drummed, sang, and danced. Ata Kwasi [the Asantehene's Abenasehene, in charge of royal cloths] was my father's nephew. He sent us "Gordon's Gin" at Nsuase. The women involved in *bragoro* drink, or the *bragoro* would not be entertaining. . . . We played until dawn, cheering.[60]

The initiate sat with her head covered with a cloth and did not drink.[61] Alcohol was poured into the sacred Subin river, which runs by the present–day Asafo Market, and the initiate was thoroughly bathed in the evening of the *bragoro*. A sheep was slaughtered, and some of the blood was collected to make *(e)kyim*, an Asante dish. Part of the meat was used to prepare the Akan dish of *fufu*. Some of the food was placed on the ancestral stools. The initiate was fed several special dishes. The desire to protect the initiate in the years ahead, and to ensure her fertility, explains the complex use of alcohol, water, and blood in Asante puberty rites. Libations of alcohol informed the ancestors of this august event and secured their blessings. The initiate was ritually bathed in a river to cleanse her of misfortune. She was served *(e)kyim*, made of sheep's blood, arguably, to make her fertile. In the Asante understanding of pregnancy, blood, which gave the fetus its physical form, came from the women.

In the politically decentralized Ga society with its numerous component wards, several different rites for girls' puberty coexisted.[62] Unlike the Asante, Ga males underwent puberty rites, which consisted mainly of initiation into the *asafo* (military companies). Resonant of the connections between alcohol, the ancestors/gods, and political power, rum was used in libation by the officiating priest to secure blessings for the initiant. The absence of a powerful central figure who could summon an army into the field necessitated some mechanism for mobilizing men for military purposes, and the *asafo* companies served this need. Male initiation thus facilitated a steady growth in the Ga fighting strength. Among the related Adangme-speaking Krobo, the law of circumcision (the essence of male initiation) was identified with the war–gods *Nadu* and *Kotoklo*.[63]

---

[59] Ibid., 23.

[60] AFN: Interview with Afua Pokua, August 18, 1994. She was in her late eighties when the author interviewed her. The social use of liquor by women during nubility rites is confirmed by Sarpong, *Girls' Nubility Rites*, 25.

[61] AFN: Interview with Afua Pokua, Kumase, August 19, 1994.

[62] The seven Ga "towns" include several quarters of immigrants, aside from the social influences of the autochthonous Kpesi. For an examination of some Ga puberty rites, see Field, *Religion and Medicine*, 185–91; and Madeline Manoukian, *Akan and Ga–Adangme Peoples* (London, 1950), 91–92.

[63] Huber, *Krobo*, 26.

Marriage Rites

In marriage ceremonies, alcohol featured more prominently as the coming together of two families expanded the range of human and ancestral witnesses and participants. Marriages often cemented alliances between male elders, and the exchange of drinks in the presence of witnesses and the pouring of libation to the gods and ancestors were enough to establish the validity of marriage. It is the marriage contract that has witnessed dynamic change from the nineteenth century in its definition.[64] Marriage was an important institution for it mediated the acquisition of women as producers and reproducers in society. It was the institution which starkly portrayed the object status of women. With the introduction of export agriculture in the nineteenth century, a demand for labor rose in the Gold Coast. Most agricultural labor was done by women, and trade in palm oil, rubber, and cocoa transformed the material transactions in marriage.[65] Although the impact of cocoa on gender relations has been widely documented, it is difficult to imagine that earlier export crops had no impact on gender relations and marriage.

The centrality of biological reproduction to marriage is evident from the marrying age for women. Rattray mentioned that in Asante, females got married immediately after reaching the stage of puberty.[66] Ellis commenting on the Fante, observed that the "natives seemed to judge of a girl's fitness for the married state by the development of the bosom, than by the fact of menstruation having commenced. . . ."[67] Both indices are, however, signs of fertility; procreation being the most important goal of marriage. Menstruation signals the onset of ovulation, a developed bosom the ability to suckle a newborn babe. Victoria Tashjian points out that some Asante women opted out of marriage on attaining menopause. This decision not only underscored the importance of procreation to both men and women, it also expressed the unwillingness of women to continue to labor for men when they perceived no clear benefits to themselves.[68]

It is evident from the accounts of de Marees, Barbot, and Bosman that marriage transactions among the coastal Akan between 1600 and 1705 were very simple. Very little money was exchanged, and the immediate expenses revolved around the marriage party or feast. The groom paid no significant amount to the bride's family, and the bride brought no dowry.[69] This had changed among the coastal Fante by the 1880s when Ellis wrote.

> Contracts of marriage are made by the payment of a certain sum to the relations of the bride, and this sum varies according to the rank of the girl . . . from 18s. to £7 5s. The amount thus paid is called by Europeans "head–

---

[64]   See Chapter 3.

[65]   See, in general, Robertson and Klein, *Women and Slavery in Africa*. On female labor in Asante between 1800 and 1950, see Austin, "Human Pawning." Bosman complained that men do little but gossip and drink palm wine while their wives labor in the fields for the money that bought their husbands' palm wine. W. Bosman, *New and Accurate Description of the Coast of Guinea, Divided into the Gold, the Slave, and the Ivory Coasts* (London, 1705), 199.

[66]   Rattray, *Religion and Art in Ashanti*, 76.

[67]   Ellis, *Tshi–Speaking Peoples*, 235.

[68]   Tashjian, "You Marry to Beget."

[69]   De Marees, *Gold Kingdom of Guinea*, 19–20; Hair et al., *Barbot on Guinea II*, 502; and Bosman, *New and Accurate Description*, 198.

money," or "head–rum," which terms are literal translations of the native ones, *Etsi siccah*, and *Etsi r'ensa*. Amongst the very poor, however, the man and woman sometimes live together without any head–money having been paid, or perhaps with only one or two bottles of rum given to the family to drink. In such cases the husband generally resides with the family of his wife, and gives his services towards their common support.[70]

The centrality of alcohol in the marriage rite was underlined by the fact that the ceremony even took its name from *nsa*. It originally emphasized the reproduction of the community. Indeed, just the exchange of drinks cemented the marriage contract among the inland Asante.[71]

The focus in marriage had somehow shifted in the nineteenth century to express a concern for ample financial compensation for lost female labor or the substitution of the prospective husband's labor. Even in Asante, an elaborate schedule, regulating the various monetary amounts required for socially–ranked *tiri aseda* (head–wine), emerged.[72] Economic demands and social status spawned two co–existing forms of marriage. The first was marked by *tiri nsa, tiri sika* or *tiri aseda* (head–wine, head–money). The second involved *tiri ka* (head–debt), in which the bride's family requested the man to pay a "debt" on their behalf. The man literally "bought his wife," acquiring more rights than the traditional privileges to exclusive sex.[73] The colonial government's abolition of slavery in the colony in 1874 and in Asante in 1896 coincided with the take–off phase of the cocoa industry. The intense demand for labor would activate a "hunt" for wives.[74] Wife–pawning became widespread, and *tiri ka* a common feature in marriage transactions.[75] By the turn of the twentieth century the Fante legalist, Mensah Sarbah, could actually argue that the exchange of drinks was not necessary in contracting a valid marriage among the Fante.[76]

Alcohol, Funerals, and Ancestorhood

In the observation of funeral rites, the intimate relationship with the world of ancestors—into which the deceased was about to enter—necessitated an extensive use of alcohol. According to Bosman, a death was signaled by the lamentation of women in the deceased's house.[77] The family then washed the corpse and laid the body in state. Sympathizers came to pay their respects, bringing presents like gold, brandy, and fine cloth.

---

[70] Ellis, *Tshi–Speaking Peoples*, 281.

[71] Rattray, *Religion and Art in Ashanti*, 84; and Rattray, *Ashanti Law and Constitution*, 25.

[72] Rattray, *Religion and Art in Ashanti*, 81.

[73] Ibid., 78. In "buying" a wife, the wife became the pawn (*Twi: awowa*) of her husband. In matrilineal Akan societies, this gave a husband legal rights to the wife and children, whereas they would have belonged to the wife's matrilineage.

[74] Takyiwaa Manuh, "Changes in Marriage and Funeral Exchanges Among the Asante: A Case Study from Kona, Afigya–Kwabre," in *Money Matters: Instability, Values and Social Payments in the Modern History of West African Communities*, ed. Jane I. Guyer (Portsmouth, 1995), 188–201.

[75] Austin, "Human Pawning in Asante," 138.

[76] John Mensah Sarbah, *Fanti Customary Laws* (London, 1897), 40.

[77] Bosman, *A New and Accurate Description*, 228–29.

During this Ingress and Egress of all sorts of people; Brandy in the morning and Palm–Wine in the afternoon are briskly filled about; so that a rich
Negro's funeral becomes very chargeable. . . .[78]

Burial often took place on the same day the body was laid in state, accompanied
by the discharge of musketry. However, the funerals of chiefs were more prolonged.[79]
After the burial, sympathizers often repaired to the house of mourning, "to drink
and be merry, which lasts for several days successively; so that this part of the
mourning looks more like a wedding than a funeral."[80] In nineteenth–century Cape
Coast, the funerals of the educated elite rivaled, if not surpassed, those of the traditional aristocracy.[81] In contemporary Ghana, the social aspect of funerals has become more prominent and funerals provide the living with an avenue for making
status statements.[82]

The ritual importance of alcohol in transforming a deceased into an ancestor is
very striking in Asante funerary practices. When a person was on the deathbed,
relatives kept close watch and "at the moment the soul leaves the body . . . pour a
little water down the throat of the person who is dying. . . ."[83] The Asante placed
great importance on the last rite of administering water, because in order to reach
asamando a steep hill must be climbed. This last drink of water was to help the
struggling, panting soul up the steep incline.[84] It appears that water, instead of
palm wine or rum, was administered because the dying person was still in the
living world. Also, the arduous task of climbing the hill required a "cool" drink
(water), not a "hot" drink (alcohol). The relatives of the deceased must inform the
chief of the village of the death before wailing can commence. The corpse was
washed and dressed:

The washers and dressers of the corpse are paid in wine which is known
as *nsa ye de yi no gware ye* (the wine which is used to bathe him). Rum is
poured down the throat, with the idea, I believe, of staying the process of
decomposition; a small quantity is also poured down the ground for the
spirit.[85]

What the living sought to gain through a proper funeral was the successful transition of the deceased from the world of the living into that of the dead. The "other
worldliness" of this phase de–emphasized money as appropriate compensation for
washers and dressers of corpses, and value was placed rather on the spiritual potency of alcohol. The dressed body was laid in state and the funeral wailing begun.

---

[78]   Ibid., 230. Bosman's account represents one of the earliest descriptions of life in the Gold Coast which
emphasizes the popularity of brandy. It appears, however, that brandy's relevance was restricted to convivial social occasions, and Bosman does not mention the use of brandy in libations.

[79]   Ellis, *Tshi–Speaking Peoples*, 239.

[80]   Bosman, *New and Accurate Description*, 230.

[81]   See Marcus Allen, *The Gold Coast* (London, 1874), 114–18.

[82]   Manuh, "Changes in Marriage and Funeral Exchanges," 198.

[83]   Rattray, *Religion and Art in Ashanti*, 148.

[84]   Ibid., 149.

[85]   Ibid. Among the Ga, eminent persons were laid in state for several days, and camphor dissolved in
rum was sometimes poured into the corpse through all available openings to slow down decomposition.
Field, *Religion and Medicine*, 199.

Throughout the funeral ceremony, alcohol was used to stay in touch with, and bid farewell to, the deceased. After the body has been dressed and laid in state, relatives "must now fast, but palm wine may be drunk."[86] Sympathizers came to share the grief of the bereaved family, and a "wake" was kept day and night till the body was buried. The body is buried in the clan burial ground, the permission of the earth goddess being sought through libation before the grave was dug. After the burial, wine was poured on the grave with the words: "So–and–so, here is wine from your family, do not cause any of us who have carried you to fall ill."[87] The family and clansmen, the only persons present at the burial, drank some of the wine, and all returned home. Libations and drinking were also featured in subsequent funeral observations on the eighth day, the fifteenth day, the fortieth day, and the eightieth day. A one–year anniversary rounded off the rites associated with funerals. By the expiration of the year, the deceased would have been fully transformed into an ancestral spirit, well connected to those left behind through libation and the consumption of spirits.

Two factors help to explain the pervasive use of *nsa* during funerals. First, the dead person was in a liminal state: neither a spirit nor a living being. The corpse represented an anomaly: the physical intrusion of the "spirit" world into the physical world. Funeral rites may be seen as the attempt of the deceased's living relatives to sever the liminality of the corpse by ensuring its successful entry into the spirit world. Margaret Field argued that the keynote of funeral ceremonies among the Ga was to "sever the ties between the living and the dead without giving offence to the latter."[88] "Sever" does not capture the essence of the funeral rite, for the living rather sought to "transform" their relations with the deceased—a potential ancestor—to their advantage. It was natural that in this close contact with the spirit world, *nsa* would be the most potent symbol and medium of communication. Thus those who bathe and clothe the corpse were paid in *nsa*, and the very contributions of sympathizers at the funeral were termed *nsa*.

Secondly, alcohol was important in funerals for it numbed the feeling of grief.[89] Paradoxically, drinking at funerals was, at the same time, an expression of grief and solidarity among the living. The "fact that a man or woman completely abstained from drink at the funeral custom of a relative, would be regarded by the mourners with the gravest suspicion."[90] The level of intoxication was also high because funerals were marked by fasting.[91] Hence, funerals were one of the few occasions amongst Akans in which intoxication was actually encouraged.[92] This did not occur during the rites of naming, nubility, and marriage because these were unambiguously joyous occasions. With death the cycle of life, as a progression from the spiritual world through the living world and back into the spiritual world, was completed. The ancestral spirit now awaited reincarnation through birth.

---

[86]   Rattray, *Religion and Art in Ashanti*, 150.

[87]   Ibid., 163.

[88]   Field, *Religion and Medicine*, 199.

[89]   Cruickshank, *Eighteen Years*, 217–18.

[90]   C. A. Armitage, Commissioner of Southern Province, Ashanti, to the Chief Commissioner of Ashanti, April 3, 1909. National Archives of Ghana (NAG), Kumasi, ROA 022.

[91]   Ellis, *Tshi–Speaking Peoples*, 239.

[92]   Ibid., 238; Rattray, *Religion and Art in Ashanti*, 151.

Festivals and Festivities: Alcohol, Ostentation, and Power

Festivals

But the dead were not banished until reincarnation, for festivals like the Akan *adae* and the Ga *homowo* provided for their regular commemoration. To facilitate the communication necessary in this context between the living and the ancestors, the family of the deceased lineage head, or the *wirempefo* (court functionaries in charge of ancestral stools) on the death of an Asante king or chief, created a stool which was named after the deceased.

> For this purpose the favourite chair [stool] of the deceased, generally a small one, which was in constant use by him, is cleaned then rubbed all over with the blood of sheep, and finally smeared with a mixture of soot and eggs. The stool is afterwards wrapped in some skin and safely kept. During this consecration, libation is made and prayers are freely offered for the prosperity of the family. . . .[93]

These stools became "shrines" of the ancestors and were kept in sacred rooms (Twi: *nkonguafieso,* "stool house"). In Asante special feast days, such as the *adae*, were specifically set aside for the veneration of the ancestors.

The *adae* (a day of rest) was set aside to propitiate the spirits of departed rulers and to solicit their favors. It took place every forty–two days according to the Asante calendar: a minor *adae* on a Wednesday (*wukudae*), and a major *adae* on a Sunday (*akwasidae*).[94] The important rituals were performed in the stool house. A sheep was slaughtered and some of its blood smeared on the ancestral stools. Blood, in this context, was associated with life, and smearing the ancestral stools with blood reinforced the perception that the ancestors continued to live in another form. Some of the meat was cooked and placed on the stools. *Eto* (mashed plantain or yam) was also prepared and some put on the stools. Libation was poured with liquor and the ancestors were left to their meal. In the evening, the food was removed from the stool room, and it was considered especially potent for barren women who desired children.[95]

Homowo, the most important Ga festival, was celebrated in August. *Homowo* means "hooting at hunger," although its significance transcended that of a harvest festival.[96] In Margaret Field's opinion, "one–ness with their living brethren and one–ness with their dead fathers is the keynote of this great gathering together."[97] It was also a day for mourning those who had died during the year, for the festival

---

[93]   Sarbah, *Fanti National Constitution*, 12. The Ewe also kept ancestral stools and approached the ancestors through these. Manoukian, *Ewe–Speaking Peoples*, 23. Although the Ga borrowed the use of stools from the Akan, they did not adopt the idea of a stool being the repository of an ancestral spirit. Manoukian, *Akan and Ga–Adangme Peoples*, 99. This reflected the prominent role of religious priests, rather than political chiefs, in decentralized Ga societies, and spirit mediums provided channels for contacting the ancestors.

[94]   On the Asante *adae*, see K. A. Busia, *The Position of the Chief in the Modern Political System of Ashanti: A Study of the Influence of Contemporary Social Changes on Ashanti Political Institutions* (London, 1968), 27–29; and Rattray, *Ashanti*, 92–108.

[95]   AFN: Interview with Afua Pokua, August 18, 1994.

[96]   AFN: Interview with Nii Amarkai II.

[97]   Field, *Religion and Medicine*, 47.

marked the approach of the Ga new year. The ritual food of *homowo, kpekpei,*[98] was prepared from the old year's corn, and none of this old corn was to be left over into the new year. The ceremony began just after noon. Field recorded that:

> Before any one else partakes of it the oldest person in the house, man or woman, goes all round the house sprinkling some of this food with rum for the ancestors, inviting them aloud to come and eat and drink and asking them to continue to protect the house from sickness and misfortune. The *mantse* [chief] and the *mankralo* [town–guardian] go round the town, or send their representatives to the various quarters of dead elders and give them food and rum. No salt or pepper is added to the food for the dead.[99]

The Ga Mashi *homowo*, the author witnessed on August 13, 1994, conformed to Field's outline. It began at the space between Ussher Fort and the old slave market, where the Gbese *Mantse* poured libation facing the sea. The gathering proceeded to the Ga *Mantse*'s old palace, where the chiefs and elders exchanged greetings amidst drumming and the firing of guns. Different parties of chiefs and elders went around the town sprinkling *kpekpei* and pouring libations of schnapps . It ended with the Ga *Mantse* and his chiefs sitting in state to watch the dancers and to receive homage. Through festivals such as *homowo* the living renewed their kinship ties with the dead, seeking their protection and blessings. These festivals endorsed the conception of community as encompassing the living, the dead, and the yet unborn.

Social Drinking

It is in the less ritualized social drinking that one sees the connections between alcohol, generosity, patronage, wealth, and power. As an old Twi proverb states: *wunni ntramma, na wuse nsa nye de* ("when you do not have cowry shells, then you say wine is not sweet"). The powerful saw possession and wastage of abundant palm wine as an index of wealth. Commenting on the huge amount of palm wine supplied to the Asantehene's palace daily, Bowdich wrote that:

> This would have appeared too large a sum, had I not witnessed the vast consumption of it; for the vigour of an Ashantee being estimated by the measure of the draught he can drink off. . . .[100]

As male elders had control over land and labor, they had more access to palm wine. In fact, by having palm wine available at all times in his house, an elder displayed his control over land and labor—that is, political power and wealth. Although young men tapped palm wine, they did not control its consumption. Taboos banned women from working on economically important palm trees. Thus spiritual, political, and economic power complemented one another in elderly male control of palm wine and palm trees.

Royal largesse and power were reflected in the generous distribution of alcohol to all and sundry. In the early nineteenth century, Bowdich observed in Kumase

---

[98] *Kpekpei* was cooked from dough kneaded with red palm oil. It was served with palm nut soup and fish.
[99] Field, *Religion and Medicine*, 49.
[100] Bowdich, *Mission*, 292.

Celebration of *Homowo* in Accra, August 13, 1994

that every day forty pots of soup and a *peregwan* (about £8) worth of palm wine
were made available at the palace for visitors. This generosity was a strong expression of the king's magnanimity and reinforced his social standing among his people.
Bowdich noted that:

> A large quantity of palm wine is dashed to the retinues of all the captains
> attending in the course of the day; much is expended in the almost daily
> ceremony of drinking it in state in the market place. . . .[101]

To assist a chief in meeting these commitments, it appears that a law in Asante
required palm wine tappers to send the chief a pot of palm wine daily (*ahen nsa*—
"chief's drink") for entertaining his guests.[102] But royal favor was also expressed
by gifts of alcoholic drinks to the favored.[103] A patron's gifts to his clients bound
his clients to him,[104] and a symbolic fluid like *nsa* with its spiritual potency not
only invoked the obligations involved in the giving of gifts but also ensured the
loyalty of clients.

   Indeed, the use of liquor to attract followers from among one's immediate social group may have fed into the existing slave trade. The acknowledged economic
connection between the liquor trade and the slave trade had important sociopolitical

---

[101] Ibid., 292–93.

[102] Busia, *Position of the Chief*, 50.

[103] See, for examples, Thomas Birch Freeman, *Journal of Various Visits to the Kingdoms of Ashanti, Aku and Dahomi in Western* Africa, 2nd ed. (London, 1968), 24, 44, and 48.

[104] On the spiritual and material obligations involved in gift–giving, see Marcel Mauss, *The Gift*, trans. by Ian Cunnison (New York, 1967).

and spiritual dimensions. An Asante aristocrat or wealthy trader bought slaves among peoples he considered peripheral in the northern markets. As Asantehene Kwaku Dua I informed the Wesleyan missionary Freeman in 1841: "The small tribes in the interior . . . fight with each other, take prisoners and sell them for slaves; and as I know nothing about them, I allow my people to buy and sell them as they please. . . ."[105] The Asante aristocrat or trader sold these slaves on the coast for European liquor (among other things), and paradoxically distributed these drinks to those within his social group to secure Asante clients. The choice of liquor was crucial for it bound recipients socially and spiritually to its giver. It was a complex manipulation of the concept of wealth in people. Drinks and their distribution was so central to political power that it was accommodated in Asante architecture. In the palace of the Asantehene were a palm wine house (*sa fie so*) and a place for the distribution of drinks (*pato a yekye mu nsa*).[106]

For commoners, whose lack of regular contact with the Asante court may have prevented them from enjoying royal largesse, the royal court's palm wine drinking sessions at the market place brought them into contact with the power and generosity of royalty. A perusal of Hutchison's diary indicates that in early–nineteenth–century Kumase, the king of Asante and his entourage of subchiefs and court functionaries often repaired to the market place to drink palm wine.[107] Although Hutchison does not explicitly state so, these were open occasions, and everybody could join the drinking party.

These public drinking sessions were moments in which the accessibility of the aristocracy was portrayed. But these occasions also exhibited an ambiguous combination of solidarity and hierarchy. In the relaxed social atmosphere, individuals with problems could approach the king directly in the informal atmosphere of the market place. But this convivial social atmosphere, paradoxically, also emphasized social rankings and the magnanimity of the politically powerful. The Asante king drank from a calabash decorated with gold, which underscored his wealth and power.[108] More intriguing were the drinking rules that structured such occasions. The king and the aristocrats drank first. Bowdich described the manner of drinking palm wine in the market place, but left out its links to social distinctions and royal generosity.

> The manner of drinking palm wine, . . . a boy kneels beneath with a second bowl to catch the droppings (it being a great luxury to suffer the liquor to run over the beard . . .).[109]

What Bowdich failed to mention was that the palm wine collected in the gourd was shared among the lower court functionaries (*ahenkwaa*) and commoners who could not drink in the presence of the aristocracy.[110] He could not have guessed the meanings attached to the process of spilling palm wine into the second gourd as he

---

[105] Freeman, *Journal of Various Visits*, 132.

[106] See Kwame Arhin and K. Afari–Gyan, eds., *The City of Kumasi* (Legon, 1992), 8–9; and Rattray, *Ashanti Law and Constitution*, 57.

[107] Bowdich, *Mission*, Ch. 12; and Freeman, *Journal of Various Visits*, 130.

[108] Malcolm D. McLeod, "The Golden Ax of Asante," *Natural History* 93 (October 1984): 72; Freeman, *Journal of Various Visits*, 130.

[109] Bowdich, *Mission*, 277.

[110] AFN: Interview with Albert Mawere Opoku, Accra, April 30, 1992.

came to these drinking sessions as a guest of the king and departed with the king's entourage. More importantly, those who did not have the means to purchase palm wine could partake through a structured drinking pattern that simultaneously expressed royal largesse and royal power. In precolonial Asante, where the predatory nature of the state encouraged commoners to avoid frequent contacts with the ruling classes, it is noteworthy that the congenial drinking sessions of the royal court provided the most intimate glimpse several commoners had of royal wealth and power. The images of drink, wealth, and power would stay with them.

An Encroaching Market Economy:
Coastal Trade and Social Change

The links between alcohol, wealth, and power had previously privileged male elders with their control over land and labor. From the mid-nineteenth century, expanding economic opportunities spawned by cash–crop cultivation, land sales, wage–labor, and commerce dissolved the ties that bound young men to land and elder kinsmen. Indeed, the very worldview which endorsed the ritual use of alcohol came under attack from Christian missionary influence as colonial rule established itself in the southern Gold Coast from 1874. And these new economic opportunities and alternative worldviews would have a liberating effect on women and young men.

In Akan, Ga–Adangme, and Ewe societies in which age and lineage defined sociopolitical status, coastal trading communities such as Komenda, Cape Coast, Anomabu, Accra, and Anexo witnessed the rise of "new men" in the eighteenth, and especially, in the nineteenth centuries. Their wealth and power was based on commercial achievement, and they did not view the possession of land and the pursuit of traditional office as the basis of their power.[111]

And for young male migrants to coastal towns like Cape Coast and Winnebah, elaborate patterns of social drinking came to represent their new found freedom. In the mid–nineteenth century, drinking clubs like the Tiger Society proliferated among coastal young men, who took opportunity of the low cost of rum and gin to binge on alcohol—the fluid sacred to the elders.[112] The numerous economic occupations that had sprung up around European commerce had afforded these young men an independent source of income, and their quest for power based on new–found wealth was expressed in the abuse of the very fluid to which they had been denied access by the elders.

It was against the young men's threat to the elders' monopoly of alcohol use, that an indigenous temperance ethic was developed by coastal male elders and it is, perhaps, no coincidence that the myths of the origin of palm wine, and the tragic

[111] See the example of the Brew family of Cape Coast and Anomabu in Priestley, *West African Trade and Coast Society*; the fascinating fortunes of the Lawson family in Amenumey, *Ewe in Pre–Colonial Times*, 86–94; and the careers of merchant princes like the Akrosan brothers of Fetu and Johnny Kabes of Komenda in K. Y. Daaku, *Trade and Politics on the Gold Coast, 1600–1720* (Oxford, 1970).

[112] Augustus Casely-Hayford and Richard Rathbone, "Politics, Families and Freemasonry in the Colonial Gold Coast," in *People and Empires in African History: Essays in Memory of Michael Crowder*, ed. J. F. Ade Ajayi and J. D. Y. Peel (London, 1992), 149.

consequences of alcohol abuse, were first transcribed into writing in the late nineteenth century—maybe they originated in that period. A person who frequently got drunk was labeled a *kowensanyi* (literally "someone who lives off alcohol"), a term of ridicule. Nana Ewua Duku II informed the author that among the Ahanta (an Akan group) in times past, family or clan members would speedily track down a member who was drunk and whisk him away before the latter made a nuisance of himself. Such a person would be strongly censured when sober. It was easy for a whole family to be stigmatized as drunkards, just because of the escapades of an individual member.[113]

Nana Ewua Duku strove to make a subtle, but important, distinction between the word *nsa*, which he always used when referring to the ritual uses of liquor, and "alcohol," which he used when he discussed drunkenness and antisocial behavior.[114] It would be accurate to state that the Akan, Ga–Adangme, and Ewe saw liquor itself as good; it was what the individual used it for that could be harmful. What had emerged over the course of time were two categories of socially approved and socially disapproved uses of alcohol. The socially approved uses of alcohol coincided with its public and ritual use. In this respect, drink united and strengthened the community—both through social interaction among the living and through communication with the spiritual world. Socially disapproved drinking coincided with private drinking, a trend which encouraged isolationism, social divisiveness, and alcohol abuse.

Alcoholism was seen as having a spiritual cause,[115] and it is instructive that male elders often accused young men of abusing alcohol. For young men, whose use of alcohol was restricted in precolonial Gold Coast, to usurp unlimited access to alcohol was to subvert elderly male power, and to dangerously experiment, socially, with a fluid that contained such potent spiritual power. In fact, alcoholism was a result of "social misadventure," and the fact that young men were often pointed out as alcoholics within a community was a strong caution to them to stay away from the elder's fluid.

Conclusion

The ritual use of alcohol in communicating with the gods and ancestors made libation central in rites of passage, festivals, and other aspects of human life. Ritual provided chiefs and male elders with an early form of social control over women and young men. Rites of passage and festivals reinforced social hierarchies in precolonial southern Gold Coast. But alcohol was also important in social life.

---

[113] AFN: Nana Ewua Duku II, March 3, 1992.

[114] The uneasiness about the use of "alcohol" in discussing Akan culture, and a preference for the use of *nsa*, was also exhibited by Albert Mawere Opoku. AFN: Albert Mawere Opoku, April 30, 1992.

[115] Illness was seen as two-dimensional: a spiritual cause with a physical manifestation. Treatment was directed at both dimensions, and the spiritual potency of alcohol made it an important ingredient in herbal medicine. Herbal preparation was seldom complete without a dash of rum or gin, for alcohol not only dissolved dry medicinal herbs, its spiritual power attacked the ailment at its roots. To trifle with such a powerful fluid was obviously to invite dire consequences on the imprudent person—or so the elders claimed.

Bosman, in the early eighteenth century, noted the conviviality that characterized drinking circles in coastal villages and towns.

> At the time when the palm–wine comes from the inland country, they go in the Afternoons together, viz. slaves and all as companions, to the publick market–place, where they sit down and drink sociably; every one that pleases, bringing his own stool, adds himself to the crowd. . . .[116]

However, in more centralized societies like Asante, drinking patterns came to reflect social ranks. The drinking sessions of the Asantehene's court at the Kumasi marketplace gave the impression of royal accessibility, but also underscored the connections between drink, wealth, and power. As young men migrated to towns from the late nineteenth century, they took with them the images of alcohol and conviviality, and alcohol and power. These images would inform the construction of social life in the colonial towns.

---

[116] Bosman, *New and Accurate Description*, 189.

3

Urban Migrants, Social Drinking, and the Struggle for Social Space: The Young Men's Challenge, c.1890–1919

Bergedof

Begye wo dofo

"Come and get your lover"[1]

One of the ironies in the social history of colonial Gold Coast is that European liquor, that coveted fluid of rural elders, constituted one of the cheapest commodities in coastal towns. In the light of alcohol's association with power and wealth, European liquor represented one of the goods that young male migrants in coastal towns could usurp easily to express their new autonomy. The proliferation of drinking clubs among young men in coastal towns, and their excessive abuse of alcohol, would encourage a new, forceful form of temperance organization by coastal chiefs and elders, and middle–class Fantes—often the products of mission education.[2]

An important aspect of social formation in coastal towns was the increasing assertiveness of women. Women had long been viewed in the Gold Coast as social and jural minors, who proceeded from the custodianship of their fathers or uncles

---

[1] The above epigram is an Asante pun on Bergedof beer, one of the most popular brands of imported beer in the Gold Coast in the first half of the twentieth century. The pun significantly links two pillars of social life in the emerging towns: social drinking and male–female relationships. AFN: Interview with Mawere Poku, April 30, 1992.

[2] See Chapter 4.

to that of their husbands. Marriages were contracted on behalf of women by male elders who hoped to cement social alliances or accumulate wealth through bride price. In the ideology of wealth and power that evolved in precolonial societies, women were considered an "economic and status good."[3] The accumulation and consumption of wives or women was seen as an index of wealth and political power. From the 1880s, court records reveal an increasing tendency in coastal towns for women to contract marriages without the support of male kin. Indeed, women even began to contest the right of men to collect *ayefere sika* (adultery money) with its connotations of women as economic property and adultery proceedings as a monetary transaction between men. What was being contested was the very definition of sexuality and the obligations of marriage.[4]

Opportunities for women to acquire wealth and to gain some degree of autonomy in towns and villages were generated by the simultaneous operation of colonial rule, the dual judicial structures of British and customary law courts, rural cash crop cultivation, urban capitalist production, urbanization and migration, and missionary activity.[5] Capitalist production promoted the growth of mechanized mining and railway towns. The low wages paid to male laborers, the unequal sex ratio in such working–class towns, and the absence of the "comforts of home" granted women a special place in the social reproduction of urban wage labor.[6] As sellers of cooked food, retailers of alcoholic drinks, and prostitutes, women lubricated the engines of capitalist production and urban social formation. Operating in the interstices of colonial rule and the colonial economy, women became active accumulators in towns. A similar process of accumulation developed in rural areas, as some women acquired their own cocoa farms.[7]

With their new wealth, some women sought to shape gender relations and their expectations in marriage in the pre–World War II era. Male elders in villages and towns were alarmed by this female threat. The round up of spinsters in the interior states of Sefwi Wiawso and Asante, the protective umbrella of indirect rule, attempts by chiefs and educated elite to (re)define custom, and the active indoctrination of women on the roles of "wifehood" and "motherhood" sum up the response of African men and the colonial government.[8] Even the initial tightening up of indirect rule created new economic opportunities, like the distillation of *akpeteshie*.[9] But gradually the gates of patriarchy came firmly shut, and women were again subordinated to men after World War II.

[3]   McCaskie, "State and Society, Marriage and Adultery," 488.

[4]   Akyeampong, "Constructing and Contesting Sexuality."

[5]   For two excellent studies on how these processes affected women's lives in east, central, and southern Africa, see Lovett, "Gender Relations"; and Jane L. Parpart, "'Where is Your Mother?': Gender, Urban Marriage, and Colonial Discourse on the Zambian Copperbelt, 1924–1945," *IJAHS* 27, 2 (1994): 241–71.

[6]   See Luise White's excellent study, *The Comforts of Home: Prostitution in Colonial Nairobi* (Chicago, 1990).

[7]   Christine Okali, *Cocoa and Kinship in Ghana: The Matrilineal Akan of Ghana* (London, 1983); and Allman, "Of 'Spinsters,' 'Concubines' and 'Wicked Women.'"

[8]   P. Roberts, "The State and the Regulation of Marriage"; Allman, "Rounding Up Spinsters"; Allman, "Making Mothers"; and Roger Gocking, "British Justice and the Native Tribunals of the Southern Gold Coast," *JAH* 34, 1 (1993): 93–113.

[9]   See Chapters 4 and 5.

Economic and Cultural Status Goods—Drink and Women

A fascinating aspect of social life in colonial towns was how indigenous and Western lifestyles, the old and the new, were incorporated into dynamic, novel urban cultures with entirely new meanings and values. A close inspection of urban cultures from the late nineteenth century reveal traces of the old *asafo* activities, the lifestyles of the *abirempon* ("big men"), and the influence of distinct social groups like the *edwibisofo* (indigenes) of Kumase. The lifestyle of the "big man" was historically and culturally defined. It is an understanding of these culturo–historical factors that shed light on apparent contradictions, such as mission educated young men who displayed their social mobility through the conspicuous consumption of imported alcoholic drinks, or African Christians who practiced polygamy.[10]

Access to palm wine in precolonial southern Gold Coast mirrored the control of male elders over land and people. In these rural societies, young men tapped palm wine but did not control its circulation and consumption.[11] In centralized societies such as Asante, the accumulation and display of wealth was controlled by the state and made a factor of political position or appointment. The politically powerful in Asante were conspicuous in their possession of land, subjects, wives, gold dust, and liquor. The politically powerful avidly bought land and subjects from indebted chiefs, a proclivity exemplified by the career of the *osikani* (rich man) Kwasi Brantuo (c. 1791–1865), the first Manwerehene of Asantehene Kwaku Dua I (1834–1867). At his village of Adiebeba, tradition recalls that "Kwasi Brantuo used to delight in watching his granddaughters playing amidst his gold dust."[12]

But in Asante society where wealth and power were so coveted, it proved impossible to eliminate commerce as a source of social mobility for commoners. It was not uncommon for chiefs to trump up false accusations against wealthy commoners, drag them before the court and impose huge fines on them. The political solution to the entrepreneurial spirit among commoners, many of whom could also access the state's realm of accumulation by joining the retinue of the aristocracy (*ahenkwaa*), was the development of the ideology of the Asantehene's golden elephant tail. The Asantehene appointed wealthy commoners who aspired to traditional office to non–royal, service stools (*asomdwa*) or even had *abirempon* ("big men") status conferred on them through elaborate ritual and ceremony. But such appointees could forfeit their self–acquired wealth to the Asantehene on their death through heavy death duties (Twi: *awunnyadee*) and inheritance duties (Twi: *ayibuadee*), hence preventing a hereditary, non–royal class of property owners.[13] The ideology of state

---

[10]   On multiple social loyalties in nineteenth– and twentieth–century Gold Coast, see Roger Gocking, "Competing Systems of Inheritance before the British Courts of the Gold Coast," *IJAHS* 23, 4 (1990): 601–18; and Casely–Hayford and Rathbone, "Politics, Families and Freemasonry." For an illuminative biographical study, see Stephan F. Miescher, "Boakye Yiadom—The Life History of a *Krakye*: Gender, Identities and the Construction of Manhood in Colonial Ghana" (paper presented at the University of Michigan, January 1995).

[11]   Charles Ambler, "Alcohol and Disorder in Precolonial Africa" (Boston University African Studies Center, Working Paper No. 126, 1987).

[12]   ACBP/PCS/51, Kwasi Brantuo, in *Asantesem: The Asante Collective Bibliography Project Bulletin* 7 (June 1977): 17. See also T. C. McCaskie, "Office, Land and Subjects in the History of the Manwere *Fekuo* of Kumase: An Essay in the Political Economy of the Asante State," *JAH* 21, 2 (1980): 189–208.

[13]   See Ivor Wilks, "The Golden Stool"; and McCaskie, *State and Society*, 42–49.

appropriation through granting political recognition to wealthy commoners worked so long as commoners perceived traditional office as their social referent. An important index of wealth and power was the possession of women. In the Asante example, McCaskie comments:

> That the accumulation of women was one among a number of indicators of differentiation (being quantitatively a prerogative of those participating in the power of the state) was and is recognized by numerous Asante. A fundamental maxim decreed that no Asante might aspire to marry as many wives as the Asantehene [customarily put at 3,333 wives]. A disgraced member of the political elite was stripped customarily of office, gold, land, subjects, all but a few of his slaves, and all but one wife—the retention of one or two body servants and a single spouse constituting perhaps the state's rule–of–thumb definition of minimal citizenship.[14]

Nukunya, Huber, and Field attest to the existence of polygamy, and its correlation to wealth and power, among the Ewe, Adangme, and Ga respectively.

More revealing of the concept of women as economic goods was the speculation in their sexuality by wealthy men. Writing on the coastal Fante in 1853, Brodie Cruickshank remarked:

> It is customary for these [wealthy men] to keep a number of women, whom they call their wives, among whom are included pawns and slaves, as well as free women, for whom dowry money has been paid, and who are in consequence, to be considered the most legitimate wives. But as far as answering the purpose of establishing a charge of adultery, the pawns and slaves are as serviceable as the most legally–married women in Christendom.
>
> Indeed, it is notorious that many of these women are maintained for the express purpose of ensnaring the unsuspecting with their blandishments, and carry on their infamous trade with the connivance of their husbands, who frequently bestow upon them a portion of the fine of the damages imposed, as a reward for their successful enterprize, and an encouragement for future infidelity.[15]

In early–nineteenth–century Asante, wealthy men arranged child–marriages (*oyere akoda*), a sure means of entrapping on adultery charges unsuspecting men who even affectionately touched the infant.[16] Indeed, in precolonial Asante, there was an impression that no woman was "free." An Asante proverb states: *mmea se, `wo ho ye fe' a, ene ka* ("When the women say (to you) `you are a handsome fellow,' that means you are going into debt").[17]

Alcoholic drinks played a key role in status politics. Poor commoners did not have the wherewithal to indulge in the lavish distributions of drinks by a patron to his followers and potential clients. It would be considered *ahomaso* ("to raise yourself"; pride) for commoners or young men to even indulge in such a display. Judi-

---

[14] McCaskie, "State and Society, Marriage and Adultery," 486–87.

[15] Cruickshank, *Eighteen Years*, 325–26. See also Dupuis, *Journal*, 37.

[16] Bowdich, *Mission*, 302.

[17] R. S. Rattray, *Ashanti Proverbs* (Oxford, 1916), 133.

cial processes would quickly cut them down to size. There were, however, structured exceptions in which young men or commoners could participate in social
drinking. One was by way of *asafo* activities.

The *asafo* played an important role as a military organization in precolonial
Gold Coast: they were the foot soldiers of the established order.[18] War warranted
deeds of valor and bravery, and a "hot" fluid like alcohol encouraged male ex-
ploits. Thus, alcoholic drinks—palm wine and rum—were reckoned as important
in military logistics.[19] Commander Glover, who was in charge of an African contingent (including the Manya Krobo) in the British expedition against Asante in 1874,
recognized this crucial role of alcohol in military warfare:

> To help the paramount chiefs overcome their apprehension, Glover thought
> it necessary to reward them for their support in advance from War Office
> funds. Powder and shot, rum, and silver coins were sent to the paramount
> chiefs.[20]

By extension, alcohol became important in *asafo* social activities, as these activities
involved military parades and the display of flags. This was the young men's "loop-
hole" to participating in liquor consumption in precolonial southern Gold Coast.
Even as the spread of *Pax Britannica* from 1830 gradually eliminated warfare as an
active pursuit in southern Gold Coast, Fante *asafo* groups made their ceremonial
appearances at Christmas and funerals subject to their receipt of rum and tobacco.[21]
And deprived of an external outlet for their martial spirit, the coastal towns and
villages often witnessed an implosion of violence sparked by inter–*asafo* competition, and often fueled by alcohol.[22]

The colonial police and military that succeeded to the military role of the *asafo*
seemed to have inherited this partiality for drink. Although the Gold Coast military and police were called "Hausa forces" after the Muslim Hausa of northern
Nigeria, they were seldom either Hausa or Muslim.[23] The name stuck because of a
Hausa contingent that had been brought in to assist the British invasion of Kumase
in 1874. Drinking and affairs with women represented the main leisure activities
for these forces.[24] The West Indian Regiment stationed in the Gold Coast in the
early colonial period could not resist this infectious lifestyle.

> On Christmas evening [at Cape Coast in 1882], especially, the behaviour
> of the people was disgraceful; but we must admit that they were the least
> to blame. Free license seems to have been given to the soldiers of the West

[18] On *asafo* political activities, see H. M. Feinberg, "Who are the Elmina," *Ghana Notes and Queries*, 11
(June 1970): 20–26; Jarle Simensen, "Rural Mass Action in the Context of Anti–Colonial Protest: The *Asafo*
Movement of Akyem Abuakwa, Ghana," *Canadian Journal of African Studies* 8, 1 (1974): 25–41; and Larry
W. Yarak, "'A Man with Whom We Can Do as We Please': Inventing Kingship (and the State) in Elmina"
(paper presented at the African Studies Association annual meeting, Toronto, 1994).

[19] See, for examples, Reindorf, *History of the Gold Coast and Asante*, 103 and 255.

[20] Wilson, *Krobo*, 124.

[21] Cruickshank, *Eighteen Years*, 1, 250–51.

[22] See, for examples, *Gold Coast Times*, June 17, 1882; *Gold Coast Times*, October 16, 1884; and *Gold Coast
Leader*, February 28, 1903.

[23] On the Gold Coast military and police forces, see Anthony Clayton and David Killingray, *Khaki and
Blue: Military and Police in British Colonial Africa* (Athens, GA, 1989), 175–91.

[24] Ibid., 186–89.

India Regiment, and they used the license to annoy all whom they met who were not in the same state of drunkenness as themselves.[25]

And some of the Hausa constabulary and soldiers were even arrested for stealing liquor from shops.[26] In 1882, the *Gold Coast Times* declared the Ada police "as useless; they are generally seen sitting outside grog–shops and strive to escape work."[27] The frequent court cases of drunken disorder involving northerners ("Hausa") may have contributed to the growing impression that northerners could not handle their liquor.[28]

Another group of commoners, the *ewibisofo*[29] of precolonial Kumase, were allowed to incorporate social drinking into their lifestyle because they were a special client group of the Asantehene.

> The people who had Kumasi as their only village were a special group in the population, called the Edwibisofo. The *Edwibisofo* lived near the main market (near the present Kingsway store), filling their days as butchers, traders, and palm wine sellers. These carefree fortunates were described by informants as having no village but Kumasi and no chief but the Asantehene and as being free to enjoy their palm wine and the favors of local women . . .[30]

Kumase was a "princely" city and it was the center of politics in precolonial Asante, not a preferred place of residence. Indeed, many Asante avoided Kumase because of the avariciousness of the resident aristocracy and the rapid changes in their political fortunes.[31] The residents of Kumase became a unique social group, beneficiaries of state–pursued social differentiation within Asante. McCaskie points to the growing contrast from the early nineteenth century between the agricultural industriousness that the state sponsored around Kumase and the life of "leisure" within Kumase. He cites the observation of W. West, a Wesleyan missionary living in Kumase in 1862, that "the people [in Kumase] seem to have but little to do," and "their time is chiefly occupied in eating, and drinking, public processions, and custom making."[32] In the nineteenth century there were emerging distinctions between "urban" and "rural" life in Asante that encouraged the lifestyle of social groups such as the *edwibisofo*.[33]

Models for urban social life in the colonial era were derived not only from the coastal examples of European officers and Fante merchants and lawyers,

---

[25]   *Gold Coast Times*, January 7, 1882.

[26]   See, for examples, *Gold Coast Chronicle*, July 28, 1894, and April 30, 1895.

[27]   *Gold Coast Times*, July 8, 1882.

[28]   See, for examples, NAG, Accra, SCT 38/5/1, C.O.P. [Commissioner of Police] vs. Mahamadu (Koforidua, May 4, 1910); SCT 38/5/7, R. vs. Moshie and Bukari Moshie (Nsawam, December 24, 1914); and SCT 38/5/9, IGP vs. Tenga Moshie (Adoagyiri, January 10, 1917).

[29]   The *Edwibisofo* are described by James Brown as the "indigenes" of Kumasi, who claimed Kumasi as their only home. The etymology of the word is not clear, and Brown did not offer an English translation. James Wilson Brown, "Kumasi, 1896–1923: Urban Africa During the Early Colonial Period" (Ph.D. diss., University of Wisconsin, 1972), 32.

[30]   Ibid.

[31]   Mcleod, *Asante*, 41.

[32]   McCaskie, *State and Society*, 33.

[33]   See K. Arhin, "Peasants in 19th–Century Asante," *Current Anthropology* 24, 4 (1983): 471–79.

but also from emerging indigenous notions of urban life in political capitals like Kumase. Indeed, the celebrations of new organizations like the friendly societies and the temperance societies in the colonial era were very reminiscent of the *asafo*, as they put "on their regalia and march[ed] assertively through the towns in order to impress non–members, young women and, no doubt, one another."[34]

New Social Groups, New Lifestyles

Colonial rule removed the control of traditional rulers over the accumulation of wealth. The spirit of acquisitiveness had been encouraged among individual commoners from the 1830s, when George Maclean's treaty with Asante secured peace south of the river Pra. The expanding market economy revolutionized agriculture—promoting the export of palm oil, rubber, and later cocoa—and introduced railways and mechanized mining. Successful African merchants became the new role models. Christianity and Western education provided competing new ideologies, while "Western lifestyles" served as fertile grounds for social innovation. With the dispersion in wealth, new social groups and new lifestyles emerged.

The Winnebah Tiger Club

Among young migrants in coastal towns, drinking circles replaced the family and kin networks abandoned in rural areas, and provided a platform for demonstrating their newly acquired wealth. Key influences in these developments were European officers and merchants, another group of migrants whose isolation in the late nineteenth–century Gold Coast encouraged their social drinking; and the effective advertising of merchants with their mind boggling array of imported alcoholic drinks. An 1882 *Gold Coast Times* editorial pointed out that: "Over one half of the European gentlemen who come out to the Gold Coast, with all due respect, invariably lead 'fast–lives.' Some individuals have been known to consume £3 worth of liquor in one week."[35] As late as 1930, A. F. L. Wilkinson (the district commissioner stationed at Dunkwa), apprising a new recruit to the colonial administration on the cost of living, could state:

> It is impossible to discuss the question of the cost of living in the Gold Coast without mentioning *Alcohol* [emphasis in the original]. This factor, naturally, is the one which varies most, depending as it does not only on one's personal taste in beverages but on that of one's friends and acquaintances. For everyone who wishes to budget his expenditure it is the principal item to consider, because of its great variation according to one's way of living.[36]

And even in the late nineteenth–century Gold Coast, there was a wide variety of alcoholic beverages to choose from.

---

[34] Casely–Hayford and Rathbone, "Politics, Families and Freemasonry," 148.

[35] *Gold Coast Times*, July 1, 1882.

[36] Letter from A. F. L. Wilkinson to Captain Norris, March 29, 1930. *Wilkinson Papers*, Rhodes House Library, Oxford University.

The 1898 front page advert of T. P. Williams and Company Merchants in the *Gold Coast Chronicle* listed:

"Egg Brandy" and excellent "pick–me–up" Brown's 4 crown Scotch Whisky, Old Tom Gin, Sloe Gin, cherry Whisky, cherry Brandy, Cognac several Brands, Punch Sote, Champagne Cognac, Pints Special Cuvee 1889 Champagne and other brands in quarts, Spanish wines, various kinds, Burgundy, Claret, Sparkling Hock Sherry, Manzanilla, Moscatel, Madeira, Port, Guinness Extra Stout, Bass' India Pale Ale, Lager Beer, several brands Dark and Light.[37]

This was indeed a bacchanalian feast, and in the late nineteenth–century Gold Coast, where rum and gin were often sold cheaper than water, young men had the opportunity to indulge themselves.

Drinking clubs like the Tiger Club of Winnebah emerged in this context from the 1860s.

At a time when good, fresh drinking water was often in short supply, the *African Times* reported with no little disgust that drinking water could be bought in markets at a greater price than gin or rum. A year before that report, the same newspaper had noted the existence of the Tiger Club. This was a collection of young men, who, taking advantage of the low price of hard liquor, had sought to outbid one another by drinking enormous quantities. The club was disbanded in tragic circumstances after two of its members had died while drinking, one by drowning and another from a fall.[38]

What had made drinking clubs like the Tiger Club possible was the independent incomes of its members. Like *nouveaux riches* in a crass display of new wealth, young men in coastal towns adopted drinking patterns that fell below the "sophisticated" pattern of the Fante educated elites they sought to emulate. But one detects the spirit of Bowdich's comment in 1817 that "the vigour of an Ashantee . . . [is] estimated by the measure of the draught [palm wine] he can drink off. . . . "[39] Drink, masculinity, and wealth went together. But a new element had been introduced into social drinking, and this was the extreme abuse of alcohol that even resulted in fatalities. This tendency towards extreme intoxication was previously associated with melancholic Europeans who could not deal with the extreme loneliness of life in the forts and castles.[40]

African merchants involved in rubber and liquor trade exemplified this new pattern of binge drinking in coastal towns. Mischlisch, a Basel missionary in the Volta District in 1897, sent an interesting report to Basel that touched on rubber and liquor trade and the lifestyle of African migrant merchants.

Reports the death of an Akim merchant in Katsenke—died while drunk and everyone believed that he had died because of the drink [schnapps]. His two wives were there and had shaved their heads. The corpse was

[37] *Gold Coast Chronicle*, August 31, 1898.
[38] Casely–Hayford and Rathbone, "Politics, Families and Freemansonry," 149. See also *African Times*, December 23, 1862 and November 23, 1863.
[39] Bowdich, *Mission*, 292.
[40] Albert van Dantzig, *Forts and Castles of Ghana* (Accra, 1980), 85.

wrapped in a 'coloured heathen cloth,' with a large silver chain round the neck, and silver coins by his side. M[ischlisch] went round the alleys of the town to invite people to preaching— 'everywhere I met small groups of merchants, singing and lamenting.' At the entrance to the town 4 drunken merchants were dancing around the grave of another merchant who had died several weeks before—tho[ugh] M[ischlisch] spoke to them earnestly they were prepared only to pour away the Schnapps they had in their glasses—not the whole bottle. . . . It is above all the Akim merchants who bring it—several chiefs have asked M[ischlisch] to write to the Kaiser to ask him to stop the trade in spirits, but part of the trouble is that the local people coin their own money—20x3cm. balls of rubber will buy a bottle of Schnapps.[41]

Rum and schnapps shops proliferated on the coast and in interior Asante,[42] and Gold Coast newspapers often commented in the late nineteenth century on the lucrativeness of the American trade in rum.[43]

The Asante Akonkofo

Even Asante, the stronghold of traditional rule, was not exempt from these new social influences and the growing assertiveness of commoners. From the Maclean Treaty of 1831 and the era of peace it initiated between the British on the coast and the Asante state, trade in Asante ceased to be the preserve of state functionaries and a "host of private individuals had their horizons shifted to the vision of the man of wealth."[44] Concurrent with the spread of the entrepreneurial spirit among Asante commoners was an increase in the exactions of the Asante state under Asantehene Kwaku Dua I (1834–1867), initiating emigration of commoners with ambitions of acquiring wealth or consolidating their wealth. In the 1870s and 1880s the conflict between state mercantilism and *laissez faire* reached its climax in Asante, degenerating into civil war in the 1880s, the dethronement of Asantehene Mensa Bonsu in 1883, the seizure of political power by the young men (*nkwankwaa*) of Kumase and increased emigration to the coast due to insecurity.[45] British annexation of Asante in 1896, and the exile of Asantehene Prempeh and his principal chiefs to Seychelles completed the breakdown of traditional authority in Asante and in Kumase in particular.

Among the exiles to the coast were rich Asante traders in rubber, and some young men of Sawua who had discovered and appropriated gold looted from the royal treasury by the fleeing Mensa Bonsu.[46] These new men of wealth came to

[41] Mischlisch to Basel, September 16, 1897 (No. II. 211). Paul Jenkins, "Abstracts Concerning Gold Coast History from the Basel Mission Archives" (n.p., n.d.).

[42] See, for examples, *Gold Coast Times*, November 25, 1882, on the rum shops along the coast; and the Basel Mission's 1898 Kumase Station Correspondence on the concentration of "schnapps–bars" in Bantama. Ramseyer to Basel, September 28, 1898 (No. II. 162) in Jenkins, "Abstracts."

[43] See, for example, *Gold Coast Times*, August 12, 1882.

[44] McCaskie, "Accumulation, Wealth and Belief, I," 35.

[45] Agnes A. Aidoo, "The Asante Succession Crisis 1883–1888," *THSG* 13, 2 (1972): 163–80; Ivor Wilks, "Dissidence in Asante Politics: Two Tracts from the Late Nineteenth Century," in *African Themes*, ed. Ibrahim Abu–Lughod (Evanston, 1975), 47–63; Wilks, *Asante in the Nineteenth Century*, Chs. 12 and 13; and McCaskie, "Accumulation, Wealth and Belief in Asante History: Part I."

[46] McCaskie, "Accumulation and Belief, II."

constitute a new social elite, the *akonkofo* ("rich men," "gentlemen").[47] Though illiterate, the *akonkofo* enthusiastically endorsed British influence, for it had broken the fetters on social mobility for commoners. The *akonkofo* promoted British imperialism in Asante and resettled in Kumase following the British military defeat of Asante in 1896. Establishing themselves as money lenders, real estate developers, and store owners, the *akonkofo* added to the growing local perception of Kumasefo (Kumase people) as being "enlightened" and urban.[48] Several of these *akonkofo* ascended to traditional political office from 1900 as collaborators of British rule in Asante. Encouraged by the protection of the British administration and the traditional political vacuum created by the exile of the Asantehene, the emboldened *akonkofo* around 1900 actually formed a social club called the "Kumasi Gentlemen." The group was led by two wealthy merchants, Kwame Kyem and Pankroso Kankam.[49] And so influential were these new men in Kumasi politics that in the early decades of the twentieth century, to be a successful businessman had become the surest way of gaining *obirempon* status. To become an *akonkoni* came to represent "the Asante dream" in this period.

The *akonkofo* usurped aspects of the lifestyle of the traditional *abirempon* that emphasized the accumulation and display of gold jewelry and the lavish consumption of alcoholic drinks.

The "Kumasi Gentlemen" consisted of a group of wealthy Asante who organized themselves into a society whose primary qualification for membership was wealth. No such society would have been permitted in precolonial Asante. Furthermore, these wealthy men, who held no traditional offices, arrogated to themselves certain of the former prerogatives of chiefs, particularly the lavish display of gold jewelry and other symbols of wealth. Their activities included such things as attending funerals as a group, bringing their own drinks in drums—contrary to the accepted practice of being provided with drinks by the bereaved family.[50]

In their wealth, the *akonkofo* endorsed European individualism by catering for their own drinks at funerals, and they also rejected the social and spiritual obligations that were associated with receiving gifts of alcohol.[51] Through the medium of alcohol, the *akonkofo* declared their autonomy.

Much excitement surrounded the activities of the *akonkofo* in Kumase. Obaa Panin Afua Pokuaa, whose father Adu Brankro was among the *akonkofo*, recalled those days. Many of these men had made their wealth through the rubber trade. Appellations were composed in their honor:

Akonkofo doo so, akwegyuma ye de
Pinanko junction aye petepee

---

47   Arhin, "A Note on the Asante Akonkofo," 26.
48   Arhin, "Peasants in Nineteenth-Century Asante."
49   Brown, "Kumasi, 1896–1923," 197.
50   Ibid.
51   See Chapter 2.
52   AFN: Interview with Afua Pokuaa, August 18, 1994. Pinanko junction was the Kumase version of "downtown."

Akonkofo are numerous, come and see them display
Pinanko junction is turning over[52]

The *akonkofo* were not only connoisseurs of drink, they also wore beautiful cloths.

They wore beautiful cloths. In those days, *ntoma po* [12 yards] was *ponko
ne sreko* [£1.1s]. [F & A] Swanzy introduced female European manne-
quins. Everybody came to see "Swanzy Saman" ["Swanzy's ghost"],
and that was the occasion for the *akonkofo* to come and buy cloth and
be admired.[53]

The *akonkofo* were admired by commoners because they had succeeded in sabotag-
ing the rigid sumptuary laws in precolonial Asante. Even among the Asante chiefs,
differences in insignia or emblems marked important distinctions in political rank
or power. The state regulated which chief used a silk or cotton umbrella, and
whether his page boys carried elephant or horse tails.[54] The direct challenge this
lifestyle of wealthy commoners presented to established traditional authority is
evidenced by the fact that the "Kumasi Gentlemen's" club was disbanded in the
mid–1920s by Asantehene Prempeh when the latter returned from exile.[55]

As colonial rule became firmly established and chiefs found they could no
longer restrict the accumulation of wealth, they moved to curtail consumption patterns that underscored the new wealth of commoners. In the early twentieth century, traditional states would pass rules regulating the amount of money and drinks
that could be spent in marriage rites and funerals. As Kwame Arhin observed concerning the Asanteman Council's 1935 regulations for marriages:

> Costs were a minor consideration to the Council in making these regula-
> tions. As in the previous century, the source of political concern was lest
> payments made by the new–rich for commoner women should exceed
> those for royalty.[56]

The Council also regulated that the "expenditure on funeral rites for a 'commoner'
should not exceed £G10."[57]

But a new social group of young men was emerging in colonial Ghana, for
whom liquor did not represent a pretentious lifestyle but provided escape from the
harshness of industrial labor and the social alienation of colonial towns. These were
the wage laborers who worked the European–owned mechanized mines and the
colonial–owned railways. They also represented a new development that would
have tremendous social and political import for the future: the group of those who
could never become rich. For them, the contrast between their social lives and that
of the educated coastal elite and Europeans who frequented the Rodger Club in
Accra or the Optimism Club in Sekondi was stark and real. The Optimism Club
counted notable personalities such as Casely Hayford, C. W. T. Menson, and Governor Frederick Guggisberg (1919–1925) among its members.[58] The imposing ce-

---

53 Ibid.

54 Ramseyer and Kühne, *Four Years in Ashantee*, 307.

55 Brown, "Kumasi, 1896–1923," 198.

56 Kwame Arhin, "Monetization and the Asante State," in *Money Matters*, ed. Jane I. Guyer, 104.

57 Ibid., 105.

58 NAG, Sekondi, No. 246 "African Clubs."

Optimism Club, Sekondi, built in 1915

ment wall that surrounded the Optimism Club symbolized a world commoners could never participate in.[59] These wage laborers would come to identify their restricted mobility as a product of colonial rule.

Drinking and Industrial Labor

Social drinking among young men in towns became more pronounced with a growing sense of anomie generated by harsh industrial labor in new industries like mechanized underground mining and railway construction. These new industries were sited in places with natural resources which did not always coincide with populous settlements. Migrant labor was crucial to the development of some colonial towns. Old towns such as Accra and Kumase also expanded in this period, but not as centers of industry. Accra owed its importance to its choice as the colonial administrative capital in 1876, and Kumase as the commercial entrepot of the interior. Although the ethic of economic migration was common by the turn of the twentieth century, young migrants were unprepared for the alienating nature of industrial labor. The rigors of migration help to explain the predominance of males

---

[59]   AFN: Interview with Opanin Kofi Twi, Opanin Kweku Makuronka, Agya Ekow Baidoo, and Opanin Nketsia. These elderly informants remembered the Optimism Club as the preserve of *akrakyefo* ("gentlemen," or the educated elite). On the Optimism Club, see also NAG, Sekondi, No. 140.

in early migration. Migrant workers began to use alcohol as an avenue of escape from unpleasant working conditions, and to create some semblance of control or normalcy in their social lives.[60]
Railway construction in the Gold Coast began in the coastal town of Sekondi in 1898. Rail lines were constructed by the colonial government to link interior mines with the natural harbor at Sekondi. The result was the transformation of the small Ahanta fishing village into a bustling cosmopolitan town. Railway equipment used at the workshop at the Sekondi location was very heavy, and, after an arduous day in the blacksmith's workshop, metal workers who used the furnace felt a restorative was necessary. For these blacksmiths and other railway workers who did exerting work, like laying and maintaining railway tracks, drinking became a way of life, a means of overcoming the physical demands of backbreaking labor.[61] The early twentieth century was the time of the steam locomotive engines, operated by only two workers—the driver and the fireman. The fireman sat behind a coal–powered engine, shoveling in coal through a trap door for the duration of the journey; and the driver stood directly in front of the heat generating engine. It is not surprising that it was generally believed that train drivers hid liquor on the trains,[62] a suspicion confirmed when drivers were occasionally caught and dismissed for drinking on the job.[63]
Obuasi owed its existence and growth to the Ashanti Goldfields Corporation (AGC), founded on the initiative of the Englishman Edwin Cade in 1897 to exploit the gold resources of the region.[64] Workers in the Obuasi underground mines continuously grappled with the reality of staying underground for hours engaged in physical labor. During the early development of the mining industry between 1870 and 1906, tasks assigned to miners were arduous, dirty and dangerous.[65] In 1882, a *Gold Coast Times* editorial criticized the vigorous labor regime at the Tarkwa gold mines.[66] The psychological relief of coming out alive after each work shift and the hot and humid conditions in the shafts which resulted in the loss of body fluids during work combined to generate a deep

---

[60] The strong connection between industrial labor and liquor in Africa is explored in Crush and Ambler, eds., *Liquor and Labor*; Charles van Onselen, *Chibaro: African Mine Labour in Southern Rhodesia* (London, 1976); and Patrick Harries, *Work, Culture, and Identity: Migrant Laborers in Mozambique and South Africa, c.1860–1910* (Portsmouth, 1994).

[61] Intoxicants were also closely associated with strenuous trades in nineteenth–century Britain and America. See Harrison, *Drink and the Victorians*, 41; and John W. Frick, "'He Drank from the Poisoned Cup': Theatre, Culture, and Temperance in Antebellum America," *Journal of American Drama and Theatre* 2, 2 (1992): 21–41.

[62] AFN: Interview with Abaka–Amuah, Public Relations Officer (Ghana Railways Corporation), Takoradi, March 10, 1992.

[63] See, for example, Public Records Office (PRO), London, Colonial Office (CO) 96/597/18243—dismissal of two engine drivers for alcoholism in 1918–19.

[64] G. W. Eaton Turner, "A Short History of the Ashanti Goldfields Corporation Ltd., 1897–1947" (London, 1947).

[65] Jeff Crisp, *The Story of an African Working Class: Ghanaian Miners' Struggles, 1870–1980* (London, 1984), Ch. 2.

[66] *Gold Coast Times*, October 14, 1882.

thirst among underground miners that they satisfied with alcoholic drinks.[67] Frequent deaths among underground miners working in unsafe conditions in the early twentieth century reinforced the anxieties of miners, and in 1923 the Gold Coast administration acknowledged the problem by conducting an inquiry into the death rates of mine laborers.[68]

Communal drinking to assuage anxiety created by hard industrial labor was encouraged by the absence of kin and family networks in the new colonial towns. Migration was often conceived as a temporary strategy to secure specific economic goals, like capital to set up as an independent trader, making individual migration the norm. But the workers' inability to control wage rates often prolonged the migrants' sojourns in the town, and drinking circles or clubs[69] emerged to fill the social vacuum by promoting friendships in the multiethnic colonial towns. The growing cosmopolitan nature of colonial towns is illustrated by the railway town of Sekondi, which in the early 1900s had an "Accra Town," due to an early settlement of Ga carpenters; a "Kru Town" dominated by Krus from Liberia, who did most of the lighterage and stevedoring; a "Lagos Town" composed of Yorubas and "Chekrees" (Calabar area), and a neighborhood for Mendes from Sierra Leone.[70] Drinking circles in the towns came to transcend barriers of ethnicity and age, particularly with the advent of European style drinking bars with their doors open to anyone who had the means to purchase a drink. Unlike the earlier rubber trade, organized by close knit groups of Asante or Akyem, industrial labor cut across ethnicity and age and homogenized the socioeconomic circumstances of wage laborers.

It was in these urban centers, that the beginnings of a popular culture began to emerge among workers.[71] In addition to drinking bars and circles, new forms of dances and music emerged that would later give birth to highlife music. In African societies where music and dance have always been integral aspects of life, these leisure activities were extended to express the process and experience of urbaniza-

---

[67] AFN: Interview with Dr. B. Domakyaareh, Medical Officer in charge of the Government Health Center, Obuasi, April 4, 1992; and interview with Y. B. Amponsah, Industrial Relations Officer (Adansi Shaft), Ashanti Goldfields Corporation, Obuasi, April 9, 1994. Crisp points out that the early twentieth century witnessed struggles over the use of alcohol between African miners and European management trying to inculcate in Africans "rigid temperance" and other virtues of Victorian capitalism. Failure to impose prohibition on mining compounds led to the setting up of spirit shops by mines management in an endeavor to control drinking and the social life of miners. See Crisp, *Story of an African Working Class,* 16 and 36.

[68] PRO, CO 96/647/29611.

[69] European–style beer bars did not become common until World War I, and drinking circles based on work or residential ties provided the convivial atmosphere of the drinking bar.

[70] K. B. Maison, "The History of Sekondi" (B.A. thesis, University of Ghana, 1979), 39.

[71] From the late nineteenth and early twentieth centuries, notions of "leisure time," as distinct from "work time," solidified with the extension of wage labor. The imposition of European time and work discipline on African labor made leisure—especially over the "weekends"—a cherished possession for workers. Urban workers and residents filled leisure time with recreational activities that enlivened their nonworking hours. See Phyllis M. Martin, *Leisure and Society in Colonial Brazzaville* (Cambridge, 1995); and van Onselen, "Randlords and Rotgut." On the interaction of "African" and "European" time and work ethics in nineteenth–century Natal, see Keletso E. Atkins, *The Moon is Dead! Give Us Our Money! The Cultural Origins of an African Work Ethic, Natal South Africa, 1843–1900* (Portsmouth, 1993).

tion.[72] Musical genres and dance styles like *ashiko* (or *asiko*), *osibisaba*, and *konkomba* became popular in coastal towns from the late nineteenth century. Music and dance came to depict and mirror social stratification. Konkomba music provides a good illustration.

> About a hundred years ago [c.1890s], a type of African brass–band music called adaha became very popular with the many brass–bands in the Fanti areas of Ghana. Within a short time the whole of the south of Ghana was swinging to this music, and every town of note wanted to have its own brass–band.
>
> When local musicians couldn't afford to buy expensive imported instruments, they made do with drums, voices, and plenty of fancy dress. This poor man's brass–band music, which included drill–like dances, became known as konkomba or konkoma music.[73]

In the poorer areas of port towns like Sekondi, local musicians learned to play the sailors' instruments.[74] Kru immigrants in Sekondi, a maritime people, were renowned for their musical skills.

Young men in the towns had begun to use drink, music, and dance as forms of protest against traditional and colonial authorities by the early twentieth century. These forms of protest are captured in a 1909 court case, Commissioner of Police vs. Kwamin Antwi and Oblamawuo, at the District Magistrate's court at Nsawam. According to the arresting corporal Soalla Kangaga:

> On the 30th July 1909 in the morning I was walking towards my house. I hear some people play osibisaba. I ask who is the house master for the place they play. I asked Kwamin Antwi and he show me the house master [Obamawuo?]. I asked him if you could not play anything except osibisaba, and I tell him it was against the law to play it. I tell him he must stop it or I go to make palaver. . . . He says as he get leave to play from the Commissioner, he play what he like then he began to abuse me. And as he was drunk I went and fetched the other policemen.[75]

A scuffle ensued when the police attempted to arrest Kwamin Antwi and Oblamawuo. In fact, the police needed extra help to arrest the two men. They were jailed six months each with hard labor. It is evident that the colonial authorities had detected a connection between these early pillars of popular culture and social protest. Their attempts to nip popular culture in the bud would fail, and a mature popular culture would provide the basis to critique colonial rule from the 1930s.[76]

The introduction of the guitar into coastal areas of the Gold Coast gave young men an additional social badge, and a boost to their musical creativity and leisure activities. The guitar and palm wine became closely associated, giving birth to a

[72] A good parallel is the development of the *Beni* dance–societies of East Africa in the late nineteenth and early twentieth centuries. Terrence Ranger, *Dance and Society in Eastern Africa, 1890–1970: The Beni Ngoma* (London, 1975).

[73] John Collins, *West African Pop Roots* (Philadelphia, 1992), 18.

[74] Ibid.

[75] NAG, Accra, SCT 38/5/1, District Magistrate's Court (Nsawam). Commissioner of Police vs. Kwamin Antwi and Oblamawuo, July 31, 1909.

[76] See Chapters 5 and 6.

new genre of music known as palm–wine music. On its origins, John Collins commented that:

palm–wine music emerged from low–class seaport dives and palm–wine bars. In fact the guitar became so closely associated with this African beer, brewed naturally from the palm tree, that anyone playing the guitar was considered to be a drunken rascal.[77]

The symbol of the guitar came to inform the old generational struggles between male elders and young men.

When the chiefs and elders of Bekwai (Asante) moved to destool their young *omanhene* (paramount chief) in 1920—Kwame Poku had been enstooled while he was in elementary school—they included an interesting charge.

That he has been in the habit of fighting in the streets, and besides roaming throughout the streets all over Town in European clothes absolutely intoxicated; with a guitar in his hands, playing and singing. Going from place to place to the educated classes "CADGING" for drinks. A disgraceful habit for an Omanhene.[78]

Local chiefs and elders in inland and coastal towns found the new drinking patterns among young men, and their lifestyles in general, disruptive to order and the maintenance of their authority. In fact, pronounced social drinking among the young men was a reminder to the elders of the decline in their authority under the colonial order. In the late nineteenth century, a group of wealthy Asante commoners in exiles on the coast could boldly state:

What is an African King? . . . The poorest Englishman is wealthier than 1,000 of them; an Englishman's pair of trowsers [sic] is more valuable than their state appearance in full costume.[79]

The town elders, naturally, found the increasing waves of young migrants very disconcerting. And even women seemed to be taking advantage of the colonial regime to declare their independence of men and custom.

Gender Relations in Colonial Towns

The historical evidence is less clear for women in the emerging towns, and their imprint on urban social life—including social drinking and ongoing social conflicts between 1890 and 1919—is more difficult to reconstruct. The material becomes more abundant from the 1930s, but even then the focus is more on inland villages and burgeoning towns. The nature of urbanization created economic and social opportunities for some women between 1890 and 1920. The sexual imbalance among the populations of working–class towns opened up important economic opportunities for women as sellers of prepared food and providers of domestic services, including sex. To take the example of the railway town of Sekondi, the male population

---

[77]   Collins, *West African Pop Roots*, 32.

[78]   NAG, Accra, ADM 11/1/773. Bekwai Native Affairs (1920).

[79]   Wilks, "Dissidence in Asante Politics," 59.

in 1901 was 3,469, compared to the female population of 626.[80] This gives us a ratio of five men to every single woman. Old towns like Accra, Cape Coast, and Kumasi had more sexually balanced populations. But as migration expanded, in the wake of mechanized mining and cocoa cultivation, even rural areas began to show an imbalance in sexual ratios. The census officer in 1911 commented that "in the mining and agricultural districts it appears that the imported labourers are unaccompanied by their women."[81] The social reproduction of this migrant male population was the task of women.

Unlike east, central, and southern Africa, women in the Gold Coast did not experience the severe restrictions imposed on female urban immigration in white settler colonies.[82] Rural elders did attempt to prevent young women from migrating, but they lacked the institutional support of pass laws and similar obstacles that hindered mobility in southern Africa. Also, women were often already in the Gold Coast towns, as many of these towns predated colonial rule. The ability of colonial rulers to shape urban space was relatively limited. Important towns like Accra, Kumasi, Sekondi–Takoradi, and Obuasi did have European residential areas for European employers and colonial administrators. Gold Coast towns such as Sekondi and Obuasi, that emerged as a result of colonial economic activity, did reflect the colonial endeavor to shape urban space.[83] In Sekondi, railway workers were housed in compounds at Ketan. In Obuasi, the Ashanti Goldfields Corporation and its affiliate, the Ashanti Obuasi Trading Company (AOTC), struggled to control the activities of even traders.[84] But here the imprint was that of capital, not the colonial state. However, there was an important commonality and continuity in the roles of urban women in colonial Africa: they were expected—by African men, colonial rulers, European capitalists, and white missionaries—to maintain their rural roles of production and reproduction.[85]

Women migrated to Sekondi from the 1890s. Initially, most were from Liberia or Nigeria. Later, Nzima and Fante from Cape Coast also joined the growing ranks of women in Sekondi.[86] One of the ways in which some of these women subsisted in towns was through prostitution, and Nkontompo, on the outskirts of Sekondi, would emerge as the quarter for prostitutes.[87] Prostitution in towns was a vital initial strategy for newly arrived women. The sale of sexual favors could secure migrant women their first, temporary place of residence. Unlike the sale of foodstuffs or liquor, prostitution did not necessarily require start–up capital. Eventu-

[80]   Gold Coast Colony, *Census of the Population, 1901,* 55. NAG, Accra, ADM 5/2/2.

[81]   Gold Coast Colony, *Census of the Population, 1911,* 30. NAG, Accra, ADM 5/2/3.

[82]   White, *Comforts of Home;* La Hausse, *Brewers, Beerhalls and Boycotts;* Lovett, "Gender Relations"; and Parpart, "Where Is Your Mother?"

[83]   On the struggle to shape urban space in colonial Africa, see Frederick Cooper, ed., *Struggle for the City: Migrant Labor, Capital and the State in Urban Africa* (Beverly Hills, 1983).

[84]   See, for examples, NAG, Kumasi, ROA 001 and ROA 414 (Regional Administration files), on the activities of AOTC between 1904 and 1915.

[85]   Martin, *Leisure and Society,* 73; Parpart, "Where Is Your Mother," 257–63; and Allman, "Making Mothers."

[86]   AFN: Interview with Opanin Kofi Twi, Opanin Kweku Mukuronka, Opanin Kweku Nketsia, and Agya Ekow Baidoo.

[87]   AFN: Interview with Anita Mensah, Takoradi, August 16, 1994.

ally, the prostitute could move to her own lodgings. The need for security and social networks encouraged prostitutes, often from the same ethnic groups, to settle close together. K. A. Busia's social survey of Sekondi–Takoradi in the late 1940s revealed 127 known prostitutes, only nine of whom were from the indigenous Ahanta ethnic group.[88] Although the colonial government disapproved of prostitution, the vagueness of the law on prostitution for the most part of the colonial era militated against the prosecution of prostitutes.[89] But prostitution never received the official encouragement that was extended in French Congo, especially during World War II.[90]

Some women sold liquor in the coastal and interior towns, and there is evidence for this early period that liquor sales were providing women with an economic niche in the colonial towns. Male elders interviewed in Anarfo (Sekondi), provided the author with a contrasting (idealized?) picture of social life for indigenes and migrants. The local Sekondi people were fisherfolk by occupation. They did not take to liquor and frequent bars. When they drank, it was palm wine. The immigrants did drink and go to bars. But on Tuesdays, a day tabooed for fishing, *osibi* or *osibisaba* provided popular entertainment.[91] In other towns during the early colonial period, court records indicate that women were active as retailers of liquor. On February 14, 1898, Abba Muria, Adjua Mannu, Adjuah Moshi, and Abba Yewuh were found guilty for selling liquor from their living quarters and were deprived of their licenses in the Kumasi District Court.[92] Animah was on July 23, 1909, fined £5 for selling liquor without a license in the town of Nsawam.[93] It appears social drinking was also prominent among female migrants from Nigeria and Liberia in the early colonial period.[94] That the Wesleyan Methodist Missionary Society found the formation of a female League of Abstainers in Accra in 1918 "very gratifying" indicates that female drinking may not have been insignificant.[95]

The cultivation of cocoa, which intensified the exploitation of rural women, may have encouraged rural–urban migration. The lucrativeness of the new cocoa industry, coming on the heels of the abolition of slavery, created a labor shortage. Marriage transactions became increasingly commercialized as male kin sought to cash in on the widespread demand for wives and labor.[96] Men were increasingly

---

[88] K. A. Busia, *Report on the Social Survey of Sekondi–Takoradi* (London, 1950), 107–108. Akyeampong, "Constructing and Contesting Sexuality," provides a detailed study of prostitution in precolonial and colonial Gold Coast.

[89] See, for example, NAG, Accra, ADM 11/1/922 (1925): "Unsatisfactory state of law [concerning] prostitution."

[90] Martin, *Leisure and Society*, 139.

[91] AFN: Interview with Opanin Kofi Twi *et al.*

[92] NAG, Kumase, SCT 204/1, Regina vs. Abba Muria, Adjua Manuu, Kwamin Ansah, Adjuah Moshi, Abbah Yewuh, Eilu, Quaye (Kumasi, February 14, 1898). Retail liquor outlets were regulated by Ordinances 18 and 19 of 1887.

[93] NAG, Accra, SCT 38/5/1, C.O.P. vs. Animah (Nsawam, July 24, 1909).

[94] AFN: Interview with Laurence Cudjoe, J. K. Annan, Joseph Kofi Ackon, and Arhu, Sekondi, May 27, 1992.

[95] Wesleyan Methodist Missionary Society (WMMS) Archives, deposited at the School of Oriental and African Studies (University of London). 1918 Gold Coast Synod Minutes, West Africa, Microfiche Box 11.

[96] Roberts, "The State and the Regulation of Marriage"; Manuh, "Changes in Marriage"; Austin, "Human Pawning in Asante."

asked to "buy" their wives in the early colonial era, and the combination of women's productive and reproductive functions led to the distinct feminization of pawnage.[97] Beverly Grier emphasizes that women—as wives, nieces, pawns, porters—bore the brunt of the Gold Coast's remarkable emergence as a world leading producer of cocoa in the early twentieth century.[98] The intense male exploitation of female labor in the cocoa industry may have encouraged female porters to "desert" to the towns. As porters to the inland and coastal towns, they were exposed to a first-hand experience of assertive urban women. But Grier's vivid portrayal of women as "victims" may apply particularly to the early years of cocoa cultivation. In matrilineal Akan societies, men's dependence on the labor of their wives and children generated expectations of inheritance that were sometimes met, but which conflicted with the norms of matrilineal inheritance.[99] Gareth Austin points out that some women acquired their own cocoa farms and gained autonomy in their relations with men through their wealth.[100] Penelope Roberts and Jean Allman depict the 1920s and 1930s as a period of socioeconomic opportunity for some rural women.[101] Indeed, they argue that the successful accumulation of wealth by some women, especially single women, sparked off the roundup of spinsters in the interior states of Sefwi Wiawso and Asante in the late 1920s and 1930s.

It is in the sphere of gender relations in the colonial towns that the impact of women was very visible. It is evident that women were taking advantage of the changing social order under colonialism, even in rural areas, to redefine their relations to men. This development was aided by the coexistence of native tribunals (customary law) and British courts (English commom law), and their distinct spheres of jurisdiction in this period of colonial rule. Importantly, the colonial government recognized customary marriage and marriage by the ordinance, mandating the latter as monogamous. This duality provided women with room to maneuver in the reinterpretation of marriage obligations, sexuality, and appropriate custom.[102] What is striking in the court cases of the early twentieth century was the assertiveness of some women in their relations to men, their determination to contract their own marriages, their interpretation of their rights and privileges in marriage, and their increasing insistence on male fidelity.[103]

It is clear that financial independence gave women more choice in their selection of marital partners in the towns. The influence of male elders in arranging marriages for their junior kinswomen was weakened in the towns. To secure their

---

[97] Austin, "Human Pawning in Asante."

[98] Grier, "Pawns, Porters, and Petty Traders." It is striking that in land-poor Anlo society, the intense exploitation of the labor and sexuality of young women (free and unfree) extended back to the eighteenth century. That century witnessed the influx of refugees into Anlo and the intensification of the slave trade on the Upper Slave Coast. Sandra E. Greene, *Gender, Ethnicity, and Social Change on the Upper Slave Coast: A History of the Anlo-Ewe* (Portsmouth, 1996).

[99] Okali, *Cocoa and Kinship*; and Okali, "Kinship and Cocoa Farming in Ghana," in Oppong, *Female and Male in West Africa*, 169–78.

[100] Austin, "Human Pawning," 143.

[101] Roberts, "The State and the Regulation of Marriage"; and Allman, "Rounding up Spinsters."

[102] See Gocking, "British Justice and the Native Tribunals."

[103] In 1933, at the Awunu Eire headman's court in Accra, a woman sued another women for damages for committing adultery with her husband. This was a novel, female version of *ayefere*. Gocking, "British Justice and the Native Tribunals," 109.

personal choices, women were willing to assist their suitors with the expenses involved in marriage rites, a radical departure in custom and gender relations.[104] An aspect of this growing independence on the part of women was a desire to protect their reputations. Women individually sued men who defamed their characters, seeking legal satisfaction and protecting their social reputations.[105] Women wanted to remove their object status and their position as jural minors.

In 1911, Araba Abakuma, in spite of the existence of male relations, personally brought a suit against J. A. Mason at the Cape Coast native tribunal for seducing her daughter, Esi Botsiwah.[106] Roger Gocking perceptively points to the enhanced role of the native tribunals as law "modifiers" and "amenders of customary law," and the instrumentality of literate court registrars—in the case of the Cape Coast tribunal, W. Z. Coker—in this process.[107] The state of Fante (and Akan) customary law had been rendered more confusing by the attempts of Fante scholars, such as Mensah Sarbah and J. E. Casely–Hayford, to transcribe or compile customary law.[108] The authoritativeness or otherwise of these texts encouraged lively debates in the Cape Coast native tribunal.

Literate youngmen were also eager to take advantage of the contested state of customary law. In October 1914, W. F. Walker brought a charge of seduction against Alfred Halm. Alfred Halm's defense was remarkable in its attempt to use English common law and "customary law" against customary law.

> Complainant has no right to sue for seduction assuming that I had seduced complainant's wife his right is to take an action against me for satisfaction [ayefere]. An action for seduction is taken by either a father, mother, family of the girl or a guardian and before they could take such an action they should get that from the girl that I had seduced her. Complainant is out of count both in the English Law and Fanti Customary Law. In support of my plea I cite page[s] 79–85 Fanti Law Report Solomon Ackah v. Arinta (Fanti National Constitution), Yaw Penin v. William Duncan page 118 of the Fanti Customary Law, 1904.[109]

Halm was seeking to draw a distinction between seduction (of a minor) and adultery (with an adult), arguing that the case ought to be thrown out on this technicality for he had been sued on the wrong charge. But Halm had met his match in the Cape Coast native tribunal registrar, Coker. He was found guilty and fined £7.4s. with 49s.6d as costs. Although it was not made explicit in the tribunal proceedings, the case of W. F. Walker vs. Alfred Halm raised the issue of who controlled women's

---

[104] See, for example, Akosua Oobil vs. Grabbah, at the native tribunal in Cape Coast, *Gold Coast Times*, August 22, 1884.

[105] See, for examples, Accosuah Fynbah vs. Quabinah; and Akosua Oobil vs. Grabbah before Cape Coast native tribunal. *Gold Coast Times*, August 22, 1884.

[106] NAG, Cape Coast, ADM 71/1/1/1, Araba Abakuma vs. J. A. Mason, Native Tribunal of Tufuhene Coker, Cape Coast, January 16, 1911.

[107] Gocking, "British Justice and the Native Tribunals," 106.

[108] Sarbah, *Fanti National Constitution*; Sarbah, *Fanti Customary Laws*; and J. E. Casely–Hayford, *Gold Coast Native Institutions* (London, 1903).

[109] NAG, Cape Coast, ADM 71/1/1/6 (Acc. No. 315), W. F. Walker vs. Alfred Halm, Cape Coast native tribunal, October 29, 1914.

sexuality. It is clear from the proceedings that neither party nor the tribunal members considered it the woman's prerogative.

It is necessary to emphasize the limits of what might be seen as an unfettered period of opportunity for women. A 1913 court case cited by Jean Allman underscores the unchanging object status of women, even before the colonial authorities. In September 1913, a case was brought before the Commissioner of the Western Province of Asante. The chief of Senase filed for adultery compensation on his female slave and mother of one of his children. This woman had run away to Sunyani, and was living with a clerk with whom she had another child. Since slavery had been abolished in Asante, the slave woman assumed that her master's hold on her—including sexual access—had been terminated. The chief commissioner of Asante thought otherwise. He argued that

> once you have done away with 'slavery' the status of wifehood must be one and the same. I make them or their paramount pay satisfaction on the same scale as regular wives—indeed, I now don't differentiate between them [and] would ask you to introduce the same rule.[110]

Women's room for maneuver had been created by the contradictions within colonial rule and the colonial economy. But as ex–slaves, pawns, wives, nieces, and daughters, women remained firmly subordinated to men in the pre–World War I era.[111] The war would bring an opportunity for male elders to regain their control over young men.

Hope for the Elders? The Prospect of British Prohibition

Hope for the elders, in their social struggle with the young men and women, was raised from an unexpected quarter. Britain in 1919 proposed the prohibition of European liquor traffic to the Gold Coast. In the impending peace talks, Britain believed the abolition of liquor traffic in her West African colonies would improve her bid for the ex–German colonies.[112] Male elders were elated, for the prohibition of the European liquor traffic would take away the liquor that had become central to the lifestyle of young men and women in the towns. A reversion to palm wine would be in the elders' favor, as land was still under their control. Responses by chiefs and elders from the Colony and Asante to the government's inquiry of their position on prohibition revealed their enthusiastic support for prohibition. To strengthen their case, they linked liquor to disorder and crime.

But a careful reading of the testimonies submitted by chiefs and elders indicates that what the male elders wanted was not total prohibition but any measure that would eliminate cheap spirits affordable to most young men. It is also significant that areas like Busua (Western Province), not plagued by conflict between elders and young men, were opposed to prohibiting European liquor.

---

[110] As cited in Allman, "Of 'Spinsters,' 'Concubines,' and 'Wicked Women,'" 180–81.

[111] In fact, as late as the 1930s, female relatives were still being pawned to raise loans. Grier, "Pawns, Porters, and Petty Traders," 319.

[112] See Chapter 4.

Considering the fact that European liquor had been incorporated into religio–cultural uses, some adjustment by male elders would be necessary in the event of prohibition. As Nana Amonu V, Paramount Chief of the coastal town of Anomabu, opined:

> Although alcohol is a poison in all quantities, as a medicine it takes the place of medical remedies, with little disadvantage to the suffering community. The quantity should be regulated . . . price made "sky high," dealing thus dependent on pecuniary ability. . . . In 9 cases out of 10 the commission of heinous crimes, disturbances, riots, bloodshed, and many suicidal practices amongst the inhabitants of the colonies result very solely from intoxicants.[113]

Nana Amonu overtly linked disorder to cheap imported spirits, but chose not to single out the young men for condemnation although their indictment was implicit.

The paramount chief of Mampong and his principal chiefs and elders were less tactful, citing drinking among the young men as the source of social disorder.

> And after a long and deepest consideration we discovered that an alcohol [sic] is a thing always leads most youngmen into a greatest temptation and therefore we do confirm of your Worship's suggestion [to prohibit European liquor].[114]

The chiefs of the Volta River District were overjoyed.

> Here there is a very strong majority in favour of liquor prohibition, in fact every chief interviewed expressed the view that the stoppage of drink would 'draw the young men into better ways and cause them to work, whereas now they spend their time drinking, playing band and adulteration' (sic); the later I understand indicating lapses from moral rectitude rather than an adulteration of spirituous liquors.[115]

Prohibition of European liquor would undermine those activities of young men that elders found most threatening: binge drinking and womanizing.

But events did not materialize as anticipated by the chiefs and their elders. The British government decided to compromise on prohibiting the traffic in European liquor because of the dependence on liquor revenue by the governments in the British West African colonies.[116] The change in British intentions convinced chiefs of the need to ally with the expanding Western style temperance movement. Henceforth, chiefs would actively seek to influence colonial liquor legislation. And liquor policy would become one of the most politicized arenas in the 1920s and 1930s. Between liquor revenue and the temperance concerns of chiefs and elders, a colonial agenda was forged that strove to balance revenue needs with social control. In the 1920s, when the colonial policy of indirect rule was more actively pursued in the Gold Coast, the colonial government would firmly come down on the side of the chiefs in their struggle with women and young men.

---

[113] PRO, CO 96/601/45430.

[114] Ibid.

[115] Ibid.

[116] See Chapter 4.

Conclusion

The period from 1890 to 1919 represented a significant phase in the endeavor of young men and women to overthrow the rigid social control of rural and urban male elders. The coexistence of customary and British law courts, the fluidity of early colonial rule, cash crop cultivation, and urban capitalist production were important resources for young men and women. In urban centers, social drinking, music, and dance became the pillars of an emerging popular culture. New social groups like the *akonkofo* and urban wage workers used alcohol to express their new found wealth and independence. As rural cash crop producers, retailers of alcoholic drinks, and prostitutes in towns, some women became active accumulators and sought to shape their relations with men. Chiefs and male elders struggled to curb this social threat from young men and women. The chiefs and elders leaned towards the colonial government for support to shore up their declining patriarchal authority. The chiefs' interest in social control intersected with the importance of liquor revenue for the colonial government. Liquor legislation became the sphere for mediating the concerns of liquor revenue and social control. But negotiating the colonial agenda was not the exclusive preserve of the colonial government and African chiefs. The metropolitan temperance movement eagerly tracked liquor traffic to the Gold Coast, and the colony was also subject to international liquor conventions. These developments are important in understanding how an agenda came to be forged that threatened the livelihood and lifestyles of urban commoners, and their emerging popular culture. These processes are explored in the next chapter.

4

Negotiating the Colonial Agenda: Temperance Politics and Liquor Legislation in the Gold Coast, 1919–1930

Significant in the negotiation of the colonial agenda was the parallel importance of alcohol and water in the Gold Coast, and British conceptions of secular and sacred power. Alcohol, the powerful ritual fluid for Gold Coasters, became a major source of colonial revenue, just as it had been in the metropolitan economy. This provided a common ground for chiefs and the colonial government in their deliberation over liquor policy. But whereas chiefs desired that the young men's access to liquor be curtailed, the colonial government sought to benefit financially from liquor imports. As the British colonial government adopted indirect rule through chiefs in the late 1920s, it compromised on its financial considerations where liquor imports were concerned, and moved towards strengthening the social control of the chiefs. Although women and young men would be severely affected by the colonial agenda, they had no official role in its composition. But their responses to the colonial agenda could not be ignored.

The purifying quality of water was common to indigenous religions in the southern Gold Coast and Christianity. This similarity encouraged African conversion and reinforced old notions of equalitarianism. It also facilitated the temperance alliance against the "corruptive power" of alcohol. The significance of liquor revenue and temperance in the Gold Coast and Britain subjected the meanings of alcohol and water to fierce contentions that bolstered, and sometimes transformed, existing generational and gender conflicts. The fluid political, economic, and social conditions of early colonial rule accentuated these tensions.

Context

In their struggle against the young men, some Gold Coast chiefs and elders had come to the conclusion by the beginning of the twentieth century that liquor imports could be stopped only at the source: Europe and the United States. What the chiefs sought to prohibit were brands of cheap liquor popular among the young men. Their ideal objective was a legislation that ensured their access to liquor for ritual and social purposes, but severed the young men's access to liquor. It was a policy of "partial prohibition." In 1897, Volta District chiefs had requested the Basel missionary, Mischlisch, to write to the Kaiser to halt schnapps exports to the Gold Coast.[1] The Wesleyan Synod meeting of 1906 reported the receipt of a message from the chief of Krobo, soliciting their assistance in suppressing the importation of Elephant Gin.[2] Since liquor was imported from Europe, the chiefs shrewdly decided to seek the missionaries as allies in their crusade against the young men and drink. The chiefs also reckoned that, since the young men were emulating Western drinking patterns, the remedy to the young men's challenge might lie in Western-style temperance.

But just as multiple meanings were attached to alcohol in Gold Coast societies, so did Western temperance assume multiple meanings and attract various adherents for different reasons. For several mission-educated young men, temperance went with missionary education. Most of the early educated young men, particularly in interior states like Akyem Abuakwa and Asante, were of lowly social origin, since the aristocracy remained suspicious of Christianity and Western education. For these early Gold Coast Christians, Christianity's elevation of the sacred power of water—in baptism and confirmation—meshed with indigenous conceptions of water as a sacred and equalitarian fluid.[3] Just as Onyame could be approached directly through the ritual use of water, the Christian did not require intermediaries like the male elders and ancestors, nor libation in order to communicate with God. Most gratifying to these early Christians was the fact that in Christianity water represented spiritual wealth.[4] And in a Christian hereafter (heaven) where all drew close to God—which differed from the indigenous representation of life-after-death as a replica of the inequalities of life on earth—early Gold Coast Christians found strength and comfort. They, with missionary support, would come into direct conflict with chiefs over the ritual use of alcohol; indeed, over the very meaning of alcohol.[5]

Conflicts between Gold Coast Christians and chiefs over traditional obligations and customs (including the ritual use of alcohol) made the temperance movement appear as a refuge for subjects who wanted to defy the authority of chiefs—even those who did not believe in abstinence. Likewise, several young men not

---

[1] See Chapter 3.

[2] WMMS (West Africa) Archives, 1906 Gold Coast Synod Minutes, Microfiche Box 4.

[3] See Chapters 1 and 2.

[4] The presence of the Holy Spirit in Christianity is symbolized by water. For some relevant verses on water and spiritual wealth, see, Isaiah 44:3; John 4:14; and John 7:37-38.

[5] As will be shown later, the conflict between the African ritual use of alcohol and the missionary desire to de-emphasize the ritual importance of alcohol in Christianity in the Gold Coast could have encouraged the Methodist attempt to ban wine in communion.

committed to abstinence saw in the temperance movement a symbol of "social progress" and "modernity." This impression was supported by the fact that most important coastal families were members of temperance societies. In the coastal towns like Cape Coast and Anomabu, to join the temperance movement was an indication of social mobility. In fact, the temperance movement was only one of numerous social associations that proliferated from the 1850s in the Gold Coast, and for many urban and rural Africans the temperance movement was just one more resource to be utilized in their endeavor for social mobility. Conversion to Christianity and temperance were social decisions that were carefully evaluated for social benefits, not just a personal declaration of faith.

A cursory examination of the Western temperance movement gives the impression that it was opposed to chiefly or traditional authority. But, there were compatible interests that made an alliance between chiefs and temperance missionaries mutually beneficial. Struggling for converts, even the nominal adherence of chiefs represented an important gain for missionaries, as such adherence allayed the fears of subjects wary of conversion for fear of the chiefs' wrath. And nominal adherence by chiefs could be the precursor to genuine conversion.[6]

Also the Christian churches themselves, in the face of Gold Coast cultures, were struggling to define proper Christian life for their congregations, and polygamy, the customary celebration of rites of passage, and other aspects of African cultures—in which the ritual use of alcohol was central—had to be tackled delicately. The Catholic church in the Volta River District, for example, found it unrealistic to uphold total abstinence among its congregation, settling instead for moderation. Thus the Christian churches in the Gold Coast could not agree whether "temperance" meant "moderation" or "abstinence," and debates over "total prohibition" and "partial prohibition" came to characterize discussions on the "liquor question." For missionaries to define temperance as moderation brought them closer to chiefs and laid the basis for temperance cooperation.

But by the early twentieth century, liquor revenue had established itself as the single, leading contributor to the colonial government's finances. The centuries of ritual and social use of alcohol among the peoples of the southern Gold Coast had created a large demand for imported European liquor. Tariffs on imported liquor, in addition to licensing fees for liquor outlets, constituted as much as forty percent of the government's revenue in the 1910s. Domestic wealth generated by palm oil, rubber, and cocoa exports underpinned the demand for imports, and local hostility to direct taxation made indirect taxes—such as customs duties—the most reliable source of government revenue. The Gold Coast colonial government, obviously, would not willingly prohibit liquor traffic, considering the financial ramifications. The ensuing tussle over liquor legislation transformed colonial liquor policy into a contested terrain between chiefs, their educated African allies and the colonial government. Indeed, the surest way to gain official attention for new claimants to political power was to attack liquor revenues. Between 1919 and 1930, temperance politics and liquor legislation became important avenues for negotiating the colonial agenda.

---

6   The Manya Krobo *Konor* Odonkor Azu's relationship with the Basel missionaries in the mid-nineteenth century exemplifies the opportunistic relations between chiefs and missionaries. Wilson, *Krobo*, 141–49.

Chiefs and the Victorian Temperance Movement

It is noteworthy that the first Western temperance society in the Gold Coast was formed in 1862 by someone who became a paramount chief, King Ghartey IV of Winnebah. Ghartey had just returned from a trip to England, where he had become connected with a temperance society.[7] Ghartey's background and social activities raise intriguing questions about his motives for establishing a temperance movement, and his understanding of temperance.

As a royal, versed in the ritual use of alcohol, it is doubtful that Ghartey espoused total prohibition. As K. A. Busia, a royal, Christian, and scholar, was to point out later in the 1950s:

> No one could be a chief who did not perform the ritual functions of his office. There have recently been elected chiefs . . . who are both literate and Christian. But they have an obligation to perform the ritual acts of their office. They were enstooled in the stool-house, where they poured libations to the ancestors whom they had succeeded.[8]

Ghartey became king of Winnebah in 1872, and it is definite that he performed rituals involving libation. A chief ran the risk of losing his legitimacy by cutting himself off from the basis of his authority—his link to his ancestors.

Casely-Hayford and Rathbone view Ghartey's temperance society as reacting in a new way to a very traditional complaint: the use and abuse of alcohol by young men. In this case, the precipitating factor in Ghartey's decision to establish a temperance society was the activities of drinking clubs like the Tiger Society in Winnebah.[9] Ghartey's temperance society can be seen as part of the ongoing effort by chiefs and elders to exclude young men from the use of a fluid that was so closely tied to the exercise of their power. What was new about Ghartey's endeavor was his formation of an organized, Western-style temperance movement to do it.

Also, Ghartey perceived the temperance society as a novel instrument for implementing social change. Ghartey was aware of the immense appeal that being "Western" held for young men and women in the towns, for he, himself, had been subject to that pull as a young man. Before he was enstooled as king, Ghartey had been apprenticed as a cooper with the Dutch firm of Stooves Brothers in the Gold Coast, through which, being illiterate, he hoped to "pick up something of the . . . [whiteman's] language."[10] His service at Stooves Brothers included a stint at Shama where the firm was manufacturing soap and distilling rum as an experiment, thus he probably even knew how to distill liquor. In fact, prior to setting up the temperance society, "King Ghartey had several rum shops [at Anomabu] and did a very good business."[11] He had actually contemplated establishing a distillery to manufacture rum in the Gold Coast. On his return from his 1861 trip to England, Ghartey, then a wealthy man, introduced

---

[7]   Magnus J. Sampson, *Gold Coast Men of Affairs* (London, 1969), 115.

[8]   Busia, *Position of the Chief*, 38.

[9]   Casely-Hayford and Rathbone, "Politics, Families and Freemasonry," 149.

[10]   Sampson, *Gold Coast Men of Affairs*, 114.

[11]   *Gold Coast Chronicle*, October 6, 1894. According to this report, King Ghartey converted to temperance through a chance encounter with some temperance literature from the United States.

the "*kabasrotu*" (a corruption of the English "Cover Shoulder" dress) among the women of his household to cover their nakedness.[12] What can be inferred from these glimpses into Ghartey's complex life was that he was adequately equipped to manipulate aspects of Western civilization to the service of temperance and the maintenance of traditional authority. The young men wanted to establish their independence as well as portray their subscription to Western ideas on social comportment and economic development. Ghartey was subtly redirecting them from emulating Western social drinking to other channels of Western influence. The use to which he put his temperance society underscores the observation that it was conceived as an instrument of social change:

> After a year's activity the members were able to report with pride the establishment of a temperance hotel, and a temperance goldsmith's shop, each with a light outside: "the first lamp posts ever erected in any streets of any town in the Gold Coast."[13]

And the membership of influential coastal families, who represented social role models for young men and women, in the temperance movement—the Brews, the Abadoos, the Fergusons, the Insaidoos, the Amissahs, and the Fynns of Winnebah and Anomabo—strengthened Ghartey's strategy.[14] Like Ghartey, many Africans came to associate the temperance society with progress and social mobility.

In 1877, three years after the Gold Coast had been declared a British colony, the first church-linked temperance society, the Good Templars, was established in Cape Coast by the Wesleyan Methodist Missionary Society. By the 1870s, the prohibition drive in Britain had diminished in strength because of internal divisions among the nonconformist churches.[15] For the derailed prohibition movement, the British colonies held brighter prospects.[16] Instrumental to the establishment of the Good Templars in the Gold Coast was a leading Methodist layman, J. P. Brown, and the commanding officer of the Cape Coast garrison.[17] Thus, Christianity, individual improvement—Brown was a leading educationist involved in promoting education and self-improvement—and political influence were associated with the Good Templars from its inception. Ambitious young men and women flocked to the Good Templars in coastal towns.

The conception of the temperance society as a network facilitating social mobility was strengthened by its introduction with a host of other social associations run by mission-educated Africans in post-1850 Gold Coast. Women's clubs, literary clubs, debating clubs, masonic lodges, and temperance societies flourished alongside ethnic associations in the growing towns as migrant Africans sought new social networks, platforms for political activity, and a general

---

[12]   David Kimble, *Political History* (Oxford, 1963), 134.

[13]   Ibid., 146.

[14]   Casely-Hayford and Rathbone, "Politics, Families and Freemasonry," 149.

[15]   See A. E. Dingle, *The Campaign for Prohibition in Victorian England: The United Kingdom Alliance 1872–1895* (London, 1980).

[16]   See H. A. Wyndham, "The Problem of the West African Liquor Traffic." WMMS Archives, West Africa, Microfiche 31.

[17]   Sarpei, "Coastal Elite," 106; and Kimble, *Political History*, 147.

sense of connectedness.[18] Literacy was a requirement for membership in most of these "Western-style" associations, and urban educated Africans, products of missionary education, emulated Western social standards drummed into them in the mission schools.

Western dress and manners became the norm, and some societies like the Ladies Mutual Club founded in Sekondi in 1904 carried it to absurd lengths by fining members who went out in "native" cloth or dress.[19] "Dress ladies" anxiously sought to distinguish themselves from "cloth women," and affluent husbands expressed their social status by ensuring that their wives and female household members were often seen in European dress. As Phyllis Martin points out in a recent study, in colonial Africa "dress conveyed identity, status, values and a sense of occasion."[20] Speaking English in public was a rule that even semiliterates tried to uphold in imitation of the snobbish Fante anglophiles.[21] But the loyalty of these anglicized coastal Africans to temperance was divided, as some, in imitation of the traditional *abirempon* and the colonial administrators, also viewed drinking expensive imported liquor as evidence of superior social status.

While most of these Western-oriented societies collapsed after a few years, probably due to pecuniary difficulties, the temperance and masonic societies survived into the beginning of the twentieth century and grew in strength. This was, at least in part, because of their external links to European organizations and financial support. The international ties of the temperance movement made it more attractive to socially conscious Africans. Its admission of women and juveniles, excluded from the masonic lodges, and the absence of large membership fees and dues also increased its popularity. The Good Templars had established twenty-one lodges and juvenile temples by the end of the nineteenth century.[22]

The Young Men and Temperance Societies

The young men were quick to realize that the temperance movement, linked to Christian missions that were antagonistic to indigenous religions and cultures, could be used as a tool in their struggle against the chiefs and elders. Perhaps, considering the antagonism of the paramount chief of Akyem Abuakwa to missionary activities, it is not coincidental that young men in his domain used mission-linked temperance societies to challenge his authority. The years from 1907 to 1909 witnessed increasing conflict between chiefs in Akyem Abuakwa and Akyem Kotoku and their subjects who had joined the Good Templars Lodge in the coastal town of Winnebah. Events between 1907 and 1909 illustrate the appeal of temperance societies for coastal as well as inland young men, their conception of what belonging

---

[18] See Kimble, *Political History*, Ch. 3; and Casely–Hayford and Rathbone, "Politics, Families and Freemasonry."

[19] Kimble, *Political History*, 134.

[20] Phyllis M. Martin, "Contesting Clothes in Colonial Brazzaville," *JAH* 35, 3 (1994): 401–26.

[21] The "Africanist" Kobina Sekyi (1892-1956) satirized the social life of Gold Coast anglophiles in *The Blinkards* (London, 1974), a play written in 1915.

[22] Kimble, *Political History*, 148.

to the Good Templars meant, and the interconnections between coastal and inland politics.

In 1907 Kwasi Abrokwa of Akropong, on whom the oath of the *Omanhene* of Akyem Abuakwa had been sworn summoning him to the chief's court in Kyebi, scurried to Winnebah and joined the Good Templars. He later sent a message to Omanhene Amoako Atta II that: "he had gone to Winnebah and joined lodge [sic] there, and that I [Amoaka Atta] had therefore no authority to require his attendance at my court."[23] Amoako Atta had Abrokwa arrested, tried him in May 1907, and sentenced him to a month's imprisonment for wilfully neglecting the chief's oath. Abrokwa's flight to the Christian temperance movement was not an isolated incident, and Amoako Atta commented that "[s]ince last year a good number of Akim men have gone to Winnebah and joined the Good Templars Lodge . . . called [the] the Star of Hope Lodge Number 8." These men then declared themselves beyond the jurisdiction of the *Omanhene*'s court.

The response of the Winnebah lodge to Abrokwa's arrest reveals the novel political claims being made by this particular lodge. The *Omanhene* of Akyem Abuakwa received a letter from the Star of Hope Lodge, signed by Rev. Daniel Acquah.

> One of our brothers at Akropong by named [sic] Kwesi Aborokwa has been imprisoned in your cell . . . which we the members of Star of Hope Lodge No. 8 Independent Order of Good Templars, beg your honour for full statement and . . . together with his charges, that we may be able to repeat same to our District Chief Templar Brother W. Z. Coker at Cape Coast who will deal hardly with this case according to the powers invested on [sic] him by the Grand Lodge of England.[24]

Assuming the Amoako Atta II was ignorant of the powers of the Good Templars Lodge, the letter advised the *Omanhene* to release Abrokwa and restore to him his confiscated certificate of membership before W. Z. Coker showed up in person in Kyebi. Amoako Atta forwarded this letter to the secretary for native affairs, querying the mandate of the large and exclusive powers claimed by the Good Templars Lodge at Winnebah. The government came out in support of Nana Amoaka Atta, and the secretary for native affairs in a letter to Daniel Acquah explicitly stated the subordination of temperance members to traditional authority.

> I am directed to inform you that the Government will not tolerate the interference of local Lodges with the decisions of the courts under the Native Jurisdiction Ordinance, and to add that, if persistence is shown in the present attitude, it will be necessary to take steps that may lead to the dissolution of such Lodges.[25]

---

[23] NAG, Accra, ADM 11/1/1388, letter from Amoako Atta II to the acting Secretary for Native Affairs, dated June 15, 1907. The author came across only one file in the National Archives of Ghana (Accra) on the Good Templars Order and the early temperance movement.

[24] NAG, Accra, ADM/11/1/1388, letter from Members of Star of Hope Lodge No. 8 to Amoako Atta, dated June 7, 1907 and signed by Rev. Dan Acquah.

[25] NAG, Accra, ADM 11/1/1388, letter from acting Secretary for Native Affairs to Daniel Acquah of Star of Hope Lodge No. 8, dated July 17, 1907.

But the issue did not end there, and the next open confrontation between a chief and members of the Good Templars surfaced at Wenkyi in western Akyem Abuakwa.

A Good Templars Lodge had been established in 1908 at Wenkyi by W. Z. Coker on a trip inland, and members of this lodge also declared themselves beyond the chief's jurisdiction and refused to attend summons in the chief's court. Those fined refused to pay, and lodge members assaulted the bailiff of the district commissioner of the Birim District. An alarmed Chief Atcheri solicited the assistance of the colonial administration.

> Herewith I sent [sic] you this bearer to report to you that your bailiff has received a severe flogged [sic] by the Lodge of the Good Templars and brake [sic] his right hand. And I beg your Worship that if you doesn't [sic] try to sent [sic] people down here, then the consequence [sic] will be serious.[26]

Chief Atcheri reported the presence of Rev. Daniel Acquah in the neighborhood and rumors that members of the Good Templars Lodge were planning an attack on Wenkyi. In early 1909 *Omanhene* Attafuah of Akyem Kotoku was also reported to be having problems with members of the Good Templars Winnebah Lodge who were refusing to pay their share of debts incurred by the stool, to take part in the clearing of the roads, or to acknowledge the authority of the chief's oath.[27]

How did the Winnebah lodge of the Good Templars Order come to assign such large powers to itself? Why had temperance societies in inland Akyem become the rallying points of dissent against chiefly rule? Who were the members of these inland temperance organizations? An inquiry, ordered by the government into the structure and activities of the International Order of the Good Templars (Gold Coast), following their disturbing activities sheds light on some of these questions.

There were two separate orders of the Good Templars in the Gold Coast: American and English orders. Both had their district lodges in Cape Coast. The American order had moved its headquarters to Glasgow, and District Lodge no. 1 in Cape Coast was directly under the Glasgow Grand Lodge. Other local lodges could be established in the Gold Coast by charter from the district lodge, to which the local lodges paid a percentage of their subscription fees, which in turn remitted a fixed percentage to Glasgow. Most of the local lodges of the American order were defunct, with only the branches in Cape Coast, Elmina, Aburi, Dodowah, Obuasi, and Bibianaha being active.[28] The more active English order had a similar structure, and it was to this order that Star of Hope Lodge No. 8 of Winnebah belonged. It is apparent from the letter of the Chief Templar in the Gold Coast to the commissioner for the Central Province that

---

[126] NAG, Accra, ADM 11/1/1388, letter from Chief Atcheri of Wenkyi to D.C. Birim, dated March 5, 1908. It should be mentioned for the benefit of Chief Atcheri that this letter was written by a professional letter writer.

[27] NAG, Accra, ADM 11/1/1388, letter from Commissioner of the Central Province to the Secretary for Native Affairs, dated February 21, 1909.

[28] NAG, Accra, ADM 11/1/1388, letter from Daniel Sackey, Office of the District Secretary (International Order of Good Templars), to the Commissioner for the Central Province, dated January 23, 1909.

the Winnebah lodge had arbitrarily assigned new powers to itself.[29] The key to this development may lie in the activities of its two prominent members: W. Z. Coker and Rev. Daniel Acquah.

W. Z. Coker was *Tufuhen* (commander of the *asafo*) of Cape Coast, and he appeared to be building himself into a political heavyweight—using the Good Templars Order in which he had been active from the 1890s. The fact that the Winnebah lodge never sent the names of the Akyem members recruited in Coker's inland drive nor remitted a part of their subscription fees to the district lodge suggests impropriety.[30] Roger Gocking highlights Coker's acquisitiveness:

> As the only literate person on the [Cape Coast] tribunal, he kept a written
> record of its proceeds, and he collected the monies paid in fees and fines.
> Along with his labor-contracting operations, which his position as *Tufuhen*
> facilitated, the money that came his way by monopolizing the judicial pro-
> ceedings of the Tribunal contributed to a considerable income. It was clearly
> much more that he would have made as the Supreme Court Registrar,
> and by the turn of the century he was one of the wealthier members of
> Cape Coast society.[31]

Indeed, Coker had lost his previous appointment as the registrar of the Supreme Court of Accra through his embezzlement of funds.[32]It is obvious that Coker was utilizing the Winnebah temperance lodge for his personal financial and political ambitions.

From 1907 to 1919, he was Grand Master of the English Lodge of the Order of Good Templars, and in this position, he was able to exercise control over western educated young men who felt that by joining such fraternal organizations, they had freed themselves from allegiance to their chiefs, and more specifically, from attendance at their courts.[33]

He quit the temperance movement when it drew the colonial government's ire.[34] Coker's activities in Cape Coast politics, where he was instrumental in destooling the paramount chief of Cape Coast in 1916, illustrates the force he had become in local politics.[35] Not much is known of Rev. Daniel Acquah but his pastoral occupation may account for his readiness to do battle against chiefly authority. It is possible that the Rev. Acquah was also using his occupation and membership in the temperance society to forward unstated political interests.

It is clear that young men or commoners of Akyem Abuakwa were manipulating membership in the Good Templars in their struggles against local chiefs. Whether they were explicitly encouraged in this by Coker is not clear, but political condi-

---

[29]   NAG, Accra, ADM 11/1/1388, letter from J. P. Brown to the Commissioner for the Central Province, dated January 23, 1909.

[30]   Ibid.

[31]   Gocking, "British Justice and the Native Tribunals," 104.

[32]   Roger Gocking, "Indirect Rule in the Gold Coast: Competition for Office and the Invention of Tradition," *CJAS* 28, 3 (1994): 427.

[33]   Ibid., 429–30.

[34]   Personal communication from Roger Gocking, July 15, 1994.

[35]   Augustus Casely–Hayford, "The Cape Coast Stool Dispute of 1916" (SOAS, African History Seminar, April 24, 1991).

tions in Akyem Abuakwa shed light on these developments. Between 1900 and 1915, internal conflicts in Akyem Abuakwa were intensified by the commercialization of land because of cocoa and mining activities, unilateral land sales by chiefs and their elders, and heated contests over chiefship due to its renewed lucrativeness. The atmosphere was strained further by the Native Jurisdiction Ordinance of 1910, which made the native tribunals compulsory courts of first instance, providing chiefs with a powerful instrument against commoners. The extension of the railway line through Akyem Abuakwa in 1912–13, and the labor demands chiefs made on the young men, under directives from the colonial government, worsened the situation.[36] The young men responded with the destoolment of chiefs. As the young men sought to mobilize themselves against the chiefs, *asafo* organizations and temperance societies came in handy.

J. K. K. Greenway, district commissioner of Birim, believed that the temperance members of Wenkyi had explicitly joined the Good Templars in order to defy the political authority of their chief. He pointed out that few of the members he interviewed even knew what the Good Templars really stood for.

> I afterwards addressed the Templars in their Lodge and discovered that they had no idea that their society was a Religious Temperance Organization. Only two out of the 40 members were Christians, the remainder were frankly pagan and consequently quite ineligible for membership. The Lodge was simply used for political purpose the main object being apparently to be a law unto themselves and to foment dis-obedience to the chief and customs.[37]

The commoners had incorporated the temperance movement into a political struggle with the chiefs that dated from the late nineteenth century.[38] The 1908 Annual Report of the Basel Mission confirmed that temperance organization was being diverted to local ends: "societies call themselves temperance unions, usually with a core of lapsed Christians, and soon become agitators and political revolutionaries, with banners of Nationalism and Ethiopianism."[39]

Liquor Revenue and the Gold Coast Colonial Government

The origins of British taxation in the Gold Coast date to the 1850s, and the controversies that characterized initial British attempts to introduce taxes bequeathed a legacy of African animosity that bedeviled subsequent debates on taxation for the entire colonial period. Long before the imposition of colonial status on the southern Gold Coast, the informal extension of British influence from the early nineteenth century generated administrative expenses and the need for revenue. In 1850, the administration of British settlements on the Gold Coast was detached from Sierra Leone, and the Gold Coast acquired its own governor and legislative and executive councils. The Gold Coast received a parliamentary subsidy of £4,000 per

---

[36] Simensen, "Rural Mass Action," 29–33.

[37] NAG, Accra, ADM 11/1/1388.

[38] See Chapter 3.

[39] Brokensha, *Social Change at Larteh*, 124.

annum, but this was insufficient to meet the cost of even the rudimentary administration of that time.[40] Taxation was a tricky issue, for British officials could not
directly tax a people over whom they had no formal jurisdiction. They faced a
dilemma on justifying the tax and gaining consensus about paying the tax. The
British decided on two solutions: creating some representative assembly of the
people, constituted of their chiefs, and getting them to pass the tax; and inserting
in the tax ordinance an explicit commitment to direct most of the tax receipts into
internal development as a justification of the levy.[41] Taxation, representation, and
internal development were thus linked in the 1850s and would remain linked in
"the African mind" for the entire colonial period.

In 1852 poll tax was introduced in the area that would become the Gold Coast
Colony and Protectorate in 1874 (excluding the territory then under Dutch influence), and the prospect of internal development unified the chiefs, the educated
elite, and the young men in their willingness to pay it. But the decade between
1852 and 1862 witnessed increasing African antagonism to collection of the poll
tax. This reached open conflict between British forces and the young men of the Ga
town of Christianborg, and the result was an eventual repeal of poll tax in 1862.
The Ga historian, Reindorf, points out that the first collection of the poll tax in 1852
was "quietly and cheerfully given. . . ."[42] It was not that the chiefs, educated elites,
and the young men could not afford to pay the tax; what irked them and led to
their resistance was the manner in which the original agreement on the collection
and use of the poll tax was abused. Chiefs, who assisted in its collection, were
cheated out of their agreed stipends, and the educated elites and the young men
did not see any benefits in terms of roads, sanitary improvements, hospitals, or
schools. The disillusionment left a permanent legacy of resentment, "and it set the
pattern for a century of strenuous, if intermittent political opposition to taxation in
any shape and form."[43]

In spite of the strong protests of European and African merchants, whose grievances the colonial administration dismissed as personal and self-serving, the British administration succeeded in introducing customs duties in the Gold Coast in
the second half of the nineteenth century. Increasing imports of liquor quickly made
liquor duties one of the important constituents of the colonial government's finances.[44] Unlike the British colonies in eastern Africa (Kenya) and southern Africa
(the Rhodesias) where the security concerns of white settlers entwined African alcohol consumption with issues of law and order,[45] the Gold Coast (and West Africa
in general) had no significant white settlement, but did have a history of liquor

---

[40]   Kimble, *Political History*, 169.

[41]   See for detailed discussions, Kimble, *Political History*, Ch. 4; Mensah Sarbah, *Fanti National Constitution*, 100–103; and Casely-Hayford, *Gold Coast Native Institutions*, 160–63.

[42]   Reindorf, *History of the Gold Coast and Asante*, 331.

[43]   Kimble, *Political History*, 191.

[44]   There were periods of united opposition to increases in customs duties, and in 1874 European and
African merchants, chiefs, African petty traders, and retail dealers of spirits in Accra and the Eastern
Province came out against an increase in the duties on spirits. The traders succeeded in getting the sup-
port of the chiefs, as the latter were "concerned about the cost of their customary fines and presents."
Ibid., 306.

[45]   See Ambler, "Drunks, Brewers and Chiefs"; and West, "Equal Rights for All Civilized Men."

TABLE 1
Contribution of Liquor Revenues to Total Government Revenue, Gold Coast, 1910-1913 (in pounds sterling).

Year	Import Duties	Liquor Duties	Railway Revenues	Total Revenue*	% of Liquor Duties to TR
1910	610,602	384,538	248,981	1,006,633	38
1911	663,071	421,970	294,650	1,111,632	38
1912	735,470	470,144	329,399	1,230,850	38
1913	779,593	502,429	357,329	1,301,566	39

Source: PRO, CO 554/41/19073; and PRO, CO 96/692/657, *1930 Commission Report,* Appendix III.
*Other revenues included licenses, court fees, etc. Total Revenue is expressed as TR in the next column.

imports. Here, colonial preoccupation was not with the sabotage of the fragile colonial order by drunken Africans, but with the maximization of colonial revenues from duties on imported alcoholic drinks. And the colonial government's minute regulation of alcohol imports, the licensing of liquor outlets, and rigid hours of sale ensured that liquor consumption would not threaten the colonial order.[46] The duty on spirits imported into the Gold Coast would be increased gradually from 2s.6d. in 1897 to 27s.6d in 1929, partly to raise revenue, but also to limit the African demand for liquor.

By the immediate pre-World War I period, liquor duties were contributing as much as 40 percent of total government revenues in the Gold Coast. Table 1 gives statistics for the two leading sources of government revenue—customs duties and railway revenues—in the immediate pre-World War I era. Spirits, wine, and beer wholesale and retail licenses brought in a further 32,440 pounds sterling in 1910; 38,786 in 1911;. 42,362 in 1912; and 45,725 in 1913, or roughly 4 percent.[47] Huge liquor imports had been made possible by the cash profits drawn off a growing indigenous cocoa industry as the Gold Coast emerged as the world's leading pro-

---

[46] Colonial statistics on the incidence of drunkenness was spotty in the pre-1930 period. Statistics for drunkenness were sometimes given or omitted in the Annual Colonial Reports. In the 1895 *Departmental Reports,* 75, the government expressed the opinion that since drunkenness in public was not an offence under the criminal code "unless combined with violent or indecent behaviour, a table distinguishing charges of drunkenness from 'other offences' would be most misleading. . . ." NAG, Accra, ADM 5/1/71. Statistics for drunkenness disappeared into general categories such as assault and breach of peace. This could have been a defensive stance against metropolitan temperance advocates. Statistics for drunkenness suddenly reappear from 1923–24, and this coverage may have been connected with the formation of a Criminal Investigation Department. Statistics became particularly detailed in the 1930s, when illicit distillation became a widespread problem. See the annual *Report of the Police Department* for this period. NAG, Accra, CSO 1100/30.

[47] Appendix 5—"Statement of amounts collected in respect of spirit, wine and beer licenses for the years 1909, 1927–28." "Report of the Commission of Inquiry Regarding the Consumption of Spirits in the Gold Coast" (1930). Hereafter referred to as the "1930 Commission Report."

ducer of cocoa in 1911. By 1919 government officials, like the comptroller of customs, were commenting on the close connection between increased cocoa exports and increased liquor imports.[48]

Liquor legislation—apart from being linked to issues of revenue, representation, and internal development—was also implicitly linked to notions of power in the African mind, which associated control of alcohol-use with sacred and secular power. British colonial administrators had also come to view liquor revenues as essential to maintaining British political power in the Gold Coast. For the Gold Coast government and the Colonial Office, liquor revenues were opportune, for they freed them from over-dependence on subsidies from the metropolitan treasury, which would have brought undue interference in the formulation of colonial policy. For both the British administrators and Gold Coasters, to attack liquor revenues was to indirectly criticize colonial rule. Also, British colonialism, on the local scene in Africa, was represented by only a few British administrators. British concerns of order and control over the teeming masses of colonized people became entwined with forebodings of the possible effects of drunkenness on the fragile control of the colonizer.[49] Liquor legislation thus became an important factor in the extension of colonial hegemony, reinforcing the association of alcohol control with power.[50]

International Liquor Conventions and the Gold Coast

In the sphere of liquor policy, the Gold Coast colonial agenda was also subject to international regulations on liquor traffic. In 1890 an international convention at Brussels prohibited European liquor from areas in Africa without a previous history of liquor consumption. A wide belt in the interior of Africa, between latitudes 20 degrees north and 22 degrees south, was subject to this potential ban on European liquor. This definition affected the Northern Territories of the Gold Coast, when they were annexed by the British in 1901. The idea of "prohibition zones" at the Brussels conference had been proposed by Britain, and her additional demand for a duty of ten shillings on every gallon had been moderated only by the objections of the Colonial Office.[51]

The next significant international liquor convention was passed at Saint Germain-en-Laye (France) in September 1919. The events surrounding the Saint Germain convention reveal the tensions over liquor policy between the British metropolitan politicians, the Colonial Office, and the colonial governments. Without prior consultation, the governors of the British West African colonies received a telegram from Walter Long, secretary of state for the colonies, dated January 7, 1919, informing them that:

---

[48] PRO, CO 96/597/15501.

[49] These forebodings were manifested in liquor laws imposed on indigenes in the British Dominions: "The penalty of selling to a Native in New South Wales is £10, and in Queensland and Western Australia £20. Prohibition or the permit system is in force in New Zealand, the Cape Province, Basutoland, Bechuanaland and the Transkei Territories." *West Africa*, February 3, 1934.

[50] See Ambler, "Drunks, Brewers, and Chiefs."

[51] Pan, *Alcohol in Colonial Africa*, 34.

In view of the present position of the liquor traffic in West Africa and the undesirability of allowing *this German [and] Dutch trade* [emphasis added] to revive I have decided that the time has come to stop it altogether as soon as practicable by extending the system at present in force in the prohibited areas to the whole territory under your administration.[52] The question will arise at the peace conference [Versailles] where the British representatives will be authorised to urge similar action on other territorial powers.[53]

Actually, Walter Long had first made his intentions of abolishing liquor traffic to West Africa known in a 1918 election speech in England as he sought re-election as a member of Parliament. Britain had had no elections since 1910 because of the war, and in the run-up to the November 1918 elections political rhetoric was keenly tuned to the popular mood, which was explicitly anti-German.[54] Walter Long apparently hoped to harness, through the issue of prohibition in the colonies, the support of temperance advocates and the textile industry. Liquor traffic to the African colonies was portrayed as a trade dominated by Germany and inimical to the economic interests of Britain's textile producers. It also appears that Long's pronouncement was motivated by the belief "that the problem of the disposal of the German colonies [Togo, Cameroon and Tanganyika] would be helped to a solution in our [Britain's] favour if we took a strong line in the liquor question. . . ."[55]

But the colonial secretary had ridden roughshod over the revenue concerns of governors in Britain's West African colonies, which were very dependent on import duties on liquor. And quite typically, the views of the African subjects had been ignored. Governor Clifford of the Gold Coast vehemently protested against Walter Long's decision, demanding a subsidy from the imperial treasury in the eventuality of prohibition. Considering the prominence of liquor revenues to government finances in the pre-World War I period, Clifford could not envisage any viable substitute.[56]

Walter Long was appointed first Lord of the Admiralty in a 1918 Cabinet reshuffle,[57] and the question of colonial prohibition fell under a new colonial secretary, Lord Milner. Milner solicited local views on the proposed prohibition of his predecessor. On his directive, the Gold Coast governor sent a circular letter to the provincial commissioners in the colony, and the chief commissioner in Asante. The majority of chiefs eagerly recommended the prohibition of imported liquor. They linked drinking among young men to social instability and

[52] Long was referring here to the decision to prohibit liquor in Africa between latitudes 20 degrees north and 22 degrees south, reached at the international conference in Brussels in 1890.

[53] The full text of this telegram, signed by Walter Long, was reproduced in Governor Hugh Clifford's lengthy report on the potential effect of the proposed prohibition on the revenue of the Gold Coast government. PRO, CO 554/41/19073.

[54] Walter L. Arnstein, *Britain Yesterday and Today* (Lexington, 1988), 264.

[55] Colonial Office minute by S. Robinson, dated January 16, 1936. PRO, CO 554/98/33522.

[56] See PRO, CO 554/41/19073; and PRO, CO 554/41/10107.

[57] The author has not been able to establish if Long's transfer had anything to do with his pronouncements on liquor traffic. But Long did lose his seat for the Constituency of the Strand Division for Middlesex in the 1918 election, reappearing as M.P. for St. George's Westminster from 1918-1921. J. R. H. Weaver, ed., *The Dictionary of National Biography* (London, 1922-30), 517–20.

appealed to the colonial government's awareness that drinking went with disorder.[58]

Balancing the revenue needs of the colonial governments against the concern for order by the home government and African chiefs, the British government abandoned prohibition and adopted the less drastic policy of restricting trade spirits. Trade spirits were defined as cheap spirits injurious to the health of Africans.[59] This limited ban would, at least, ensure that some revenue came in from liquor imports but keep out cheap spirits the young men could afford. The decision also reflected the colonial support for the chiefs as indirect rule become more established.

The decision to ban trade spirits in Africa was enacted at Saint Germain on September 10, 1919, the colonial powers, Japan and the United States resolving that trade spirits be prohibited in sub-Saharan Africa excluding the Union of South Africa (Article 2). An import duty of 800 francs (about 80 pounds sterling in the early 1920s) was imposed on every hectoliter (about 22 gallons) of pure alcohol for permitted spirits, and no imported spirits were to be allowed in areas not accustomed to the consumption of European liquor (Article 4). The manufacture of distilled beverages of every kind for commercial purposes was forbidden (Article 5).[60]

Article 2 left the definition of "trade spirits" to the colonies, a concession that would allow great laxity in the (re)definition of trade spirits in the years to come. The Gold Coast, in consultation with the Colonial Office, passed the Spirituous Liquors Ordinance, 1920, defining trade spirits as:

> spirits imported, or of a type previously imported, for sale to natives, and not generally consumed by Europeans, and includes mixtures and compounds made with such spirits.[61]

These trade spirits, mostly Dutch geneva or gin[62] and rum (exported from New England in the United States) in their square bottles and green cases, were very common along the west coast of Africa. The Gold Coast's list of prohibited trade spirits excluded the commonly available geneva and rum. It is worth noting that the Gold Coast's list of banned trade spirits heavily limited foreign labels, a fact obviously pleasing to British distillers and interests that sought a diminution in the volume of foreign trade.

But the effect of banning geneva and rum soon proved contrary to the financial interests of the Gold Coast government. The definition that rum was to be distilled from sugar-cane products, in sugar-cane growing countries, and stored in wood for a period of three years eliminated rum imports from New England and imitation rum from Europe.[63] Table 2 illustrates the sharp drop in liquor revenues.

---

[58] See Chapter 3.

[59] PRO, CO 554/62/20621.

[60] See Raymond Leslie Buell, *The Native Problem in Africa*, II (New York, 1928), 950–53, for the text of the St. Germain Convention.

[61] See Gold Coast, *Government Gazette*, July 24, 1920; PRO, CO 96/611/15587; and PRO, CO 554/45/27790. The colonial administrations of Nigeria and Sierra Leone enacted similar ordinances. Liquor revenues were not important to tiny Gambia with its large Muslim population.

[62] Geneva is Dutch gin made in a pot-still, as distinct from the patent-still used in the manufacture of British gin.

[63] PRO, CO 554/55/51423.

TABLE 2
Contribution of Gin and Rum to the Total Customs Revenue from Spirits Imports,
Gold Coast, 1913-1921

Year	Total spirits Imports (gal)	Duties	Duties (Sterling) Gin	Rum	Gin + Rum duties as % of total
1913	1,762,850	502,429	159,404	328,965	97.2
1914	1,722,611	494,460	150,985	327,344	96.7
1919	672,462	371,431	9,083	344,208	95.1
1920	179,597	141,018	37,607	14,439	36.9
1921	283,319	283,868	93,605	14,253	38.0

Source: Appendix III, "1930 Commission Report"; and PRO, CO 554/46/21446.

Dutch gin was far cheaper than British gin, and three centuries of Dutch-domi-
nated liquor trade on the Gold Coast had definitely popularized Dutch gin labels
over British labels. Also, the British gin manufacturers failed to fill the huge vacuum
created by the elimination of geneva.

In the face of a general decline in liquor revenues in British West Africa, a
conference of governors in British West Africa was convened at the Colonial Office
in London to discuss colonial finances. It was decided in 1923 to readmit Dutch
geneva. Dutch exports of geneva were to be accompanied by a certificate from a
Dutch customs officer. This certified that the product conformed to a prescribed
mode of manufacture, deemed to be of higher standard, to counter potential temperance protests against the re-entry of inferior and injurious Dutch trade spirits.[64]
The list of banned trade spirits was abandoned for a definition of what were ad-
missible spirits.

Dutch trade agreements with Britain had been instrumental in the readmission of geneva. Lynn Pan correctly mentions pressure by Dutch distillers on the
British government and their "undertakings to improve the quality of their geneva"
as a major reason for the readmission of geneva.[65] But colonial revenue concerns
were definitely crucial to this policy change. The readmission of Dutch geneva increased imports of gin ten-fold from 83,855 gallons in 1921 to 859,160 gallons in
1925. Out of a total spirits imports of 1,312,258 gallons in 1927, gin contributed
1,181,913 gallons or 90 percent of total imports.[66] The Gold Coast had shifted from
being a rum-drinking population to a gin-drinking one.

---

[64] See Colonial Office minute on "Gin and Geneva" by J. A. Calder, September 24, 1928. PRO, CO 554/
77/4030. The new definition of standard geneva was published in the Gold Coast, *Government Gazette*,
September 22, 1923.

[65] Pan, *Alcohol in Colonial Africa*, 70. See also, PRO, CO 554/62/48092. British distillers were very dis-
pleased that Dutch geneva distillers had been "re-assigned" such a large part of the Gold Coast liquor
market and thus sought to exclude Dutch spirits other than geneva. See, for example, PRO, CO 554/66/
3063.

[66] "1930 Commission Report," Appendix 1.

Temperance Agitation and "Partial" Prohibition

The metropolitan temperance movement and the Wesleyan Mission in the Gold Coast were extremely disappointed by the British government's revision of its position on prohibition in 1919, and the government's decision to proscribe only "trade spirits." The Wesleyan Mission, struggling with the problem of drinking among its Gold Coast congregation, adopted a stringent position for prohibition. But the year 1919 witnessed the appointment of Frederick Gordon Guggisberg as governor of Gold Coast (1919–1927), and the commencement of an active phase in internal development. Guggisberg's promotion of internal development divided chiefs and the educated elite in their temperance demands. Guggisberg met African expectations of taxation, representation, and internal development. His successor, Governor Alexander Ransford Slater (1927–1932), however, reneged on these expectations, and inadvertently provided a basis for consensus among missionaries, chiefs, and the educated elites in their demand for prohibition. The ideological conflicts within the educated elite, sparked by the 1925 Constitution and the Native Administration Ordinance of 1927, and the rise to prominence of "non-cooperative" chiefs in the coastal states, further complicated African politics in this period.[67] The outcome was the decision in 1930 to gradually ban the import of gin and geneva over a ten year period.

The Missionary Front

With temperance taken out of its Victorian cultural context, Wesleyan missionaries were experiencing difficulties forging consensus on the missionary front in support of prohibition, and in imposing teetotalism on their African congregations in the Gold Coast. The two missions most active in temperance were the Wesleyan Society and the Basel Mission, but the latter had to leave during World War I because of their Germanic origin and were replaced by the Scottish Mission. The Basel Mission does not appear, unlike the Wesleyans, to have established any elaborate temperance organization. However, this did not mean the Mission was unconcerned about the liquor traffic.[68] But the Basel Mission also sold beer at its factory,[69] so their conception of temperance was close to what it meant in its European origins—moderation, and abstinence from spirits.

The fact that the Wesleyan Mission was strongly established in coastal towns may partly explain its strong demand for prohibition. The prominence of social drinking in coastal towns compelled the Wesleyan Mission, the major missionary organization on the coast, to adopt a stern policy on teetotalism. Interior-based missions, such as the Basel Mission and the English Church Mission, saw nothing wrong with palm wine, communion wine, and beer.[70] The 1909 Wesleyan District Synod meeting expressed its disappointment that:

---

[67] Gocking, "Indirect Rule in the Gold Coast."

[68] NAG, Kumasi, ROA 022, Basel Mission Resolutions passed at the General Synod of 1909 related to the limitation of liquor traffic in Ashanti and the treatment of Christians. The collective license was a system whereby a whole village, in the person of its chief, took out a single liquor license and paid a fee proportionate to its population. It reflected the lack of an adequate administrative machinery to police liquor outlets in the early days of colonialism combined with a desire to maximize liquor revenues.

[69] Rev. W. H. Maude, Wesleyan Society (Gold Coast) to Rev. Andrews, Wesleyan Society, London, dated March 19, 1919. WMMS, West Africa, microfiche 14.

the use of spirituous liquors is becoming more prevalent among those connected with the Church, and deeply regrets and strongly condemns this growing practice, and exhorts the members to abstain therefrom in accordance with the rules of the society. In order to combat this evil the Synod directs that Temperance Societies and Bands of Hope be formed in each place where they do not exist.[71]

To devalue the ritual importance of alcohol in Christian sacrament, in an attempt to discourage social drinking among Wesleyans, the 1915 Synod recommended "that non-alcoholic wine should be used for sacramental services throughout the District."[72] In 1919 the Society was still complaining that educated members of the Church were being led away by strong drink.[73]

The ritual importance of water was growing among some African Christians in the Gold Coast in this period, a development illustrated vividly by the advent of the "water carriers." In 1914, a Liberian evangelist, William Wade Harris, had toured the Ivory Coast and the Axim part of the Gold Coast, converting thousands of people to Christianity.[74] Harris converts in the Gold Coast, like Grace Tanne and John Nackabah, formed "spiritual" churches in which the use of "holy water" was significant in exorcism and healing. The churches that developed out of the Harris movement were labeled the "water carriers."[75]

The career of Samson Opong, who stirred Asante with his preaching between 1920 and 1922, highlights the growing tension between water and alcohol in the competing indigenous and Christian conceptions of spiritual power. Opong had vowed, when he converted to Christianity, not to drink alcohol again.

> Samson Opong's evil genius was his maternal uncle, a fetish priest who stubbornly resisted the appeals and persuasions of his nephew. He knew the prophet's former weakness for alcohol and he knew of his vow which made alcohol his new taboo. With satanic cunning he now set to work to make the prophet break that taboo, knowing that if he could succeed in doing so Sampson Opong would lose his power as surely as his biblical namesake lost his when through the cunning of Delilah he broke his vow.
>
> He succeeded and a bottle of crude trade spirit robbed Sampson of the mighty indwelling Spirit of God through whose power he had wrought so mightily.[76]

It is noteworthy that Opong, before his conversion to Christianity, had specialized as an *adutofo*, a sorcerer who dealt in charms.[77] This profession, which prominently engaged the use of alcohol in ritual and the payment of fees, probably explains Opong's partiality to alcohol. Even assuming that the explanation

[70] ʼ See, for example, the evidence of A. J. Hughes (English Church Mission, Kumase), and P. N. Tham (Presbyterian Mission, Kumase) before the 1930 commission on alcohol consumption. Notes of evidence attached to the "1930 Commission Report."

[71] District Synod Minutes, 1909 (Western Section), WMMS Archives, West Africa, Microfiche Box 4.

[72] Gold Coast Synod Meeting, 1915, WMMS Archives, West Africa, Microfiche Box 11.

[73] District Synod Minutes, 1919, WMMS Archives, West Africa, Microfiche Box 11.

[74] Walker, "The Message as the Medium," 9–64.

[75] Hans Debrunner, *A History of Christianity in Ghana* (Accra, 1967), 273–74.

[76] Hans Debrunner, *The Story of Sampson Opong* (Accra, 1965), 32–33.

[77] Ibid.

of Opong's loss of power is not accurate, what is significant here is the contra-distinction between alcohol and water in the indigenous and Christian defini-tions of spiritual power.

When the Wesleyan Missionary Society endorsed total prohibition in the Gold Coast in 1919, it may have been responding, in part, to the growing ap-peal of the "spiritual" churches. It is noteworthy that several of the early Afri-can churches in the Gold Coast were breakaway sects from Methodism.[78] They advocated strict teetotalism, and some, such as the Memeneda Gyidifo ("Satur-day Believers"), even used water instead of wine in communion.[79] The Method-ist church may have felt the pressure to prove its piety. The British government's suggestion in 1919 that liquor imports be banned in the colonies was timely. It encouraged the Wesleyan Missionary Society to endorse prohibition in 1919. The change in British official policy was galling, and the Native Races and Li-quor Traffic United Committee singled out the Gold Coast government for se-vere chastisement.[80] Its secretary, A. E. Blackburn, concluded after a fact-find-ing trip to the Gold Coast that trade spirits were still being admitted into the Gold Coast. From 1919, the Gold Coast government and the Colonial Office were continuously plied with memoranda from this body and the Wesleyan Missionary Society.[81]

By the 1920s the Gold Coast had become the focus of the metropolitan tem-perance movement because Southern Nigeria, the other British colony with sig-nificant liquor imports, had been given a clean bill of health. The Mackenzie Chalmers' commission on the consumption of spirits in southern Nigeria in 1909 had concluded that southern Nigeria did not have a drink problem.[82] Mission-ary criticism about excessive consumption of European spirits among southern Nigerians had led to a metropolitan directive that a commission of inquiry be established. Whether the conclusion of the Chalmers' Commission was accu-rate or not, the liquor question in southern Nigeria was seen to be technically resolved. The Gold Coast had not yet received a clean bill of health, and "the fact that the importation of spirituous liquors into this colony far exceeds that of all the other West African colonies put together" made the Gold Coast the obvious choice for metropolitan temperance agitation.[83]

---

[78]   C. .G. Baeta, *Prophetism in Ghana: A Study of Some "Spiritual" Churches* (London, 1962).

[79]   Ibid., 72.

[80]   This body had been formed in Britain in the 1880s as an umbrella organization for missionary and temperance societies.

[81]   See, for examples, the Memorial of the Native Races and Liquor Traffic United Committee to Ramsay MacDonald in 1924 demanding the prohibition of spirits for all races in the African colonies. PRO, CO 554/62/20621; and the 1926 Memorandum of the Gold Coast Wesleyan Society to Governor Guggisberg deprecating the government's reliance on liquor revenues to finance its development plan. PRO, CO 96/681/6204.

[82]   Southern Nigeria, *Report of the Committee of Inquiry into the Liquor Trade in Southern Nigeria* (London, 1909).

[83]   Memorandum by the WMMS to Governor Guggisberg, March 9, 1926. PRO, CO 96/681/6204. The minutes of the 1929 conference on temperance in West Africa convened by the Native Races and Liquor Traffic United Committee in England reveals the preoccupation with the Gold Coast. WMMS Archives, West Africa, Microfiche Box 31.

Liquor Revenue and African Politics

What is striking is that, in spite of surging imports of gin from 1923, no organized protest emerged in the Gold Coast until 1928. Growing imports of liquor troubled the educated elites and the chiefs. It is significant that the first memorandum (1919) of the new political movement of the educated elites, the National Congress of British West Africa (NCBWA) to the secretary of state, had as its fifth resolution the total abolition of liquor traffic throughout West Africa.[84] J. E. Casely–Hayford, one of the leading spirits behind the NCBWA, and editor of the *Gold Coast Independent*, criticized the redefinition of geneva and the rise in geneva imports from 1923.[85] The prominent role of educated paramount chiefs such as Nana Ofori Atta of Akyem Abuakwa (r. 1912–1943) and Nene Mate Kole of Manya Krobo (r. 1892–1939), products of the Basel Mission, in temperance underscored the fact that temperance politics was still important. But the chiefs and educated Africans were also keenly interested in internal development. Thus, during Guggisberg's tenure as governor, temperance politics took a back seat to economic development.

Guggisberg initiated a costly Ten-Year Development Plan on his arrival in the Gold Coast in 1919, setting ambitious goals for socioeconomic development.

This was to involve a total expenditure of £25 million; £2 million was earmarked for the construction of a harbour, £14.5 million for railways, £1 million for roads, £1.9 million for water supplies, £1.9 for town improvements and drainage, £2 million for hydraulic and electric works, £1 million for public buildings including Achimota [college], £90,000 for posts and telegraphs, and £200,000 for maps and surveys.[86]

Apart from an external loan of £4 million, Guggisberg met the financial demands of this project mostly from internal sources—customs duties. Today, Achimota College, Takoradi harbor and township, and Korle Bu Hospital are national monuments and a tribute to Guggisberg's administration. But in the 1920s Guggisberg had to forge ahead with his project in the face of strong criticism from the Colonial Office and the Gold Coast press that his development plan was overambitious. Guggisberg met the expectations of chiefs and the educated elite on internal development linked to the taxation they endured.

A central aspect of Guggisberg's Ten-Year Plan was the Africanization of the civil service and the expansion of African representation in the legislative council, which was fast becoming the focus of African politics since the admission of the first African in 1886. Africans had occupied important positions in the British administration in the Gold Coast in the mid-nineteenth century. James Bannerman even became lieutenant governor in 1850. But racial discrimination had set in from the proclamation of the Gold Coast Colony in 1874, and from the turn of the twentieth century there had been a deliberate policy to eliminate Africans from senior posts.[87]

---

84 PRO, CO 96/598/14867.

85 *Gold Coast Independent*, July 3, 1926.

86 Albert Adu Boahen, *Ghana: Evolution and Change in the Nineteenth and Twentieth Centuries* (London, 1975), 110.

87 Kimble, *Political History*, 97–105. Not coincidentally, the second half of the nineteenth century also witnessed the popularity of Social Darwinism in Britain. See Douglas A. Lorimer, *Colour, Class and the Victorians* (Leicester, 1978); and Kuklick, *The Savage Within*.

Guggisberg reversed this trend, and he made plans to increase the number of educated Africans in European posts to 29 in 1926, 76 by 1931, and 229 by 1945. The 1925 Guggisberg Constitution increased unofficial African representation on the legislative council, giving six seats to the municipalities of Accra, Cape Coast, and Sekondi, for which the educated elite could vie for election, and also set up provincial councils for chiefs. The Native Administration Ordinance of 1927 strengthened the position of chiefs in the indirect rule partnership with the colonial government. A surveyor by profession, Guggisberg differed from the ordinary colonial official in that he valued efficiency and transcended racial prejudices in his pursuit of it. Guggisberg met, perhaps exceeded, Gold Coast anticipations of representation and internal development in return for taxation. Reflecting on Guggisberg's administration in the early 1930s, the staunch temperance advocate, Nana Ofori Atta, confessed that: "I make one claim, and that is, the Government of 1919-1927 has been a Government of cooperation, as far as any government can justifiably be of that nature."[88] And even Casely–Hayford, whose strong views against the European liquor traffic were set out in his *Ethiopia Unbound*,[89] adopted a pliable attitude to liquor imports. Guggisberg's policies thus disarmed the educated elites and chiefs, who would have preferred a drastic cut-back in African consumption of imported liquor. Where liquor policy was concerned, he secured the cooperation of African legislative council members between 1919 and 1927.

Guggisberg's successor, Governor Slater, shelved Guggisberg's costly development plan and reversed his predecessor's policy of Africanizing the senior civil service.[90] Slater had strong racial views on African ability. As early as 1919, when he was colonial secretary in the Gold Coast, a petition signed by practically every government clerk in Accra had been forwarded to the secretary of state requesting the recall of Slater because of his "Negrophobist" tendencies.[91] Slater drastically curtailed social and economic development with the onset of depression from 1929. The last political act of Casely–Hayford, who died in 1930, was to sign a petition to the secretary of state opposing Slater's attempt to reduce the salaries of African government officials.[92] And the failure of post-Guggisberg administrations to fulfill the hopes and promises of the 1920s became an important source of political resentment among the chiefs and the educated elite.

The Call for Prohibition

The chiefs and the educated elite in the legislative council strongly opposed the Slater administration's continued dependence on liquor revenues. If Slater did not want to respect the "conventions" attached to taxation, representation, and internal development, he could not expect liquor revenues to continue. African members on the legislative council began to demand a commission of inquiry to exam-

---

[88] As cited in Jonathan H. Frimpong-Ansah, *The Vampire State in Africa: The Political Economy of Decline in Ghana* (London, 1992), 70.

[89] J. E. Casely–Hayford, *Ethiopia Unbound* (London, 1911).

[90] See Andrew Roberts, "The Imperial Mind," in *The Colonial Moment in Africa*, ed. A. R. Roberts (Cambridge, 1990), 75.

[91] Kimble, *Political History*, 103.

[92] F. Danquah,"Introduction," in Magnus J. Sampson, *Gold Coast Men of Affairs* (London, 1969), 37.

ine the reasons behind the huge gin imports and to recommend solutions to reverse this trend. They argued that such huge imports could only be detrimental to African health and finances.

The occasion of a legislative council meeting on March 1, 1928, provided the opportunity for the chiefs and the educated elite to launch a formal attack against colonial dependence on liquor revenues. The government (in the person of the comptroller of customs) introduced a new ordinance increasing the import tax on liquor from £1.5s. to £1.7s.6d., an increase of 10 percent.[93] African representatives capitalized on the motion to critique liquor policy as a whole. Casely–Hayford posed a series of penetrating questions to the comptroller of customs. He demanded to know if it was "true that half of the imports duty last year was collected on gin,"[94] and if

> the attention of government [has] been drawn to the fact that such consumption of gin cannot be good for the health and welfare of the people of this country, and will consider the advisability of taking steps to minimise the evil?[95]

Casely–Hayford's antagonism to the government's dependence on liquor revenues set the tone on discussions of the liquor question for the day.

Nana Ofori Atta I, Omanhene of Akyem Abuakwa, applauded the decrease in duties on imported provisions and attacked the proposed increase in liquor tax.

> if I believed that the increase of duty on spirit would help to decrease consumption, I would vote for this motion without hesitation, but I am convinced that the higher the price becomes, the more impoverished the people will be, whilst *quantity* will not suffer.
> All the money we get in cocoa goes back to revenue and the gin trade account.[96]

Gold Coast chiefs and the educated elites had become very sensitive to the exploitation of Africans by non-Africans, and the appropriation or repatriation of wealth by European firms, and the colonial government. If socioeconomic development in the Gold Coast was being curtailed, the government had no need for a further increase in liquor taxes—unless it was just to benefit the British colonial officials.

The metropolitan temperance movement, closely watching developments in the Gold Coast, added its voice to African demands for curtailing liquor imports. In his trip to England in 1928 to be knighted, Ofori Atta had detoured by the Liverpool Chamber of Commerce to lobby for the chamber's assistance in halting liquor traffic to the Gold Coast in a remarkable address.[97] This further publicized the Gold Coast liquor issue in England.

Assailed on the local and metropolitan fronts, Governor Slater announced the formation of a committee in April 1928 to consider the Spirit License Ordinance and its amending ordinances which regulated the wholesaling and retailing of spir-

---

[93] To ease the passage of the ordinance, the increase in liquor tariff was tied to a decrease in the import of all provisions except salt and sugar.

[94] Gold Coast, *Legislative Council Debates*, March 1, 1928.

[95] Ibid.

[96] Ibid.

[97] *Gold Coast Times*, November 23, 1929.

its.[98] The committee was comprised of the secretary for native affairs, H. S. Newlands (chairman), the acting solicitor-general, the inspector general of police, Nana Ofori Atta, J. Glover Addo, and J. W. Campbell. The committee eventually recommended an increase in the retail license fee for spirits from £20 to £60 per annum, a reduction in the hours of sale of spirits from 8 am to 6 pm to 10 am to 6 pm, and a ban on the sale of spirits on credit. These measures were implemented in the Spirit License Amendment Ordinance of 1928.[99] The effects of these measures were to increase the price of liquor, to cut down the number of liquor outlets and to reduce access to alcohol for the increasing ranks of urban workers who credited drinks.

The African members of the legislative council unanimously opposed the 1928 ordinance on the ground that its provisions were inadequate to deal with the gin problem:

> they urged instead that government should take steps to restrict the imports of gin in 1929 to 50% of the importations in 1928, that in subsequent years the importations should be further restricted, i.e. by 10% *per annum* and that in the six year [sic] from now gin should be prohibited altogether.[100]

The African representatives were too familiar with government increases in liquor tariffs that never seemed to discourage liquor imports and consumption. They wanted the liquor question to be tackled at its roots—prohibition, not a regulation of outlets of sale in the Gold Coast. The African representatives demanded a commission to inquire into the liquor traffic. The Gold Coast government found itself in a quandary. The governor could not ignore what appeared to be a popular demand of "the people" for the prohibition of gin, articulated by their representatives in the legislative council. Yet gin import duties continued to be the leading contributor to government revenue. Taking just the year 1929, the total revenues from import duties, the most important source of government finance, amounted to £2,040,348, of which gin contributed £734,286 or 36 percent. The second-ranking import commodity, tobacco, brought in only £286,733 (14 percent). Cocoa export duties fetched £277,746 (13.6 percent). All other items, totaling the remaining third, were individually insignificant.[101]

Governor Slater made a final ineffective appeal to save gin revenues in his address to the legislative council on February 15, 1929. He couched his appeal in the rhetoric of taxation and development that he had jettisoned in practice. In his opinion, the decision to cut down drinking should be voluntary, not enforced by legislation.

> If, however, that object were not obtained, or were only partially obtained, it would still be incorrect to say that the native was being impoverished: he would only be showing his willingness to pay a higher rate of taxation in

---

[98]   Nana Ayirebi Acquah III had drawn attention to the huge gin imports in the Legislative Council in 1927 and had recommended setting up a Commission of Inquiry. Gold Coast, *Legislative Council Debates*, March 24, 1927.

[99]   Enclosure II to the Notes of Evidence, "1930 Commission Report." See also Gold Coast, *Government Gazette*, September 29, 1928.

[100] Governor Slater's address, Gold Coast, *Legislative Council Debates*, February 15, 1929; and Slater's telegram to Secretary of State, December 18, 1928, PRO, CO 96/681/6204.

[101] Gold Coast, *Blue Book, 1933-34*.

order to satisfy one of his desires, and so far from that taxation impoverish-
ing the people generally its proceeds would be repaid to them in the form of
more water supplies, medical and sanitary improvements and the like.[102]

The African representatives of the legislative council rejected the logic of Slater's
argument because he had proved that he, himself, did not observe the claimed
connection between taxation and socioeconomic development.

Hesitantly, Governor Slater appointed the requested commission in March 1929
to examine spirits consumption in the Gold Coast. His hesitation was understandable, for previous responses to temperance agitation had been to increase liquor
tariffs. Such increments in liquor duties, ostensibly to cut down consumption, had
not prevented a continuous increase in imports. To demand total prohibition, however, was to change the name of the game entirely. And the terms of reference for
the commission underscored the Governor's dilemma.

(a) Whether any, and if so, what further action should be taken to control
the consumption of spirits in the Gold Coast, Ashanti and the Southern
section of British Togoland;

(b) in the event of action being advisable which would be likely to result
in an appreciable loss of revenue, what means should be adopted to make
good that loss.[103]

The commission consisted of Newlands again as chairman, the deputy comptroller of customs, Frank Talland, and an African representative, F. V. Nanka Bruce.
In all, 125 witnesses were examined: 64 Africans (chiefs and others), 59 Europeans,
and two Syrians. The Europeans comprised officials in the colonial government,
Christian missionaries, merchants, and mine managers.

The commission recommended, *inter alia*, that the importation of geneva should
be gradually prohibited by means of a progressive reduction in imports over a ten-
year period.[104] The duties on all spirits were to be increased and the sale of palm wine
put under license. In the opinion of the commission, the liquor problem in the Gold
Coast was confined to the consumption of geneva, there was a genuine demand for its
exclusion, and the Gold Coast had no national drink problem. It is important to note
that the liquor question, from the "African" perspective, was confined to the consumption of geneva—the leading item in African expenditure on imported liquor. Also significant was the finding that the Gold Coast had no national drink problem.

Liquor laws were enacted in 1930 to implement the commission's recommendations.[105] The Gin and Geneva (Restriction of Importation) Ordinance was intended
to gradually prohibit gin and geneva over a period of ten years, complete prohibition to be achieved after December 1939.[106] The Liquor Traffic Amendment Ordi-

---

[102] Gold Coast, *Legislative Council Debates*, February 15, 1929.

[103] "1930 Commission Report."

[104] This scheme followed closely the recommendation contained in the WMMS memorandum to the 1930
Commission. See Notes of Evidence.

[105] See Gold Coast, *Report for 1930–31*, 53–54.

[106] Gold Coast, *Government Gazette*, October 25, 1930 and November 1, 1930. The government decided to
avoid the confusion in distinguishing pot-still geneva from patent-still gin by abolishing both over the
ten-year period. In this way, Dutch distillers could not accuse Britain of discriminating in favor of British
gin distillers.

nance prohibited the importation of cheap brandy, rum, and whisky to preempt their replacing gin.[107] The import duty on potable spirits was raised 21.8 percent from 27.6d. in 1928 to 33s.6d. in June 1930. The Liquor Licences (Spirits) Amendment Ordinance imposed further restrictions on the sale of spirits.[108]

It should be mentioned, perhaps, that is was particularly propitious that the demand for the exclusion of geneva was made under the governorship of Slater, and when Lord Passfield was secretary of state for the colonies. The personal convictions of Slater favored temperance. Slater had been noted for his pro-temperance stance as governor of Sierra Leone in the 1920s before his transfer to the Gold Coast. As acting governor of the Gold Coast in 1919, he had expressed the opinion that: "I do not myself any longer entertain much doubt that the Gold Coast could, in a few years, make good the loss of revenue entailed by a prohibition policy. . . ."[109] Slater was definitely not the person to stand in the way of a "popular" demand for temperance. It was also fortunate for temperance advocates that the secretary of state, Lord Passfield, or Sidney Webb of Fabian Socialism fame, placed primacy on the demands of Gold Coast subjects in the issue of temperance. Sidney Webb's political convictions may have been responsible for his capitulation, in spite of the continued relevancy of liquor revenues for colonial administration. Indirect rule ensured that the colonial government would be sensitive to the opinions of Gold Coast chiefs.

Conclusion

Liquor legislation and the temperance movement provided an important arena for chiefs and the educated elite in the negotiation of the colonial agenda. The desire of chiefs for a selective access to liquor that discriminated against young men clashed with the colonial government's interest in liquor revenues. But as indirect rule in the Gold Coast solidified, the colonial government became more sensitive to the need to shore up the social control of chiefs. Restrictive liquor policies were enacted from 1928. The colonial agenda had been forged without the input of young men and women. This chapter has examined that upper level of negotiation that even included international conventions on liquor traffic. In implementing the colonial agenda at the local level, however, the chiefs and the colonial government would encounter opposition from women and young men. The pre-1930 era had witnessed the emergence of a new popular culture in towns and villages. Social drinking was central to this new culture. In response to restrictive liquor laws and the tightening of colonial social control, commoners would offer strong resistance through the ideology and structure of popular culture. Illicit gin, *akpeteshie*, became the symbol of this protest movement.

---

[107] Gold Coast, *Government Gazette*, November 3, 1930.
[108] Gold Coast, *Government Gazette*, November 18, 1930 and November 22, 1930.
[109] PRO, CO 96/601/45430.

5

What's in a Drink? Popular Culture, Class Formation, and the Politics of Akpeteshie, 1930–c.1945 *

Wunni ntramma na wo se nsa nye de.

When you do not have cowry shells, you say wine is not sweet

Twi Proverb

Studies of social protest in pre–1945 Gold Coast have concentrated on the rural socioeconomic revolution caused by cocoa, with its associated cocoa holdups in the 1920s and 1930s,[1] and the *asafo* as an organizational mechanism for the young men in their struggle with chiefs and their elders.[2] This chapter examines the history of the illicit distillation of *akpeteshie* (local gin) in the 1930s and 1940s.[3] It ana-

---

* An earlier version of this chapter, covering the period from 1930 to 1967, was presented at the annual meeting of the African Studies Association at Toronto in 1994, and is forthcoming in the *Journal of African History* 37, 2.

[1] In these cocoa holdups, Gold Coast farmers refused to sell their cocoa at the low prices offered by the expatriate firms.

[2] See, for example, Sam Rhodie, "The Gold Coast Cocoa Hold-Up of 1930–31," THSG 9 (1968): 105–18; Roger J. Southall, "Polarisation and Dependence in the Gold Coast Cocoa Trade, 1897–1938," THSG 16, 1 (1975): 93–115; Jarle Simensen, "Nationalism from Below. The Akyem Abuakwa Example," *Communications from the Basel Africa Bibliography* 12 (1975): 31–55; Robert Stone, "Rural Politics and the States of the Central Province," *Communications from the Basel Africa Bibliography* 12 (1975): 117–41; and Gareth Austin, "Capitalists and Chiefs in the Cocoa Hold-Ups in South Asante, 1927–1938," IJAHS 21, 1 (1988): 63–95. For detailed studies of the cocoa industry, see Polly Hill, *The Migrant Cocoa Farmers of Southern Ghana: A Study in Rural Capitalism* (Cambridge, 1963); and Gwendolyn Mikell, *Cocoa and Chaos in Ghana* (New York, 1989).

[3] *Akpeteshie* was distilled from fermented palm wine or sugar cane, and required a simple apparatus of two tins (usually four–gallon kerosene tins) and copper tubing. The fermented palm wine or sugar cane

lyzes how *akpeteshie* facilitated links between rural and urban economies, and strengthened the growing political consciousness of commoners of their exploitation by both the chiefs and the colonial state. *Akpeteshie's* illicitness unified its patrons—male and female—against the colonial forces of law and order. Its mobilizing ability transcended that of the cocoa holdups as rural cocoa farmers were divided by inequities in wealth.[4] Together, the *asafo* activities in the first half of the twentieth century, the crosscutting alliances forged between large farmers, small farmers, chiefs, brokers, and urban politicians by the cocoa holdups of the 1930s, and the growing class consciousness of *akpeteshie* patrons reinforced African political radicalism in the prelude to the independence struggle.

The spread of illicit distillation led to an irreversible decline in gin imports and the elimination of liquor legislation as a sphere for negotiating relations of power between chiefs, the educated elite, and the colonial government. The value of temperance as a political issue declined. The depression of the 1930s deepened the government's financial straits, and led to attempts to introduce income tax in 1931, a rural levy in 1932, and a Waterworks Ordinance in 1934. These revenue bills were violently resisted by commoners in urban and rural areas. The colonial government temporarily aborted the income tax and rural levy measures, but the Waterworks Ordinance and a Sedition Bill were passed in 1934. The colonial government reverted to its old dependence on liquor revenue. It attempted to revise the rigid liquor laws of 1930, it approved the establishment of a brewery by a Swiss firm in Accra in 1933—with the unfulfilled hope that excise duties from locally manufactured beer would supplant import duties on liquor[5]—and it adopted the vigorous prosecution of *akpeteshie* patrons.

The colonial onslaught on *akpeteshie* lent coherence to the political consciousness of the working classes. Indirect rule had made the chiefs obnoxious in the eyes of commoners, but it also buffered commoners from the colonial state. The direct attack on *akpeteshie* patrons confirmed the commoners' growing realization that the colonial government had always been the root cause of their political and economic impediments. Meanwhile, the alliance between chiefs and the educated elite had been split by the enhanced, independent status of chiefs under the 1925 Constitution and the Native Administrative Ordinance of 1927.[6] Embittered educated elite reached out to commoners in rural and urban centers to forge a new political alliance.[7] In these circumstances, *akpeteshie* became an important political symbol as Africans re–evaluated the colonial situation.

But for the colonial government, *akpeteshie* distillation not only threatened the government's finances, it raised the specter of crime and disorder, compromised

---

juice was boiled with a coiled copper tube running from the boiling container through a receptacle filled with cool water or a stream and into an empty container. Steam rises from the boiling palm wine or sugar cane juice, condenses as it passes through the cool water and drips as gin into the empty container. The standardized alcohol strength of *akpeteshie* today is between 40 and 50 percent by volume. Palm wine contains between three and five percent of alcohol by volume.

4   Rhodie, "Gold Coast Cocoa Hold–Up"; and Austin, "Capitalists and Chiefs."

5   See PRO, CO 96/703/7242 and PRO, CO 96/711/1933, for the origins of the Overseas Brewery beer factory in Accra.

6   See Kimble, *Political History of Ghana*, 492–505.

7   Simensen, "Rural Mass Action."

colonial concerns about urban spacing, and exposed the weakness of colonial rule. Illicit distillation eventually led the British government into the embarrassing diplomatic position of seeking an alteration of the Saint Germain Convention of 1919 that banned commercial distillation of spirits in the African colonies. By the 1940s and 1950s, *akpeteshie* had become a popular issue in nationalist politics, for legalizing illicit distillation had become an emotional issue with political and economic ramifications. But the drink also underpinned a vibrant, emerging popular culture, that sought to interpret the working–class experience, and present them with new values. Thus, the drink conjured images of class and popular protest that not only unnerved the colonial government, but also divided Gold Coast society. As a cheap drink, *akpeteshie* came to encapsulate the working–class experience; and as such it could not be ignored by the powerful or the weak.

Alcohol, Revenue, and Order in the Gold Coast: The Government's View

The terms of reference of the commission of inquiry into spirits consumption in the Gold Coast underscored the colonial government's concerns over revenue.[8] Governor Slater's attempt to link restriction in liquor imports to direct taxation alarmed some chiefs, causing some to withdraw their support for the stiff liquor laws. The paramount chief of Berekum (western province of Asante), who ended up sending two letters to the commission, is a good example. In his first letter, the chief reported with glee:

> My young men, learning of the fact that alcohol will be buried in the grave next year in Berekum Division, are keeping the funeral custom for gin and whisky to-day by swallowing as much of the "liquid dead bodies" as the capacities of their drinking organs will permit.[9]

When, on the directive of the chairman of the commission, Nana Kojo Barnieh consulted his people about introducing direct taxation to replace lost liquor revenues, opinion was against paying any tax. In a second letter to the commission, Nana Kojo Barnieh resigned himself to "freely allow[ing] the merchants to sell their liquor in my division, for my people say they will pay no tax. . . ."[10]

But the liquor laws passed, and Governor Slater prepared to introduce income tax in 1931. The reaction, in his own words, were "acts of violence" by "the uninstructed classes in Sekondi, Cape Coast and elsewhere."[11] These riots further reduced the stock of the educated elites in the eyes of the governor, for the governor believed that the Aborigines Rights Protection Society—the voice of the coastal educated elite since 1890s—fomented the riots against income tax.[12] But as Robert

---

[8]   See Chapter. 4.

[9]   "1930 Commission Report," letter received from the *Omanhene* of Berekum, November 3, 1929. By "liquid dead bodies," the *Omanhene* was figuratively referring to prohibition as the "death" of imported liquor.

[10]   "1930 Commission Report," letter received from the *Omanhene* of Berekum, November 19, 1929.

[11]   Governor Slater's address to the legislative council, *Legislative Council Debates*, March 1, 1932.

[12]   NAG, Accra, ADM 11/1/1724.

Stone demonstrates, for even the rural areas, commoners were reacting indepen-
dently to the increased exactions of the colonial state.[13] What is certain is that the
urban riots over income tax alarmed chiefs and made them reluctant to introduce
the rural levy proposed by the 1932 Native Revenue Measure.

In practice, the chiefs proved reluctant to establish the Treasuries and levy
the rates which the Government thought essential in this scheme, and so
attempts were made, culminating in the Native Administrative Authority
Ordinance of 1944, to give administrative officers more and more power
over the chiefs, both to compel them to establish Treasuries and levy rates,
and to supervise their day–to-day administration.[14]

The chiefs' loyalty to the colonial government became divided as indirect rule became more direct, and among commoners there was a "change in emphasis from
opposing the chief and *therefore* opposing a district commissioner who supported
him, to opposing a government policy and *therefore* opposing a chief who supported it.[15] For the meantime, the government would have to continue its dependence on liquor revenues.

However, the restrictive liquor laws of 1930, unlike previous increases in liquor tariffs, coincided with the depression of the 1930s and reconfigured the colonial government's financial agenda. Liquor imports plummeted, and fewer licenses
were taken for the retail of spirits. Gin imports dropped 91.4 percent from 569,746
gallons in 1929 to 49,356 gallons in 1931 although the permitted quota was 512,280.
The total revenue collected from spirit licenses dropped 82.4 percent from £68,078
in 1928–29 to £12,118 in 1933–34.[16] Government revenue and expenditure steeply
declined, as evidenced in Table 3. Officials debated whether this decline in gin
imports was due only to the temporary decrease in purchasing power because of
the fall in the value of cocoa exports in the depression or was a reflection of a new,
permanent downward trend in gin imports.

The colonial government quickly discovered, however, that Gold Coasters had
not given up gin, but that a local source of illicit gin had emerged to compete with
the old shops that sold imported gin. In 1930–31, only six cases of illicit liquor
traffic had been reported with eleven persons convicted. These offenses jumped a
hundred times to 558 reported cases with 603 persons convicted between April 1,
1933 and March 31, 1934.[17] The colonial government was astounded. As recently as
March 1926, the comptroller of customs had confidently opined that the art of distillation was largely unknown in West Africa except in Liberia.[18] The government
fumbled to piece together what was happening.

Comparing notes with Nigeria, the other British colony experiencing a rash of
illicit distillation, further alarmed the Gold Coast government. Also overtaken by
events, Governor Donald Cameron of Nigeria believed that illicit distillation:

---

[13] Stone, "Rural Politics in Ghana in the Inter–War Period."

[14] Ibid., 121.

[15] Ibid.

[16] Governor Shenton Thomas, *Memorandum on Liquor Policy* (Accra, 1934). Copy in PRO, CO 96/715/
21702.

[17] Ibid.

[18] PRO, CO 96/681/6204.

TABLE 3
Revenue and Expenditure of the Gold Coast, 1927–1933.

Year	Revenue (£)	Expenditure (£)
1927–28	4,121,522	3,618,382
1928–29	3,913,529	4,629,294
1929–30	3,397,324	3,932,022
1930–31	3,499,419	3,744,010
1931–32	2,284,299	2,823,752
1932–33	2,670,786	2,679,482

Source: Gold Coast, *Annual Report, 1932–33*, 80.

commenced as recently as May last [1931] and it is alleged that the knowledge was acquired from natives who had returned from the United States of America. I am told that the secret of distilling spirits by means of a rude still made of earthen pots (or petrol tins) and copper or other tubing is being sold broadcast for £10 in each case.[19]

Political officers in the Calabar province reported an epidemic of thefts of feed pipes from launches and cars. Even the enforcers of colonial rule were not immune to this new vice, and the commissioner of police reported a constable on duty at the Ibagwa Mill, who was found "raving and maniac drunk" from what was believed to be illicit gin.[20] Illicit gin appeared to have heralded a new dawn of crime and disorder in colonial Nigeria.

To the Gold Coast government, patronage of illicit *akpeteshie* compromised respect for law, and represented a loss of revenue as it undercut liquor imports and the taking out of retail licenses.[21] But *akpeteshie* also constituted a menace to public health because of its unrefined nature and harmful contents. One laboratory analysis in 1933 found as "much as twenty–four grains of copper and zinc per gallon of spirits in an exhibit."[22] Another *akpeteshie* sample from Saltpond in 1932 was found to contain 72.9 percent of alcohol by volume.[23] And those involved in *akpeteshie* distillation in the colonial era admit to the hazards of the trade, especially the explosion of kerosene tins used in distillation when overheated.[24]

Convictions of armed young men in the Gold Coast in the 1930s, and evidence that those involved in illicit distillation often carried guns alarmed the colonial government. In July 1931, Kobina Adjigo was found in possession of one revolver and four rounds of ammunition at Nsawam, and Odartey Quarshie was found

---

19 Governor of Nigeria to the Secretary of State for the Colonies, December 22, 1931. PRO, CO 554/89/ 4495. It is strange that the Nigerian government regarded illicit distillation as a recent phenomenon. Colonial records indicate a proliferation of illicit distillation in Nigeria around 1910. Olorunfemi, "Liquor Traffic," 241.
20 Resident of the Calabar Province, "Memorandum on the Illicit Distilling of Spirits in the Calabar Province." PRO, CO 554/89/4495.
21 Governor Slater to the Colonial Office, January 16, 1932. PRO, CO 554/89/4495.
22 PRO, CO 554/96/21446.
23 PRO, CO 96/708/1660.
24 AFN: Interview with Jeremiah Oman Ano, Sekondi, August 15, 1994.

guilty for bearing a cap gun in Mami Dede village (Accra District) without a valid license.[25] In Kumase, S. A. Onyinah and others were charged before the court for "being in possession of (a) illicit distilled liquor (b) gunpowder (c) firearm."[26] In what the government believed to be a display of defiance, persons convicted of trafficking in illicit liquor preferred to go to jail rather than pay the fines. Out of the total fines of £17,677 imposed in 603 convictions in 1933–34, only £692.10s.6d. was paid.[27] The following year was no different: only £826.12s. being paid out of the total fines of £30,157.12s. imposed in 615 convictions.[28]

Equally disturbing to the Gold Coast government was the fact that those involved in illicit liquor defied categorization. The colonial mind was a neat mind, and crime in the Gold Coast was conveniently catalogued according to "tribal" tendencies. Ewes were prone to murder, northerners to drunkenness and disorder, and Akans were often the perpetrators of fraud. A gender categorization of crime also made crime appear "orderly." Crimes with violence, for example armed robbery, were associated with men. Women often ran afoul of the Ministry of Health for leaving refuse in public places or for having open receptacles containing water at home which encouraged the breeding of mosquito larvae.[29] With illicit distillation, retail, and consumption of local gin, no regional, ethnic nor gender stereotypes seemed valid. The perpetrators lacked an organized face, but had a boldness that unnerved the colonial government.

But there was growing evidence that the Volta River District (Eweland) was emerging as the den of illicit distillers.

In January 1934, a highly successful raid was made by police in force between the villages of Kpong and Amedica, where 50 Bush Stills, 40 gallons of distilled spirits and 500 gallons of palm wine were seized and destroyed. Fines to the aggregate of £375 were imposed in respect of this raid but nothing was paid. This raid revealed the fact that the Volta River Islands afford suitable shelter for the distillers which accounts for the numerous cases of possessing trade spirits reported in the Akuse and Ada Districts.[30]

In 1938–39, the Ada–Keta district still held the record for the highest number of illicit distillation cases reported.[31] The 1930s witnessed a phenomenal increase in

---

[25]   NAG, Accra, SCT/38/5/29. Nsawam Criminal Court Record Book, IGP vs Kobina Adjigo (July 6, 1931); and IGP vs Odartey Quarshie (July 13, 1931).

[26]   NAG, Accra, CSO 15/3/01, Inspector General of Police to the Colonial Secretary, December 9, 1932.

[27]   NAG, Accra, CSO 1100/30, Vol. 5, Gold Coast, *Report on the Police Department for the Year 1933–34*, 9.

[28]   NAG, Accra, CSO 1100/30, Vol. 6, Gold Coast, *Report on the Police Department for the Year 1934–35*, 6.

[29]   These impressions are based on the author's perusal of ADM 15 files (Law Officer's Department), the CSO 15/3 files (Criminal Investigations and Reports), and the Criminal Record Book of Nsawam District (SCT 38/5) housed at the National Archives of Ghana (NAG), Accra. These "tribal" categorizations, in the author's mind, were aided by the fact that Eweland was on the border of the colonial territory, hence Ewes were seen as being free of colonial restraints; by the prohibition of European liquor in the Northern Territories, hence the belief that European liquor was culturally and chemically powerful for northerners; and by the early establishment of mission schools in Fante territory, making educated Fantes the perfect perpetrators of fraud.

[30]   Gold Coast, *Report on the Police Department, 1933–34*, 5.

[31]   Gold Coast, *Report on the Gold Coast Police Force for the Year Ending 31st March 1939*, 16. NAG, Accra, CSO 1100/30, Vol. 10.

police duties compared to the 1920s, and the Gold Coast police force was stretched thin in their endeavor to stamp out illicit distillation.

With roots in rural and urban areas, and patronized by urban men and women, *akpeteshie* also compromised the colonial government's conception of urban space. In parts of colonial Africa, governments strongly discouraged the immigration of women into the towns.[32] This was especially true of towns that sprang up as a result of colonial activity. The Gold Coast wage economy itself was very male–oriented, and the colonial government remained ambivalent about migrant women's position in towns. But the depression of the 1930s dampened rural and urban economies, and increased the movement of men and women between villages and towns in search of economic opportunities. Some urban women, strapped for cash, took to the retailing of *akpeteshie*. The colonial government found it uncomfortable that single women were discovering niches in the urban economy. The colonial government galvanized its forces to stamp out illicit gin.

Legislating Leisure? The Commoners' View

The restrictive liquor laws of the 1930s directly threatened a vibrant popular culture that was emerging in urban Gold Coast.[33] This popular culture encompassed drinking bars, popular music ("highlife") and dance, and comic opera (concert).[34] To appreciate the tenacity of *akpeteshie* patrons in their resistance to colonial forces, and what *akpeteshie* meant to them, it is necessary to examine the history and form(s) of this new urban culture.

Urbanization and economic development in southern Gold Coast from the turn of the twentieth century opened up new employment opportunities and encouraged rural–urban migration among young men and women. The period between 1900 and 1930 witnessed phenomenal economic expansion and increased urban immigration.[35] Sekondi's population of 4,095 in 1901 expanded to 16,953 by the 1931 census. The village of Obuasi was transformed by the gold mining activities

---

[32] Lovett, "Gender Relations," 27, argues that under capitalism "production increasingly came to be gendered male, while reproduction conversely became gendered female. . . ." See also Kenneth Little, *Women in African Towns* (Cambridge, 1973).

[33] "Popular culture" is used here in the sense defined by Johannes Fabian, "Popular Culture in Africa: Findings and Conjectures," *Africa* 48, 4 (1978): 315. In particular, "it suggests contemporary cultural expressions carried by the masses in contrast to both modern elitist and traditional 'tribal' culture" and "it signifies, potentially at least, processes occurring behind the back of established powers and accepted interpretations. . . ." But the use of popular culture in this paper differs from Fabian's in that it posits no inherent tension between rural and urban culture. Areas of tension may exist, but popular culture also has the potential to link or integrate urban and rural social experiences.

[34] These were not the only pillars of the new urban popular culture, other aspects included independent African churches, film and sports. But drinking– and dance–bars, with their associated paraphernalia of popular music and comic opera, were particularly relevant to the history of *akpeteshie*. From the 1940s, highlife bands doubled as concert parties. They staged plays theatricalizing urban life and punctuated with music, the lyrics of which underscored the themes in the play and with the actors as singers. This genre has been dubbed "comic opera" by scholars, but ordinary Ghanaians prefer the term "concert." Martin, *Leisure and Society in Colonial Brazzaville*, examines the importance of football, clothing, drinking, music and dance in the creation of leisure and urban society in colonial Brazzaville.

[35] Frimpong–Ansah, *Vampire State in Africa*, Ch.. 4.

of Ashanti Goldfields, and Obuasi registered a population of 7,877 in the 1931 census. The population of Accra rose from 19,582 in 1911 to 60,726 in 1931.[36] For many of these migrants, single men and women, the social lifestyles of Europeans and educated coastal elites provided important models in their construction of new social lives.[37] By the 1930s and 1940s, a dynamic popular culture had emerged, giving identity and meaning to the lives of urban commoners. World War I had been instrumental to this development. The stationing of foreign troops in towns like Sekondi and Accra during the war, and the need to entertain these troops strengthened an elite urban culture in which European–style drinking bars, dance–band music, and comic opera were becoming central. Against this bustling social background, highlife music emerged when dance bands fused Akan dance rhythms and melodies with Western instruments and harmonies.[38] Actually, the term "highlife" was assigned to the new genre of music by the urban poor excluded from elite social activities.[39] One of its earlier practitioners, Yebuah Mensah, commented on the origins of highlife:

> During the early twenties, during my childhood, the term "highlife" was created by people who gathered around the dancing clubs such as the Rodger Club (built in 1904) to watch and listen to the couples enjoying themselves. Highlife started as a catch–name for the indigenous songs played at these clubs by such early bands as the Jazz Kings, the Cape Coast Sugar Babies, the Sekondi Nanshamang, and later the Accra Orchestra. The people outside called it "highlife" as they did not reach the class of the couples going inside, who not only had to pay a, then, relatively high entrance fee of 7s. 6d., but also had to wear full evening dress including top–hats.[40]

Comic opera constituted an important part of this new social life. Commonly referred to as "concert," this genre developed at the turn of the century in coastal towns as "stylish affairs."[41] Borrowing from American minstrelsy shows, "black face" became the most striking image in concert performances.[42] Concert became popular through Empire Day drama performances and the first professional actor, Teacher Yalley, began his career in these Empire Day performances. Just like the

---

[36] Gold Coast, *Census of the Population, 1911*, 50. GNA, ADM 5/2/3; and A. W. Cardinall, *The Gold Coast, 1931* (Accra, 1931), 158–59.

[37] See Chapter 3.

[38] E. J. Collins, "Ghanaian Highlife," *African Arts* 10, 1 (1976): 62–68; and Collins, *West African Pop Roots*, Ch. 2. Kofi E. Agovi, "The Political Relevance of Ghanaian Highlife Songs since 1957," *Research in African Literatures* 20, 2 (1989): 194, points to the greater significance of lyrics over instrumentation in highlife songs. The mix of African, New World, and European rhythms, instruments, and lyrics in the French Congo gave rise to the celebrated "Congo music" of the 1950s. Martin, *Leisure and Society in Colonial Brazzaville*, 127.

[39] David Coplan, "Go to My Town, Cape Coast! The Social History of Ghanaian Highlife," in Brunno Nettl, ed., *Eight Urban Musical Cultures* (Urbana, 1978), 100.

[40] Collins, *West Africa Pop Roots*, 21.

[41] Ibid.

[42] Catherine M. Cole, "Reading Blackface in West Africa: Signs Taken for Wonders"(paper presented at the annual meeting of the African Studies Association, Orlando, 1995). Catherine Cole is conducting research on "Wandering Minstrels: A Historical Ethnography of Ghanaian Concert Parties," the subject of her dissertation for Northwestern University.

new dance bands, Teacher Yalley performed to an elite audience at places like the Optimism Club, charging entrance fees as high as 5s. in the early 1920s.[43]

Johannes Fabian has commented on the process of cultural "creolization" that characterizes the creative synthesis of African and Western influences into unique urban popular cultures.[44] David Coplan notes in the case of urban Gold Coast, that as rural–urban migration increased after 1919,

> the new elite rapidly began to serve as a reference group for more tradi-
> tional, nonliterate Africans as the new urban socio–economic reality be-
> came progressively less comprehensible to the latter and less responsive
> to mediation by traditional values and systems of social control.[45]

But the social needs of the new migrants differed from those of the educated coastal Africans. The immigrant urban workers began to construct, not imitate, a unique urban popular culture that meaningfully interpreted their urban social experience.

Working-class drinking bars like "Liberia Bar" and "Columbia Bar" were estab-
lished in Cassava Farm (Takoradi).[46] The drinking patterns of urban workers differed significantly from those of the rural palm wine bar in that they transcended barriers of ethnicity, age, and gender.[47] Unlike the elitist Optimism Club, anyone with cash was welcome at Columbia Bar. Acoustic guitar bands bridged the social gap between the rural *seprewa* (Akan lute) player and the urban dance band designed for elite entertainment.[48] Itinerant concert parties, like "The Axim Six"[49] and "The Two Bobs," toured towns and peri–urban villages, and they incorporated Ananse, the traditional spider–
hero, in their acts. Their Joker or "Bob" "took on all the mischievous aspects of Ananse."[50] These concerts became the medium for socializing new migrants and would–be mi-
grants into the urban experience through plays that dramatized urban life for a low admission fee. Popular groups like "Glass and Grant" drew crowds in towns with plays like "'Another Little Drink' (wouldn't do us any harm)."[51] And important to these new forms of recreation was cheap Dutch gin.

It was this whole complex edifice that the restrictive liquor laws of 1930 assailed. In addition to expressing the real and the ideal about the urban social experience, popular culture provided new job opportunities as bandsmen, actors, retailers of liquor, and prostitutes.[52] Urban and rural laborers felt themselves pitted against

---

[43] On comic opera, see also E. J. Collins, "Comic Opera in Ghana," *African Arts* 9, 2 (1976): 50–57.

[44] Fabian, "Popular Culture," 317.

[45] Coplan, "Go to My Town, Cape Coast," 101.

[46] AFN: Interview with Laurence Cudjoe, et al.

[47] David G. Mandelbaum, "Alcohol and Culture," 281, points out that in complex societies, "the drinking patterns of each subgroup or class may reflect its special characteristics as well as the cultural frame of the society."

[48] The guitar bands became famous for their "palm–wine music," a style of highlife that emphasized the trials of life in its lyrics. The lyrics of palm wine music contrasted with the lofty images of love, comfort, and happiness portrayed by dance bands. On palm–wine music, see Collins, *West African Pop Roots*, Ch. 3.

[49] *Gold Coast Times*, 9 August 1930.

[50] Collins, *West African Pop Roots*, 38.

[51] See *Gold Coast Independent*, January 10 and 17, 1925.

[52] The close association between drinking places like Colombia Bar and prostitution in Sekondi and Takoradi was pointed out by interviewees like Anita Mensah, Takoradi, August 16, 1994.

Distilling *akpeteshie* **in the bush**

the "discriminatory" laws of colonial rule. Ironically, the colonial onslaught against *akpeteshie* heightened the relevance of popular culture as an interpretation of the exploited existence of workers in urban Gold Coast.

Women who retailed *akpeteshie* experienced firsthand victimization in a colonial economy that was male–oriented. Women like Anita Mensah[53] and Novisi Segbedzi[54] cited the need to supplement the inadequate wages of their husbands as their reason for selling *akpeteshie* in the Gold Coast. It was difficult for the colonial regime to justify the classification of such women, who were struggling to survive in the urban environment, as "criminal elements."[55] What is striking about the women who retailed *akpeteshie* in colonial towns is the fact that many of them either came from families with a history of retailing liquor and/or were married to distillers. Anita Mensah's life history is illustrative.

Anita is an illiterate woman born in Sekondi around 1927. Her grandfather had worked in the Customs Service in the 1880s and 1890s when there was no port at Sekondi–Takoradi. Then, ships docked around Shama, and canoes were used to offload the ships. The grandfather would buy a cask of rum, and the grandmother would retail it in tots. Anita's mother went into *akpeteshie* retail-

---

[53] AFN: Interview with Anita Mensah, Takoradi, March 5, 1992.

[54] AFN: Interview with Novisi Segbedzi, Accra, June 14, 1992.

[55] Helen Bradford points out the paradox that by sexist definition, women could not be a threat to law and order. The arrest, manhandling, and jailing of women during women's demonstrations against municipal beerhalls in Natal in 1929 had the effect of bringing their men into the struggle against the government. Helen Bradford, "'We Women Will Show Them': Beer Protests in the Natal Countryside, 1929," in Crush and Ambler, *Liquor and Labor* , 208–34.

ing in the 1930s when demand for it arose in Sekondi. Anita was her mother's first born, so at the age of 13 she began to assist her mother. The mother would construct a wooden box in which Anita would carry the *akpeteshie* from, then forested, Takoradi along what is now Poase Beach road to Sekondi in the night. Anita married in 1948 and moved from Sekondi to live with the husband in Takoradi. The family needed additional income so Anita took up the family trade—retailing liquor. A first child came in 1950, and Anita decided to go into distillation to bring in more income. She bought two drums, secured land at Amanful–Kuma, hired help, and went into distillation. Anita personally assisted her hired help in the felling of palm trees. Queried whether this was not an infringement of the Akan taboo that women should not work on palm trees, Anita retorted: "who decreed that taboo? Men! Akan men knew the economic value of palm wine and the palm tree, and to establish male control claimed it was a taboo for women to work on palm trees. I have worked on palm trees for so long, what has happened to me?"[56]

Distillation was sometimes a family venture that involved males and females in colonial Gold Coast. This gender cooperation reflected the traditional division of labor by sex.

> In the distillation of *akpeteshie*, when the mash has been put into a drum ready for boiling, it is a woman who puts firewood under the drum, lights it and tends it. It is a woman who fetches water for the receptacle the pipe passes through. Distillation was often a family concern. The man did it with his wife and children. In those days, women worked strictly under their husbands instructions. But all women worked.[57]

In farming villages, *akpeteshie* could be distilled with much ease. The Police Department report for 1934–35 noted that: "The spirits are usually distilled in the country districts at a distance of 20 miles or more from the town where they are marketed, and are transported to the town in four–gallon petrol tins by motor transport."[58] Interviews conducted at Ntoaso, a village close to Nsawam, confirmed the existence of a tradition of distillation among certain families. In Ntoaso today, cement wells used in distillation have become valuable heirlooms.[59] In peri–urban villages, men dominated distillation as the proximity to large towns heightened fears of police raids. These areas were also probably new to the *akpeteshie* business, and they lacked the tradition of family distillation common in an Ewe village such as Akpefe in the Volta district by the 1930s.[60] The *akpeteshie* was smuggled into the town at night, sometimes by armed gangs, and delivered to retailers.[61]

Akpeteshie distillers often came to town to explore new retail outlets, and for single women without capital this was an opportunity to set up business. New

---

56   AFN: Interview with Anita Mensah, Takoradi, March 5, 1992.

57   Ibid., August 16, 1994.

58   Gold Coast, *Report on the Police Department, 1934–35*, 7.

59   AFN: Interview with Adotei Akwei, Ntoaso, July 11, 1992; and interview with George Blankson, Ntoaso, July 11, 1992.

60   AFN: Interview with Samuel Agbeve, Accra, February 26, 1992; and interview with Sylvester Adenyo, Ntoaso, February 26, 1992.

61   AFN: Interview with Jeremiah Oman Ano.

Akpeteshie **wells at Ntoaso**

contacts were put on a trial basis, even extended credit facilities, and supplies were increased when they showed promise.

> Distillers sold a container of *akpeteshie* (holding four gallons) for 1 pound 8 shillings when paid for immediately, and 2 pounds when purchased on credit. After resale, a retailer made 2 pounds 4 shillings on a container of four gallons—a profit of between 4 shillings and 16 shillings. The retailer informed her acquaintances in the community of her hidden cache, and social networks were essential to success in this trade.[62]

Migrant women from families and/or rural areas that had distilled *akpeteshie* were quick to capitalize on these new urban opportunities. That is how Novisi Segbedzi of Accra struck business relationships with distillers from Coaltar and Suhum in the 1930s.[63] The *akpeteshie* industry, thus, effectively linked rural and urban economies.

The production of *akpeteshie* meshed neatly with the rural economy—oral evidence suggests that cocoa farmers had knowledge of distillation from the late nineteenth century—and farmers came to distill gin as a supplementary occupation and supplied it to villages and towns. There appears to be some confusion as to when knowledge of distillation became available in the Gold Coast. It is likely that this knowledge may have existed in restricted circles, at least, by the early–nineteenth century. Dutch traders in the Gold Coast experimented with commercial

---

[62]   AFN: Interview with Novisi Segbedzi.
[63]   AFN: Interview with Novisi Segbedzi, Accra, June 14, 1992.

distillation from the early–nineteenth century.[64] As far back as the first half of the eighteenth century, Asantehene Opoku Ware I (1720–1750) had solicited Dutch assistance in the establishment of distilleries in Asante. But the Dutch jealously guarded their trade secrets.[65] Ironically, Ewe laborers, who worked on the Basel Mission's cocoa plantations in Akropong,[66] are credited by one source with learning the art of distillation from the European missionaries. Apparently, Basel missionaries distilled liquor from fermented cocoa beans for their private use.[67] In the words of Anita Mensah:

> Two of my grandfather's brothers were taken as laborers for the Basel Mission from Eweland to Akropong. These Europeans instructed my grand uncles in distillation. My grand uncles would supervise the fermentation of cocoa beans. They would then connect a pipe between two receptacles and distill. The vapor from the fermented cocoa beans turned into gin. My grand uncles developed an interest in this gin as the Europeans used to give them some to drink, although they were paid laborers. So immediately after the cocoa season at Akropong, my grand uncles would ferment some of the beans and distill it. But the Europeans used to rectify their distilled gin. But that part of the process they did not let my grand uncles witness or learn. So my grand uncles would just do the initial distillation and drink their gin. The gin aided them in their agricultural labor and it livened their social moments.[68]

As the Ewes left Akropong for other areas, they took their interest in distillation with them. The Ewes later discovered that fermented palm wine had the same qualities as fermented cocoa beans. Since palm trees grew naturally in the forest habitat, it was a cheaper raw material than cocoa. Later, distillers experimented successfully with fermented sugar cane, taking their cue from the fact that the Basel missionaries added brown sugar to the fermented cocoa beans before distillation.[69] But it appears a market for *akpeteshie* did not develop until the economic depression of the 1930s with its expanding urban population and emerging popular culture. Farmers came to use *akpeteshie* distillation from the 1930s as a source of cash in the nonproductive period between harvests.[70] The cocoa holdups of the 1920s and the 1930s may have actually radicalized cocoa farmers, encouraging them to breach colonial rule in their distillation of *akpeteshie*.[71]

The colonial attack against *akpeteshie* afforded ordinary Gold Coasters the opportunity to critique the ideology of colonial rule. James Scott points out "the

---

[64]   See Chapter 4; and Sampson, *Gold Coast Men of Affairs*, 114–15.

[65]   Wilks, "Mossi and Akan States 1500–1800," 447.

[66]   Cocoa seedlings had been introduced into the Gold Coast by the Basel Missionary Society in 1858.

[67]   AFN: Interview with Anita Mensah. Anita is from a family of distillers, and she was recounting what her grandfather told her. Susan Diduk points out that "Basel missionaries came from rural areas of southern Germany and Switzerland where they were well acquainted with home brews like *most*, prepared from fermented apples. Susan Diduk, "European Alcohol, History, and the State in Cameroon," *African Studies Review*, 36, 1 (1993): 9.

[68]   AFN: Interview with Anita Mensah.

[69]   Ibid.

[70]   See Asare Konadu, *The Wizard of Asamang* (Accra, 1988), 114–15.

[71]   Southall, "Polarisation and Dependence."

extent to which most subordinate classes are able, on the basis of their daily
material experience, to penetrate and demystify the prevailing ideology."[72] The
colonial rhetoric argued that *akpeteshie* was physically injurious to its consumers because of lead and copper contents. But for those who patronized illicit
gin in the Gold Coast, the colonial concern was really about revenue. As K. K.
Kabah, an executive member of the Western Region Distillers Cooperative, put
it:

> The white men wanted to cheat us. If they could ban our local drink, we
> would end up buying their imported drinks. We knew they were cheating
> us, but we could not say anything. So we hid in isolated places and dis-
> tilled our gin and drank our own thing.[73]

In several interviews the author conducted, none of the interviewees seemed convinced by the colonial government's altruistic arguments. Even A. A. Amartey, who
worked in the Broadcasting Corporation until 1959, affirmed that it was all about
revenue.[74]

The colonial government was disturbed that Gold Coasters, even the chiefs,
refused to see illicit distillation as a moral or legal crime. Voluntary informers were
rare. The Eastern Province commissioner in despair stated:

> I must with regret express the opinion that illicit distillation will never be
> entirely stamped out, as it has become the practice to distill in individual
> houses sufficient spirit for family needs, apart from the class of distillers
> for commercial profit. The process is so easy, the profit is clear, and the
> trade is regarded as a very venial breach of the law by the chiefs and
> people generally. It is quite obvious, however, that definite action must be
> taken by the government, who cannot remain passive under the reproach
> which is conveyed in the native name of the liquor "the whiteman's
> shame."[75]

Other names given to illicit gin capture the colonial experience of its patrons.
"Akpeteshie" is a derivative of a Ga word meaning "hide-out" because distillation
and consumption were secretive.[76] Another revealing name was *bome kutuku* ("box
me"), which described the sound of the beating the arrested culprit received from
the colonial police.[77]

A general atmosphere of "daring the state" developed, and it appears baiting
the authorities became fun. A contemporary witness in Sekondi remembered that
his father found it amusing outwitting policemen by stringing his purchased
akpeteshie bottles around his waist, and then putting on his cover cloth.[78] When the
author asked Novisi Segbedzi if the colonial police ever arrested her, she laughed
and clapped her hands, "yes" she answered. She had to secure a lawyer and go to

[72] James Scott, *Weapons of the Weak: Everyday Forms of Peasant Resistance* (New Haven, 1985), 317.
[73] AFN: Interview with the Western Region Distillers Cooperative Management Committee, Takoradi, August 16, 1994.
[74] AFN: Interview with A. A. Amartey (aka Nii Amarkai II).
[75] PRO, CO 96/715/21702. Eastern Province Commissioner's Report, December 28, 1933.
[76] *Co-op Distillers News*, No. 1 (January–March 1992).
[77] AFN: Interview with Jeremiah Oman Ano.
[78] AFN: Interview with J. K. Annan, Sekondi, May 27, 1992.

the High Court in Accra where she was fined £5.[79] Her amusement at her recollec-
tion was linked to the feeling of having "gotten away" from the state. Imprisonment constituted a real threat, and female *akpeteshie* retailers had by necessity fa-
miliarized themselves with the workings of the colonial judicial system. According
to Anita Mensah,

> if I was fined and it took my mother even a few hours to get the money, I
> was put in a small cell. If at 2:00 pm—when the court was over and the
> prisoners were being taken to jail—and my mother was not back, I would
> have to be taken to jail with the prisoners. You incurred further expenses
> getting your ward out of the prison yard. Because you were booked as a
> prisoner and you had to pay a discharge fee.[80]

For female *akpeteshie* retailers, staying out of prison and minimizing court fines
were essential. It is important to remember that these retailers were often also
mothers. Although the passage of time may have encouraged romanticized memo-
ries, it is clear that in the post–1930s, the "moral authority" of colonial rule came
under question. It became imperative that the colonial government salvage its image and repair its hegemony.

The Tail Wags the Dog:
The Colonial Government's Dilemma

Although the colonial government could not deny the "representatives" of the
people—the chiefs and the educated elite—their demand for restrictive liquor laws
(highly publicized in Britain), it did not intend to give up a lucrative and reliable
source of revenue without a fight. It believed it could out–maneuver the illicit distillers if it could reduce the price of imported gin to make it competitive with
akpeteshie. A second strategy involved the vigorous prosecution of *akpeteshie* patrons and the imposition of heavy sentences. The government hoped that both strategies combined would end the *akpeteshie* menace. Official propaganda also encouraged the consumption of lager beer with the intention of promoting the Accra
brewery, boosting the government's excise duties, and diminishing the popularity
of *akpeteshie*.

The new governor's address at the opening of the Accra brewery in 1933 presents an interesting example of the official sales pitch for lager beer:

> There are some who say that beer is bad for you. Don't you believe it.
> What is the secret of England's greatness? Certainly not lime juice. Any-
> how beer is not as bad as gin, and not nearly so bad as the liquor which is
> manufactured by certain enterprising persons of this country by means of
> two old petrol tins and a piece of copper tubing. You call it "Kelewele," or
> "Akpeteshi" which means "going around the corner." A neat word which
> seems to correspond with our English phrase "Come and have a quick
> one."[81]

---

[79]   AFN: Interview with Novisi Segbedzi.

[80]   AFN: Interview with Anita Mensah, Takoradi, August 16, 1994.

[81]   *Gold Coast Independent*, July 1, 1933; Shenton Thomas served as governor from 1932 to 1934.

Considering the "harmful" effects of gin, the governor recommended: "Why not let us go off the gin standard and go on the beer standard?"[82] From 1933, Governor Shenton Thomas petitioned the Colonial Office to relax the restrictions on liquor imports and sales passed in 1928 and 1930. He stressed the need to reduce tariffs on imported liquor, pointing out that while a bottle of *akpeteshie* was priced around 3s.6d., a bottle of imported gin cost at least 5s.[83] In rural areas such as Yabiw, in the Western Province, a bottle of *akpeteshie* cost as low as 1s. 6d. during World War II.[84] Thomas believed that illicit distillation was spawning criminal networks that could threaten colonial law and order if *akpeteshie*'s popularity was not eroded. The report of the commissioner of police in Kumasi that hundreds of bottles of *akpeteshie* had been seized from Kumasi stores in the Christmas of 1932 was very disturbing.[85] It suggested the existence of an organized production network.

Some chiefs and educated elite sympathized with the government's position. In 1933, chiefs in the Eastern Provincial Council of Chiefs requested the withdrawal of the restrictive liquor laws of 1928 and 1930 "in order that their people might be able to obtain gin at a reasonable price when they desire it."[86] An editorial in the *Gold Coast Independent* in March 1933 commented on the sad development that the attempt to curtail liquor imports had resulted in a far worse situation—illicit distillation.[87] The opinion of state councils, polled in a 1933 questionnaire distributed by the governor, supported the governor's requests for continued imports of gin and geneva, the readmission of rum in cask, a reduction in license fees, and an increase in the hours of sale.[88]

Even the Catholic mission at Keta (Volta River District) endorsed the governor's remedy of a cheaper imported alternative to *akpeteshie*, pointing out the deleterious effects of *akpeteshie* on the inhabitants of the Volta River District.

> The consumption of the spirits distilled from palm wine was started only when the natives could no more buy imported spirits. This locally distilled spirit is very harmful and it tends to increase. About 40 people around Abo (near Keta), where the stills are numerous, have died in consequence of the consumption of this native spirit.[89]

It remained for the governor to persuade the colonial secretary about the validity of his strategy. Although Thomas did not remain in office long enough to push his policy through, his successor, Arnold Hodson (1934–1941), adopted his demand for a reduction in tariffs on imported gin.

The urgency of this demand for cheap imported gin was heightened by the apparent inability of the colonial police to stem the tide of illicit distillation. Hodson

---

[82] Ibid.

[83] PRO CO 96/708/1660. Thomas to Cunliffe–Lister, January 7, 1933.

[84] AFN: Interview with Jeremiah Oman Ano.

[85] PRO, CO 96/715/21702. Report of the Senior Commissioner of Police, Kumasi, November 16, 1933.

[86] *Gold Coast Independent*, March 18, 1933.

[87] *Gold Coast Independent*, March 11, 1933.

[88] Thomas, *Memorandum on Liquor Policy*.

[89] PRO, CO 96/715/21702. Gold Coast, *Correspondence and Statistics Relating to the Consumption of Spirits in the Gold Coast* (Accra, 1934), 161. The Catholic Mission of Keta was the only mission in the Gold Coast that favored the reimportation of cheap gin.

confessed to the colonial secretary that he had been "advised that no efforts by the police can successfully deal with the problem."[90] Persons convicted for trafficking in illicit gin preferred to go to prison instead of pay the fine.[91] This was to ensure that their profits were not depleted.[92] From the colonial records, it appears that the heavy fines for dealing in *akpeteshie* were a more effective deterrent than the short imprisonment terms.[93] Some offenders, who had paid heavy fines, now restricted their activities to touring the Sekondi and Axim Districts instructing people, in return for payment, on how to make the illicit stills and manufacture the liquor.[94] The resources of the colonial police were not adequate to deal effectively with the widespread trafficking in *akpeteshie*.

But international conventions regulating liquor traffic to the African colonies limited the extent to which Britain could reduce tariffs on imported liquor. Allowing for the depreciation of the franc, the lowest duty under the Saint Germain Convention that the colonial government could levy on a gallon of imported gin was 24s. in 1936.[95] This was not sufficiently low enough to enable imported gin to outcompete *akpeteshie*. By 1939, the option of reducing duties on imported spirits to make them competitive had been ruled out by the Colonial Office.[96]

The outbreak of World War II in 1939—and the military's demands on shipping space—further reduced liquor imports into the Gold Coast, forcing the colonial government to consider the radical and embarrassing option of legalizing illicit gin in the Gold Coast.[97] Although this would involve Britain unilaterally seeking to revise the Saint Germain Convention, Britain believed it would express goodwill towards Gold Coasters in a time of national crisis, not to mention the revenue that could accrue from the distillers' fees and excise duties on *akpeteshie*.[98] In October 1942, the British War Cabinet approved in principle the proposal for local distillation of spirits in West Africa, but insisted that this should be done by a government agency. The War Cabinet asked the Foreign Office to explore the best means of revising the Saint Germain Convention.[99]

Popular opinion in the Gold Coast and Nigeria ruled out the institution of any "Durban System" in West Africa, whereby the colonial government would commercially exploit the production of an "African drink" through government agencies.[100] In South Africa, beginning with Durban in 1909, several municipal govern-

---

90   PRO, CO 554/98/33522. Hodson to Cunliffe–Lister, May 3, 1935.

91   Thomas, *Memorandum on Liquor Policy*, PRO, CO 96/715/21702.

92   See the report of the Social Welfare Committee in the WMMS's Gold Coast Synod Minutes of 1946 (Box 1241).

93   The Inspector General of Police, Bamford, argued for heavier prison sentences. The fine for a first offence was £100 or six months imprisonment with or without hard labor. Subsequent offenses could receive a fine up to £500. PRO, CO 554/89/4495 (1932).

94   PRO, CO 96/715/21702.

95   PRO, CO 554/103/33522 (1936).

96   PRO, CO 554/119/33522 (1939).

97   PRO, CO 554/127/33522/B (1943), conveys the Foreign Office's acute embarrassment at having to seek unilaterally an amendment to an international liquor agreement.

98   PRO, CO 554/127/33522 (1942).

99   PRO, CO 554/127/33522/B (1943).

100   On the "Durban System," see La Hausse, *Brewers, Beerhalls and Boycotts*.

ments monopolized the production of indigenous beer, retailed exclusively through municipal beerhalls. The West African War Council minuted that:

The products of such distilleries would be boycotted, and the present system of illicit distillation would continue. On the other hand, a system under which private manufacture was permitted under government licence would be workable. Responsibility for administering such a system would be largely decentralised on the native administration.[101]

The British government eventually approved the private distillation of local gin by Africans in 1943, and the Gold Coast and Nigeria were advised to proceed with the necessary legislation.[102] Curiously, the Nigerian Executive Council chose not to proceed with legalizing local distillation. Citing regulatory problems as a justification, the government, nevertheless, clearly stated that it did not consider "that the present is the time to embark on an undertaking that would be bitterly opposed by the missionary bodies."[103] This sudden turnabout deterred the Gold Coast government from implementing its desire to legalize local distillation.[104] The *akpeteshie* issue was thus left unresolved.

Akpeteshie, Class Consciousness and Political Protest

From the 1930s, legalizing *akpeteshie* became a potent issue in nationalist politics. On the streets, highlife songs in vernacular championed the cause of *akpeteshie*, and deprecated colonial rule in general. Highlife songs articulated a worldview that was significant in its lack of a moral commitment to colonial rule and, perhaps, to authority in general. "Ma ye adwuma aye aye tro na wode tua me ka" ("After all my labor you pay me with 3d!") by Kwaa Mensah expressed the feelings of economic exploitation laborers experienced in the colonial economy.[105] And "Nye mi nku na warrant atia me" ("I am not the only one who has fallen foul of the law"), by A. K. Mathews' Band, disparaged law.[106] The commoners' impression of the colonial order as exploitative seemed to have rationalized economic pursuits that bordered on criminality. Okaija "Coal Boy" sang in Ga, "Ka wie nakai" ("Don't say that it [*akpeteshie*] is not good"), refuting the colonial propaganda that *akpeteshie* was dangerous.[107]

"Akpeteshie," a song released by The Comets in the early 1960s, sought to recapture the *akpeteshie* controversy of the colonial period. It is revealing how the song utilizes lyrics in Pidgin–English and Fanti–Twi to highlight the need for duplicity in the colonial period. The chorus runs:

---

[101] PRO, CO 554/127/33522/B (1943). Resident Minister (Accra) to the Colonial Secretary, October 24, 1942.
[102] PRO, CO 554/127/33522/B. "Memorandum by the Secretary of State for the Colonies," dated April 28, 1943.
[103] PRO, CO 554/127/33522/B. T. Hoskyns–Abrahall, Nigerian Secretariat (Lagos), to Resident Minister (Accra), August 9, 1943.
[104] PRO, CO 554/142/33522 (1946).
[105] Zonophone JLK 1015 (NSA).
[106] Zonophone JVA 160 (NSA).
[107] AFN: Interview with A. A. Amartey, Accra, August 31, 1994.

Akpeteshie no good oh, akpeteshie no good oh,
no good oh no good oh, akpeteshie.

This was a line that definitely appealed to the colonial government. But one stanza in Fanti–Twi runs:

Meya me sika de ato nsa
awo te akyire na wobo afu
hwe wo ho yie na wo anhye me ahoroba
akpeteshie.

I have earned my money and I am spending it on drink
You, the observer, are infuriated
Be careful and do not annoy me
akpeteshie.

It was assumed that the colonial officials would not understand the Twi lyrics. As E. K. Nyame later emphasized in his comments on concert parties during the colonial era: "we minded the colonial ideology and British mind, so whatever we did in those days was in English."[108] If the government was pursuing its "selfish" interests—under the guise of public welfare—in its prosecution of *akpeteshie* patrons, the people being prosecuted did not lack guile. The argument for African economic self–sufficiency in an independent Ghana was a powerful one when applied to the legalization of *akpeteshie*. And as Richard Rathbone capably demonstrates, economics was a moving force in the Gold Coast nationalist agitation of the 1940s and 1950s.[109] Gold Coast newspapers between the 1930s and the 1950s commented on the economic potential of the *akpeteshie* industry if it was legalized and regulated to ensure good quality.[110] As early as 1933, a contributor to the *Gold Coast Independent*, under the pseudonym of "Wet," had inquired why the colonial government did not want to make a local industry out of *akpeteshie*. "Wet" argued that no severe punishment could deter the "working masses given to manual labour" from distilling and drinking their own gin.

It is to them the case of necessity which knows no law; for it is their view that it is their unquestionable right to manufacture things in their own country for themselves and so long as it is not made a crime by Government for them to drink any imported liquor they themselves [the Europeans] make.[111]

With rising rates of unemployment, "Wet" advocated that the government turn illicit distillation into a viable, legitimate industry by showing "our people the proper and most scientific ways of distilling," while levying license fees and excise taxes.

The perception of *akpeteshie* as an "African drink," a product of African ingenuity, turned it into a symbol of political discontent in the 1930s and 1940s. Official persecution was seen as a typical colonial response to African enterprise. The po-

---

[108] Collins, *West African Pop Roots*, 40.

[109] See, for example, Richard Rathbone, "Businessmen in Politics: Party Struggle in Ghana, 1949–57," *Journal of Development Studies* 9, 3 (1973): 391–401.

[110] See, for examples, *Spectator Daily*, September 14, 1939; *Gold Coast Observer*, March 5, 1943; and *Sunday Mirror*, April 4, 1954.

[111] *Gold Coast Independent*, December 23, 1933.

lice department report for 1934–35 highlighted the African complicity to shield
akpeteshie patrons.

> Motor lorries have on occasions been found to be conveying as much
> as 100 gallons illicitly distilled spirits at a time. The distribution and
> sale of such quantities of unusually potent liquor in any community
> could well be unknown even by those of the local inhabitants who nei-
> ther participate in the trade nor themselves consume the illicitly dis-
> tilled spirits; but, despite this, the fact remains that it is very rarely
> indeed that any assistance or information is volunteered to the police
> in this matter by *Africans who could, by reason of their social status or their
> education, be expected to disapprove of the trade in cheap potent illicit spirits*
> [emphasis added].[112]

But this African solidarity concealed deep social tensions across gender and
class lines, and the ambiguous meanings attached to *akpeteshie* by different social groups.

Women who retailed *akpeteshie* in the colonial era commented that they were
sometimes snitched upon by the same male patrons who came to buy *akpeteshie*.[113]
At the core of these gender tensions was what men perceived to be the increasing
"commercialization" of gender relations, or the growing materialism of women. A
highlife song by a famous male musician of this period, Kwaa Mensah, summed
up this gender conflict: "wo pe tam won pe ba" ("you like cloth but you don't
want children").[114] Colonial rule, the colonial economy, urbanization, and migration had created unintended opportunities for women to accumulate wealth through
the sale of prepared foods, alcoholic drinks, and prostitution. Women became "lu-
bricators" of urban social formation in unique ways. Their financial independence
allowed women to shape the terms of their relations with men. A parallel situation
emerged on the Zambian Copperbelt in the 1930s.

> Most of the women seem to have long deserted their parents and have
> nearly forgotten all the tribal customs. There is a daily cry among the na-
> tive villagers, wanting these women to get properly married at home, in
> order that they may have children instead of hunting for money and
> clothes.[115]

The male contemporaries of these migrant women remained steeped in patriarchal
rural values. Men feared that they were losing their control over women. From the
1940s, Anita Mensah's family, after initially criticizing her involvement in the
akpeteshie business, regularly consulted her for loans during funerals and other family emergencies. And she became the talk of the town, when she put up a large–
storey building in Amanful–Kuma.[116] The Twi proverb, *baabi ye sum na wode sika pe
ho a, eho tew* ("if money is scattered in a place which is dark, the whole place becomes bright," i.e., "money talks") applied equally to men as well as women.[117]

---

[112] Gold Coast, *Report on the Police Department, 1934–35*, 7.
[113] AFN: Interview with Novisi Segbedzi; and interview with Tsotso Alice Akwei, Accra, June 14, 1992.
[114] Zonophone JLK 1016 (NSA).
[115] Parpart, "Where Is Your Mother?," 258.
[116] AFN: Interview with Anita Mensah, Takoradi, March 5, 1992.
[117] C. A. Akrofi, *Twi Mmebusem: Twi Proverbs* (Accra, n.d.), 6.

Also, *akpeteshie* was acquiring a "class" dimension, as the cheapness of *akpeteshie* made it the commoners' drink.[118] Laborers involved in demanding manual work found *akpeteshie*'s "invigorating" effect appealing. From its origins, distillers, retailers, and consumers of *akpeteshie* were regarded as "low–class" and "filthy" people by *akrakyefo* (educated gentlemen) and *awurabafo* ("ladies"). To distill or retail *akpeteshie* entailed courting social ridicule, and *akpeteshie* enthusiasts—motivated by the industry's profits—became social nonconformists. The drink had an especially pungent scent, and people avoided the company of *akpeteshie* patrons.[119] Imported drinks were seen as symbols of social status among the upwardly mobile in the Gold Coast. Although the "upper classes" would not inform on *akpeteshie* patrons because of a sense of "African solidarity," they ostracized them socially. Patrons of *akpeteshie* found themselves involved in a two–way battle: politically against the colonial state, and socially against educated and wealthy Africans—to whom they were also bound by kinship ties. Indeed, many urban workers entertained the hopes of making it big one day. Although it would be premature to speak of a coherent working–class, what was emerging was "class struggle without class."[120]

It was *akpeteshie*'s image as the commoner's drink, that made it an indispensable platform in the party politics preceding independence. Once the Constitution of 1951 introduced universal adult suffrage, public expectations and mood seemed to propel Gold Coast politics, and manipulating popular culture became an important means of gauging and shaping popular opinion. *Akpeteshie* was integral to popular culture. From its formation in 1949, the Convention People's Party (CPP), led by Kwame Nkrumah, portrayed itself as the "commoners' party" and patronized urban popular culture. Overnight, urban popular culture gained a new saliency and political legitimacy. Highlife songs promoted the CPP and praised Nkrumah as the political savior, the Axim Trio staged plays like "Kwame Nkrumah will never die,"[121] CPP sponsored "political dances" spread the CPP's charm, and drinking bars became the foci of political organization and discussions. And legalizing *akpeteshie* was inducted into the CPP's political program. Alcohol had retained its ties to power and autonomy from the precolonial era, and as the stage was set for an independent Ghana, its multiple uses and meanings would inform the contest over who would succeed the colonial masters.

Conclusion

Knowledge of distillation in the Gold Coast predated the 1930s. But the large demand for illicit *akpeteshie* was generated in the 1930s through the combined forces

---

[118] It is interesting that today these class connotations persist among the Akan, Ga, and Ewe even though *akpeteshie* has been incorporated into ritual. The handbook on customary law in Dutch Sekondi, shown to me by Nana Ewua Duku II on March 3, 1992, stipulated the possible use of *akpeteshie* in the customary marriage rites for illiterate women. This did not apply to educated women, reflecting the old coastal divide between "cloth women" and "dress women."

[119] AFN: Interview with the Western Region Distillers Cooperative Management Committee, Takoradi, August 16, 1994; and interview with Anita Mensah, Takoradi, August 16, 1994.

[120] See E. P. Thompson, "Eighteenth–Century English Society: Class Struggle Without Class," *Social History* 3, 2 (1978): 133–65.

[121] Collins, "Ghanaian Highlife," 67.

of restrictive liquor legislation, the depression of the 1930s, the resilience of urban popular culture, and the initiative and creativity of ordinary men and women. The ineffective attempts of the colonial government to stamp out *akpeteshie* underscored the determination of men and women to subsist in towns, and the growing strength of urban popular culture. *Akpeteshie* became an important symbol in the struggle of the working classes against the snobbish upper classes, traditional authorities, and the colonial state. The dawn of mass politics and general election would give popular culture a new respectability as politicians wooed the urban masses. Political power in independent Ghana was a prize no party could take for granted. Party politics of the 1950s thus witnessed the revitalization of old forms of power in a fierce competition to succeed the colonial masters. In this struggle, alcohol, water, and blood would be plumbed for their ritual and social significance.

6

Alcohol, Popular Culture, and Nationalist Politics

The formation of the Convention People's Party (CPP) in 1949 was a significant landmark in the struggle between the chiefs—and their allied educated elite—and the young men and women. The CPP originated as a commoners' party, and its rapid rise to prominence and power was deeply satisfying to ordinary men and women. For women, this was the opportunity to reverse the decline in their socioeconomic conditions caused by the intensification of indirect rule and the enhanced dominance of expatriate firms in commerce. For the young men, an end to their long–standing conflict with the chiefs and elders seemed near. They hoped to shape the new independent state along lines favorable to them. They envisaged a more prominent role for themselves in the politics and economy of an independent Ghana. Indeed, even chieftaincy could be scrapped. The CPP's partnership with the commoners would facilitate its ascent to political power. Key to this success was the political potential of popular culture. Popular culture can be used as a critique of state or political power. It can also provide a supporting plank in the foundation of political power.

The Setting

The Gold Coast independence struggle was launched with the February 1948 riots, in which the use of alcohol in a carnivalistic fashion by young men promoted the subversion of colonial law and order. The Watson Commission of Inquiry, set up by the colonial government to investigate the causes of the riots, argued that the age of nationalism had dawned in the Gold Coast and political concessions were necessary. The emergence of the United Gold Coast Convention (UGCC) in 1947 to champion the nationalist cause, the breakaway of its youth faction in 1949 to reconstitute itself as CPP, and the introduction of the 1951 constitution with universal adult suffrage and some measure of internal autonomy set the stage for the impending political struggle. The educated elite were pitted against the Standard VII school leavers.[1]

---

[1]   A detailed historical narrative of the progress towards independence is avoided here, as several detailed studies can be consulted on this: Austin, *Politics in Ghana*; Bob Fitch and Mary Oppenheimer, *Ghana:*

The symbolism of alcohol permeated the independence struggle as political parties vied for supporters through the generous distribution of drink, turned drinking bars into mechanisms of popular mobilization, and contested the uses and meanings of alcohol in their presentation of the future political order. The ritual significance of powerful fluids such as alcohol, water and blood,[2] and the emergent popular culture[3] were all exploited for political support and legitimacy. Controlling liquor policy, advocating the legalization of akpeteshie, extending the economic benefits of retailing alcoholic drinks to ordinary Africans, and abolishing liquor prohibition in the Northern Territories all became emotional issues that informed the nationalist struggle.

What appeared to be a CPP domination of general elections between 1951 and 1954 became more complicated with the formation of the National Liberation Movement (NLM) on the eve of independence. The educated elite, the chiefs, and Asante young men united in a last ditch effort to unseat the CPP. In the renewed struggle over who would replace the colonial rulers, alcohol and disorder became linked to the unsteady transfer of power. Drinking fueled political violence in Asante, and the model colony of Britain became a political nightmare. As independence approached in March 1957, the preceding chaos and violence had left a bitter taste in the mouth of many, raising some doubts about independence as an era of hope.

Economics, Alcohol, and Nationalist Politics

The coastal elite who had been prominent in pre–World War II commerce, were being gradually eliminated by the maintenance of wartime economic controls that favored large expatriate firms. In the widespread economic discontent after the war, a group of coastal African businessmen and lawyers—led by George Grant (timber magnate), J. B. Danquah (lawyer), R. S. Blay (lawyer) and others—decided to exploit prevailing conditions by establishing a nationwide political movement, the UGCC. For these coastal politicians, economic concerns were preeminent. Rathbone has argued that the "UGCC leadership was more concerned with economics than with nationalist politics."[4] What the UGCC leadership found unacceptable was the continuation of wartime controls that had drastically reduced their share in imports and exports in the face of a booming internal economy as large expatriate firms practically monopolized trade through their formation of an Association of West African Merchants (AWAM).

But being part of the colonial mercantile economy, the UGCC businessmen did not want to destroy the colonial economy and their share in it; they strove rather to

---

End of an Illusion (New York, 1966); Maxwell Owusu, Uses and Abuses of Political Power: A Case Study of Continuity and Change in the Politics of Ghana (Chicago, 1970); David E. Apter, Ghana in Transition (Princeton, 1972); Rathbone "Businessmen in Politics"; Richard Rathbone, Murder and Politics in Colonial Ghana (New Haven, 1993); and Jean Marie Allman, The Quills of the Porcupine: Asante Nationalism in an Emergent Ghana (Madison, 1993).

[2]   See Chapter 1.

[3]   See Chapter 5.

[4]   Rathbone, "Businessmen in Politics," 394. Rathbone argues that economic considerations outweighed nationalist ideology in Ghanaian politics between 1949 and 1957. A similar interpretation is offered in Owusu, Uses and Abuses of Political Power.

open the closed colonial economy by reducing the privileges of expatriate commercial firms.[5] Steeped in the constitutional politics that had characterized Gold
Coast politics from the early–twentieth century, the coastal elite believed that their
increased political representation on the legislative council would solve their economic problems. Still smarting from the predominant unofficial[6] representation given
to chiefs under the 1925 constitution, and only slightly altered by the Burns Constitution of 1946, the coastal elite argued that their declining economic conditions
were due to the inept representation of the chiefs.[7] The UGCC advocated self–government. But the "privileged" position of its leaders generated ambivalent feelings
towards the colonial system that had favored them and hence they qualified their
demand by a gradualist approach: "self–government within the shortest possible
time."

The economic grievances of the young men demanded more radical changes,
as they, unlike the coastal elite, had a tenuous position and little to lose in the
colonial economy. From the mid–1940s, the young men were becoming convinced
that their economic prosperity could be achieved only through the abolition of colonial rule. For these young men, even setting up in the retail trade was fraught
with obstacles they believed to be contrived by the colonial government.

The rejection of applications by young men to sell imported liquor provides an example of some of the economic grievances held by the young men.
It is apparent that Africans who petitioned the colonial secretary's office, when
their applications for liquor licenses were rejected, believed their applications
were denied because they were Africans. When J. R. O. Brako's application for
a liquor license was refused in 1943, he was certainly puzzled for he had just
bought the store from a European company, Nomen and Co., which had sold
liquor from the same premises.[8] Allegedly, Brako was supposed to have taken
out a new license in his name as owner of the store, instead of seeking to renew
Nomen and Co.'s license in spite of the change in ownership. W. E. Nkansa
Tannor accused the district commissioner of Mpraeso (Kwahu District) of de-
liberately refusing him a liquor license when he had just bought his premises
from the United Africa Company (UAC), which had used the same premises as
a liquor store for eight years.[9]

A prominent sore point with young men was the distribution system of the
Overseas Breweries factory in Accra, which privileged expatriate business firms

---

[5]   Rathbone, "Businessmen in Politics."

[6]   The Clifford Constitution of 1916 allotted three seats each to the chiefs and other Africans (educated
elite) as unofficial members (non–governmental) in a legislative council of 21 members. The 1925
Guggisberg Constitution enlarged the legislative council to 29 members. Nine unofficial seats were assigned to Africans, six seats to be filled by chiefs. The Burns Constitution of 1946 introduced an African
majority in the legislative council of 32. Nonetheless chiefs continued to wield predominant influence on
the legislative council.

[7]   The 1946 Constitution marked a significant political improvement on the 1925 Constitution by including the educated elite in a three–tiered political structure: colonial government, chiefs, and educated elite.
But the socioeconomic changes during World War II rendered the 1946 Constitution (conceived in prewar
conditions) "outmoded at birth."

[8]   NAG, Accra, No. 4052/1. J. R. O. Brako to Colonial Secretary, September 1, 1943.

[9]   NAG, Accra, CSO 948/30. W. E. Nkansa Tannor, Kwahu District, to the Governor, through the Commissioner for Eastern Province (Koforidua), July 1938.

in the granting of distributorships. Domestic production of lager beer in the Gold Coast did not seem to have lessened European dominance of the liquor traffic. In May 1947, the workers at the Accra Brewery went on a ten–day strike, and it was suggested "that the 1947 strike was fomented by small African traders who resented the Brewery's policy [of] selling directly only to the large expatriate firms."[10] Ironically, the brewery itself was involved in a paradoxical relationship with the large mercantile firms, who sabotaged the factory's production by siphoning beer bottles off the local market.[11] The United African Company actually encouraged Africans to collect Overseas Brewery bottles,[12] which it redeemed at a price and destroyed, to create obstacles for the factory's production. The profit margin on imported beer was bigger than that on local beer.

The belief that big business had the overt support of the colonial government transcended the African business community. Nicholas Karabetsos, a Greek [?] trader, could not help pointing out, when he was instructed to seal his shop's back door with cement before being granted a liquor license, that several large European firms had outlets with back doors selling liquor in town and upcountry.[13] For Gold Coast young men, the whole colonial edifice seemed to stymie their economic aspirations. It is significant that when they chose to challenge the colonial order, alcohol constituted an important symbol in their struggle. Confronting colonial rule was dangerous: alcohol not only provided spiritual protection and bonding with co–conspirators, but the guise of drunkenness could provide extenuating circumstances if the challenge backfired.

The 1948 Riots: Drink and Disorder

In February 1948, economic riots broke out in Accra during which the young men, using alcohol in a carnivalistic way resonant of the *odwira* festival,[14] initiated an organized struggle against colonial rule that climaxed in the grant of independence in 1957. But this time, the inversion of the social order, unlike the *odwira* in nineteenth–century Asante, was not orchestrated from above. The inspiration was from below, and its control was unpredictable. The carnivalistic events of February 1948 bear uncanny parallels to the 1888 riots in the Swahili town of Pangani, precipitated by the German attempt to impose their authority.[15] What is most striking in both cases are the central role of the "young men" and the evidence of discipline in what appeared to be spontaneous riots.

---

[10]   R. B. Davison, "African Labour: Studies of Migrancy and Industrial Relations in a Factory in the Gold Coast" (Ph.D. thesis, University of London, 1955), 306. See also *Gold Coast Observer*, March 19, 1943, on African resentment about the factory's distributing system.

[11]   AFN: Interview with K. Attakora Gyimah, Kumasi, June 11, 1992.

[12]   Bottle collection (*pintoa*) became a full–time occupation for many Hausa and Northern immigrants in the towns.

[13]   NAG, Accra, CSO 948/30. Karabetsos to Colonial Secretary, July 10, 1935.

[14]   See Chapter 1 for details on the inversion of the social order during the *odwira* festival in nineteenth-century Asante.

[15]   Glassman, *Feasts and Riot*, Ch. 7.

Beginning in January 1948, a local Accra chief, Nii Kwabena Bonne III, organized a popular boycott against the expatriate commercial firms in protest against
the soaring prices for imported goods.[16]

> It is plain that by the end of 1946 at least, short supplies, maldistribution,
> conditional sales, pass–book customers and other devices calculated to
> impede fair distribution at reasonable prices had created among the mass
> of the population a sense of frustration and the greatest social unrest.[17]

The Africans laid the blame at the feet of AWAM, which they suspected of deliber-
ately manipulating prices. The government took no steps to resolve the issue until
February 11, 1948, when a series of meetings between the chambers of commerce,
the Nii Bonne committee and the chiefs under the chairmanship of the colonial
secretary was arranged.[18] The firms consented to reduce their profit margin on certain specified goods from 75 percent to 50 percent for a trial period of three months
beginning on February 28, and the boycott was called off on that understanding.[19]

Coincidentally, February 28 happened to be the day the Ex–Servicemen's
Union[20] had decided to present a petition to the governor detailing their economic
grievances. They demanded, among other things, an increase in their present pen-
sions to compensate for the reduced purchasing power from inflation and that "rehabilitation funds be established for those ex–servicemen who are deprived by reason of age, from entering the government service, and for those who are anxious to
start their own business, as is done in England."[21] To make their demands more
effective, the ex–servicemen planned a procession to the governor's residence at
Christianborg Castle. The commissioner of police specified a route for the ex-
servicemen's procession and stressed that the petition would have to be presented
at the secretariat for onward transmission to the governor.

But under the guise of drunkenness, the procession deviated from its scheduled route, and a confrontation with the police set off riots in which the young
men used alcohol to intensify the conflagration. In the confrontation, Superinten-
dent of Police C. H. Imray fired a rifle and killed two ex–servicemen and injured
four or five more. Imray, in his unpublished memoirs, offers insights into the prominent role alcohol played in the events of that fateful day.[22] As the crowd gathered

---

[16]   This was not the first organized boycott of European goods and the 1937 cocoa holdup, during which
African farmers refused to sell their cocoa for the low prices offered by the expatriate firms, was accom-
panied by a boycott of European goods in some districts. See NAG, Kumasi, No. 1263. Annual Report of
Obuasi District 1937–38.

[17]   Colonial Office, *Report of the Commission of Enquiry into Disturbances in the Gold Coast, 1948* (London,
1948), 34 [hereafter cited as *Watson Commission Report*].

[18]   Governor Gerald Creasy had only been sworn in on January 12, 1948, and he definitely had not found
his feet yet.

[19]   *Watson Commission Report*, 35–36.

[20]   Two organizations of ex–servicemen existed in the Gold Coast: the older Gold Coast Legion and the
Ex–Servicemen's Union, founded in 1946. See Eugene P. A. Schleh, "The Post–War Careers of Ex–Servicemen in Ghana and Uganda," *Journal of Modern African Studies* 6,2 (1968): 210. Coincidentally, the celebration of *siku ya mwaka* (the solar new year) and the Islamic festival of *Idd al–Hajj*, which fell within one day
in August 1888, provided the context for the riots in the Pangani. Glassman, *Feasts and Riot*.

[21]   "Petition Addressed to His Excellency Sir Gerald Creasy" *Watson Commission Report*, Appendix 15.

[22]   C. H. Imray, "A Policeman's Story" (Private papers Mss. Afr. S. 2053, Rhodes House, Oxford University).

at the polo grounds on February 28 to begin the procession, a dispatch rider brought information to Imray at the police headquarters that "a number of them [crowd] appeared to have been drinking." The procession began.

But then, twenty minutes or so later, there came a highly significant report: At a point near a drinking dive called the White Horse, the procession had turned about, and had been joined by a lot of local toughs carrying sticks and cudgels, who were certainly not servicemen. Many of them—went the report—appeared to be drunk and in a truculent mood. The procession was moving fast—apparently of set purpose, and directly back on its tracks. Indeed it was already approaching Victoriaborg police post.[23]

The police intervened, with fatal consequences. The controlled structure of the subsequent riots would contradict Imray's claim that the "local toughs" were drunk, and evidence supports the conclusion that the young men were the hidden but active catalysts of the February 28 riots in Accra.

Crowds had already gathered in the commercial part of Accra, waiting to see if prices for imported goods would indeed be reduced as promised by the chamber of commerce. Evidence presented to the Watson Commission suggested that among the crowds that collected in the commercial area in Accra were "men of a rough type who seemed anxious to persuade the crowds in the streets that the stores were not in fact charging the agreed prices."[24] Rioting and looting broke out, and the disorder worsened when news of the shooting of the ex–servicemen reached rioters in the commercial section of Accra. As Nkrumah commented:

> The looting and rioting seemed to be quite out of hand and many buildings, including the large stores of the United Africa Company and the Union Trading Company were on fire. As a result of this disorder, 29 people lost their lives and 237 were injured.[25]

But the rioting was not without structure, and there was a deliberate pattern to the looting that belied the chaotic scene.

> An exception must be made of A. G. Leventis & Co., a Cypriot trading firm (and no friend of the British–dominated Association of West African Merchants) which pledged support for Nii Bonne's campaign, and agreed to make "substantial reductions" in its prices. As Nii Bonne commented, the company was "duly rewarded in later weeks." When the riots took place and the big trading stores were looted it was noted that the crowds spared the firm's property.[26]

It is evident that groups of young men were present among the ex–servicemen's procession and among crowds that gathered in the commercial district of Accra,

---

24   As cited in Austin, *Politics in Ghana*, 74.

25   Kwame Nkrumah, *Ghana: An Autobiography* (New York, 1957), 77. For the two days of rioting in Accra, the Watson Commission reported approximately 15 persons killed and 115 injured, apart from the casualties of the crossroads. *Watson Commission Report*, 14.

26   Austin, *Politics in Ghana*, 71. The "virtual lack of looting" reflected the discipline of the crowds that seized power in Pangani in 1888–89. Glassman, *Feasts and Riot*, 228.

determined to direct the course of events. They appeared drunk, and some even emerged from drinking bars to join the procession, but they had the presence of mind to steer looters away from the shops of A. G. Leventis. Official investigation into the riots established the fact that the coastal elite and the UGCC were not responsible for organizing the riots.[27] The Chiefs, aghast at the breakdown of law and order, vociferously condemned the rioters and the UGCC, before the latter was absolved by the Watson Commission. The chiefs definitely did not plan the riots. The urban young men, whose ranks had been increased by migration from the 1930s, and whose solidarity had been enhanced by youth associations were the only coherent group capable of directing the Accra riots.

Liquor represented not only prize booty for the young men in the rioting that broke out in Accra on February 28 through February 29,[28] but their liberal distribution of liquor booty also seemed to fuel the intensity of the riots.

> On the morning of the 29th, one of the first stores to be broken into was the Kingsway Wholesale Stores. The looters removed spirits and alcoholic drinks of all sorts and passed them over the wall to the inmates of Ussher Fort Prison. Later a mob broke down the front gates of the prison and some prisoners, including some serving long sentences for violent crimes, by now intoxicated and in a wild mood escaped temporarily to join in the looting and general disorder. This release of convicts—and those in Ussher Fort included the most experienced and dangerous criminals—is of a pattern familiar in communist disorders when the communists are seeking to seize power.[29]

Governor Creasy seemed to link the riots to the communist scare of the 1930s associated with the West African Youth League.[30] But communism was not a factor in the riots, and Richard Jeffries argues that the socialist influence of Wallace Johnson in the Gold Coast was ephemeral.[31] The "drunken" charades that marked the inversion of the social order during the politically flavored *odwira* festival provided a more appropriate, indigenous model.[32] The liberal distribution of alcohol, and the subsequent "disorder" under the guise of drunkenness harp back to the *odwira*. And young men in youth associations, reminiscent of the traditional Akan *asafo* companies, provided the cast.

---

[27] *Watson Commission Report*, 19–20.

[28] On March 1, the rioting spread to Koforidua, Nsawam and Akuse (in the Eastern Province), and Kumasi as news of developments in Accra reached these towns.

[29] Governor of Gold Coast, "Brief Narrative of Events from the 17th February, 1948, to the 13th March, 1948." *Watson Commission Report*, Appendix 10. Prisoners were also set free during the riot in Pangani in 1888, but it was the German officials liberating the prisoners of the Omani sultan of Zanzibar.

[30] The West African Youth League was established in the Gold Coast by I. T. A. Wallace Johnson, a Sierra Leonean trade unionist who studied in Moscow in 1931–32. His intent was to organize laborers and the unemployed for the overthrow of the colonial system. His activities led to his being deported by the Gold Coast government to Sierra Leone. See A. Adu Boahen, "Politics and Nationalism in West Africa, 1919–1935," in *General History of Africa: VII Africa Under Colonial Domination 1880–1935*, ed. A. Adu Boahen (Berkeley, 1990), 271–72. See also, Leo Spitzer and La Ray Denzer, "I. T. A. Wallace Johnson and the West African Youth League," *International Journal of African Historical Studies* 6, 3 (1973): 413–52.

[31] Richard Jeffries, *Class, Power and Ideology in Ghana: The Railwaymen of Sekondi* (Cambridge, 1978), 46–47.

[32] See Chapter 1.

But the "communist" taint of the riots provided Governor Creasy with the perfect scapegoat for the disturbances: the UGCC leadership with their new communist-influenced general-secretary, Kwame Nkrumah. The Central Committee of the UGCC also lent itself to suspicion when, in a spirit of adventure, it sought to capitalize on the riots for political gain. They sent a short telegram to the secretary of state for the colonies on February 29, demanding immediate self-government with the UGCC as the interim government.[33] Six of the leading members of the UGCC—including George Grant, J. B. Danquah, and Nkrumah—were arrested and detained for their roles in the riots. When Nkrumah was arrested and searched, a communist party card and a document known as "The Circle," detailing the organization of a secret, elite revolutionary vanguard were found in his room.[34] Although Nkrumah and the UGCC had no overt role in the outbreak of the riots, the UGCC benefitted from detention, as the leaders became extremely popular and the convention a nationwide movement overnight.

But the radical political convictions of Kwame Nkrumah soon resulted in conflicts between him and the more conservative leadership of the UGCC, who feared that Nkrumah would earn them the disfavor of the colonial government. Nkrumah, who had been brought from England in 1947 by the UGCC to organize its drive to embrace the mass support of the youth associations, seceded with the Party's Committee of Youth Organization (CYO) to form the Convention People's Party.[35] On June 12, 1949, the CPP was launched at the West End Arena, in Accra, with the objective of fighting "relentlessly by all constitutional means for the achievement of full 'self–government NOW' for the chiefs and people of the Gold Coast."[36]

Popular Culture and Mass Politics

Political developments between 1948 and 1951 transformed commoners—male and female—into active participants in colonial politics, and patronizing popular culture underscored one's identification with the masses and their future hopes of material improvement. Nkrumah gave a voice, a face, and power to "the masses." George Hagan highlights how Nkrumah "identified the youth and women, the poor and the illiterate, the urban worker and the rural dweller as his target group and [how] he oriented himself to them."[37] The central place of women in CPP politics, a novel development in Gold Coast politics, is acknowledged in Nkrumah's

---

[33] *Watson Commission Report*, Appendix 13.

[34] Nkrumah, *Autobiography*, 79. These documents had come into Nkrumah's possession during his sojourn in England and it is doubtful whether "The Circle" represented an active group.

[35] The nucleus of the CYO comprised of the Youth Study Group of Accra, the Asante Youth Association of Kumasi, the Wassaw Youth Association of Tarkwa, and the Ghana Youth Association of Sekondi. The CYO came into being in Kumasi in late 1948 as a direct result of disillusionment among young men who were active members of the UGCC as well as those outside the Convention. Convinced that the interests of the UGCC leadership diverged from theirs, the young men pressured Nkrumah, whose radical rhetoric they found attractive, into leading them in a commoners' party. See Boahen, *Evolution and Change*, 168.

[36] Nkrumah, *Autobiography*, 101.

[37] George P. Hagan, "Nkrumah's Leadership Style—An Assessment from a Cultural Perspective," in *The Life and Work of Kwame Nkrumah*, ed. Kwame Arhin (Accra, 1991), 205–6.

autobiography and several accounts of the Gold Coast independence movement.[38] In carving out a political constituency, Nkrumah not only drove a wedge between the UGCC and the CPP, but his rhetoric firmly established the nationalist struggle in class terms.

> Up till that break, the ordinary people of the Gold Coast had not seen their leaders as a class apart. If they did, they did not see this as a cause for war—a class war. Now Nkrumah described the leaders of the UGCC as the bourgeois, privileged, professional group, and began to cast them in the role of enemy within.[39]

By positing the nationalist struggle in class terms on the internal front, Nkrumah appropriated popular culture for the CPP. Distillers and retailers of *akpeteshie*, market women, prostitutes, musicians, concert actors, the *asafo*, laborers all rallied to the CPP flag.[40] The party's association with popular culture would be of extreme importance in the general elections preceding independence.

The Watson Commission's recommendations for political reform was followed by the establishment of the all–African Coussey Committee to frame a new constitution. Nkrumah and his youth supporters, excluded from the Coussey Committee, took the intransigent position that anything less than full self–government would be rejected by them. The report of the committee was published at the end of 1949, and although it made far–reaching political recommendations—including a general election and an executive council with an African majority—they fell short of a demand for full self–government. In January 1950, the CPP declared "positive action" (a general strike) and several party members, including Nkrumah, ended up in prison. With the CPP leadership in prison, Governor Charles Arden–Clarke noted that other political leaders still proved unable to fill the vacuum.[41] General elections under the Coussey Constitution were scheduled for February 1951, and Arden–Clarke invited Nkrumah and the CPP to participate.

The CPP accepted the challenge, and the young party launched its campaign to mobilize supporters with dances, concerts, and other forms of entertainment that characterized urban popular culture. It was actually the local branches that raised funds for the 1951 election campaign, accepting donations at rallies and charging entrance fees at their dances, concerts, and football matches.

> A Party flag—red, white, and green; a Party salute—the uplifted arm and the open palm; and the cry of freedom; propaganda vans picked out in red, green and white; clothes, handbags, and belts in the Party's colours, the sale of framed photographs of Nkrumah, procession, picnics, dances, rallies, songs, and plays ensured that the Party was seen to exist in as personal and colourful a form as it was possible to devise.[42]

---

[38] See, for examples, C. L. R. James, *Nkrumah and the Ghana Revolution* (Westport, 1977); and Takyiwah Manuh, "Women and Their Organization During the Convention Peoples' Party Period," in Arhin, *Life and Work of Kwame Nkrumah*, 108–34.

[39] Hagan, "Nkrumah's Leadership Style," 184.

[40] Jon Kraus, "On the Politics of Nationalism and Social Change in Ghana," *Journal of Modern African Studies* 7, 1 (1969): 118, described the CPP's ideology as "diffuse populism" and the party as an "open-ended omnibus" which sought to latch onto existing grievances.

[41] Sir Charles Arden-Clarke, "Eight Years of Transition in Ghana," *African Affairs* 57, 226 (1958): 33.

[42] Austin, *Politics in Ghana*, 127.

In the new era of mass politics, the CPP party with its young men and women strategically positioned itself to benefit from urban popular culture. Comic opera actors and highlife musicians, working class people themselves, joined the CPP and integrated political themes into their plays and music. The Axim Trio Concert Party staged amusing political pieces like "A D.C.[District Commissioner] and His Good Friend,"[43] and serious pieces like "Kwame Nkrumah will never die"[44] and "Kwame Nkrumah is Mightier than Before."[45] Albert Ocran, one of the Sekondi Railwaymen who supported the CPP in its early days, emphasized the relevance of these plays in explaining the nationalist ideology to illiterates.[46] Numerous highlife songs praising Nkrumah came out in the 1950s. Kumasi Dramatic Choir's, *CPP Wobedzi Kunyim* ("CPP will emerge victorious");[47] and after CPP's 1951 election victory Kojo Bio and his Band composed *Ko hwe CPP Assembly ho* ("Go and look at the CPP in the Legislative Assembly!").[48]

Political rallies were invariably accompanied by a highlife band or a propaganda van with a public address system blaring highlife music. After a large crowd had been attracted to the rally venue by the highlife tunes, CPP activists would then deliver the CPP message which, in short, was latching on to any manner of local grievances:

> We promised the CPP would put all things right. This is what we told the people. We would go to the village by lorry, a group of us, fifteen or twenty. Sometimes we would have a band to attract the people. . . . When we had preached CPP to them, we would leave that village and go to the next.[49]

"Preaching CPP" was a powerful experience for those who attended CPP rallies. The simple, commonsense political messages delivered at these rallies are still remembered by old CPP activists.

For disadvantaged groups like women, CPP granted them an active role in the political process and the promise of a more equitable distribution of economic resources. Ataa Baasi, a famous prostitute in Kumasi and leader of the "Baasifuo Community" (an organized band of prostitutes living in Adum), became a CPP stalwart.[50] She even became a speaker at CPP rallies.[51] Anita Mensah, the *akpeteshie* seller, recalled Nkrumah's appealing rhetoric.

> He explained how the whitemen were cheating us. How they exported our resources to build their country. How Britain was actually poor in resources but exploited her empire. That we should come together to pro-

---

[43] DCs invariably addressed chiefs as "My Good Friend."

[44] Collins, "Ghanaian Highlife," 67.

[45] Austin, *Politics in Ghana*, 127. A member of the Axim Trio, E. K. Dadson, would be elected to the legislative assembly in the 1951 election.

[46] AFN: Interview with Albert Ocran, Sekondi, August 15, 1994.

[47] Zonophone JZ 5442 (NSA).

[48] Zonophone JVA 158 (NSA).

[49] Austin, *Politics in Ghana*, 131–32.

[50] On the Baasifuo, see NAG, Kumasi, No. 2339.

[51] See *Ashanti Pioneer*, April 27, 1955.

tect what we had left before the British depleted everything. If someone is coming to take away all your father's or mother's property, won't you be alarmed? So the women in the Western Region flocked to the nationalist banner.[52]

Women became active supporters of the CPP cause. Women contributed in cash and kind, and Anita Mensah often carried cold water during rallies to refresh the speakers. Reflecting on those days, Essie Aluah, a cloth seller who became the CPP Women's Leader in Takoradi, confidently opined that without women the CPP would not have won the general elections and self–government.[53] The mass appeal of the CPP was irresistible. The commoners' party won the 1951 election, sweeping thirty–four of the thirty–eight popularly contested seats.[54] The only viable opposition party, the UGCC, won three seats. The CPP formed the first African government with Nkrumah styled the leader of government business.

But it did not take long for the opposition to regroup. The educated elites in the UGCC formed a new party in 1952, the Ghana Congress Party (GCP) under the leadership of K. A. Busia. Shortly after its inception, personality conflicts developed within the leadership of the Ghana Congress Party, and Obetsebi Lamptey broke off to form his Ghana Nationalist Party (GNP). In British Togoland two parties emerged: the Togoland Congress (TC), and the Anglo Youth Organization (AYO). By January 1954, when Nkrumah pushed through a new constitution in which all the 104 seats in the Legislative Assembly were to be popularly elected, six major parties were in existence: CPP, GCP, GNP, TC, AYO, and the Gold Coast Muslim Association.[55] Elections for the new constitution were scheduled for June 1954, and another party, the Northern Peoples Party, joined the fold in April 1954.[56]

In the general elections of 1954, the CPP plumbed popular culture with even greater confidence. Only the CPP, with its mass base, appeared able to utilize popular forms of entertainment as sources of finance. The popularity of social drinking, dances, and concerts and the sale of party paraphernalia continued to be major sources of funding in the 1954 election campaign. Political dances proliferated in 1954, and appearance at these occasions of CPP cabinet ministers lured adoring fans, and their money, to these affairs. The year started off well for the CPP with significant victories in municipal council elections.[57] A grand victory dance was celebrated at "Tip Toe," in Accra, with Nkrumah in attendance. Photos in newspapers showed Nkrumah dancing to the popular highlife tune, "Nkrumah Special."[58]

Drinking was an important aspect of CPP dances as a CPP dance announcement illustrates:

---

[52] AFN: Interview with Anita Mensah, August 16, 1994.

[53] Communication from Essie Aluah, aka Charlotte Morrison, Takoradi, August 16, 1994.

[54] A total of 74 seats were set aside for African representatives in the legislative assembly under the Coussey Constitution which came into effect in 1951.

[55] The Muslim Association was subsequently renamed the Muslim Association Party.

[56] See *Daily Graphic*, June 15, 1954, for the political manifestos of the parties.

[57] For example, the CPP won 14 of 21 seats unopposed in the Sekondi–Takoradi municipal election in February 1954. *Daily Graphic*, February 17, 1954.

[58] *Daily Graphic*, March 8, 1954.

CPP calling. Ebeye Dwe![59] Ebaafee Gbeyei![60] It will be terrible! A dance in connection with the Electioneering Campaign of the CPP will take place today 2nd April, 1954 at the Weekend–In–Havana. *An inexhaustible bar will be run* [emphasis added]. Ticket 5s. Gentlemen 2s. Ladies. Spectators 2s.[61]

Nkrumah attended several CPP dances in Accra, and the participation of the new political elite and their female partners in dances and concerts conferred respectability on the emerging urban popular culture.

Whereas drinking by urban women had originated as part of their rebellion against male attempts to define female social decorum, the endorsement of popular culture by the new political elite and their women now lent sophistication to female drinking.[62] The presence of women at dances and night clubs became accepted.

The days when only men went to bars, we were not very "enlightened." In those days it was said that a woman could not accompany her husband to a drinking bar. The husband actually had to sneak off to a bar. When Nkrumah came and "opened our eyes," then *nsa* became a social status symbol. If you did not drink, you were not "enlightened." So if we saw our female friends drinking, we felt challenged to do likewise to prove our sophistication.[63]

As a commoner's party, the CPP leaders' patronage of dances and other forms of popular entertainment seemed to strengthen the party's legitimacy. Drinking by young men and women had become an accepted, and even desirable, part of urban life. And as more people participated in drinking and dances in the towns, the ranks of the party expanded. Popular culture and CPP political support had become mutually reinforcing. The CPP again proved victorious in the 1954 election, and the party won 71 out of the available 104 seats.[64]

The triumph of the CPP was conceptualized in terms of the collapse of traditional authority, which leaders portrayed through the ritual use of alcohol. Aaron Ofori Atta, a successful CPP candidate in 1954 and minister of communications, cited the ability of the CPP to reach the "people" as the explanation for the party's electoral victory. Using his personal election victory as a contrast to the failure of his uncle, J. B. Danquah, who stood for GCP, Ofori Atta opined at a CPP victory rally at the Palladium that:

Dr. Danquah had never been able to understand human nature. During the electioneering campaign . . . Dr. Danquah was with the chiefs, who went round to pour libation, but he (Ofori Atta) was with the people.[65]

[59] *Ebeye Dwe* (Twi: "It will be sensational").
[60] *Ebaafee Gbeyei* (Ga: "It will be sensational").
[61] *Daily Graphic*, April 2, 1954.
[62] See Chapter 3.
[63] AFN: Interview with Afua Denuah, Essikado, March 5, 1992; and interview with Sabina Morrison, Essikado, March 5, 1992.
[64] 1954 Election Results: CPP 71; Independents 16; NPP 12; TC 2; GCP 1; MAP 1: AYO 1. *Daily Graphic*, June 18, 1954, and June 19, 1954.
[65] *Daily Graphic*, June 28, 1954.

The pouring of libation, a rite male elders and chiefs had controlled, harped back to the days of traditional political power. Aaron Ofori Atta argued that the old educated elites, like Danquah, could not comprehend that those days were over.

Decolonizing Liquor Policy

The gradual transfer of political power to the CPP from 1951 was accompanied by the party's growing control over liquor policy. The party's patronage of social drinking and popular culture, and its image as a commoners' party led it to champion the abolition of liquor prohibition in the Northern Territories and the legalization of *akpeteshie*. But in extending access to alcohol, the CPP was also establishing itself as a political patron in a very cultural way.[66]

Repealing Prohibition in the Northern Territories

As early as 1945–46, the chiefs and their educated allies in the Northern Territories had petitioned the colonial government to withdraw the prohibition laws applied to the north since the 1890s.[67] The international liquor treaties at Brussels and St. Germain, however, prevented the colonial government from meeting this request—in spite of its willingness.[68] In 1953, under the CPP government, prohibition for inhabitants of the Northern Territories was successfully abolished.

The legislative assembly debates that marked the repeal of prohibition in the north underscored the connection between liquor legislation and political power for the colonial government, the CPP government, and representatives of the Northern Territories. Protesting against continued prohibition in the north, A. Asumda, territorial member for the Northern Territories, explicitly linked the denial of access to liquor to the powerlessness of northerners: "Every village and hamlet in this part of the country [the south] is at liberty to obtain license to sell all kinds of liquor, but the North is deprived of it. Why?"[69] CPP legislative assembly representatives endorsed the demand of northern politicians and cited the prohibition of liquor in the north as a sore instance of political discrimination. As CPP politician, A. R. Boakye, testified:

> I have visited the North and I know that in the stores, Whisky, Schnapps and others are obtained, but I think they are sold to some particular persons. If this is what is happening, I feel that our brothers in the North are being discriminated against. We are now advancing towards self–government and we know very well that our brothers in the North are coming along with us.[70]

The fact that southern visitors to the north could purchase liquor in northern shops made the northerners feel like political minors.

---

[66] See Chapter 2.
[67] PRO, CO 96/779/31406. Governor Burns to Oliver Strachey, April 26, 1945.
[68] See Chapter 4 for the conditions established by the international liquor conventions.
[69] Gold Coast, *Legislative Assembly Debates*, February 12, 1953.
[70] Ibid.

The colonial government openly acknowledged the long–established association of the right to drink with political status when Colonial Secretary R. H.
Saloway, in introducing legislation repealing prohibition of liquor in the north,
stated:

> It is, Mr. Speaker, our aim that the Northern Territories, Ashanti and
> the Colony should go forward as equals to form part of a full self–
> governing Gold Coast . . . and I feel, Mr. Speaker, that this measure
> which I am now proposing forwards this aim, in that when it is passed
> into law our friends in the North will be able to drink level with the
> rest of the country.[71]

And the CPP government, in the person of Archie Casely–Hayford (minister of
agriculture and natural resources), hastened to remind northern politicians that
repeal had only been possible through the good offices of the CPP government.[72]

The year 1953 also witnessed the CPP government's repeal of the quota
system established under the Gin and Geneva (Restriction of Importation) Ordinance, in the face of strong opposition from chiefs, who had instigated the
restrictions in 1929.[73] For old chiefs like Nene Mate Kole, who, with Nana Ofori
Atta I, had been instrumental in securing the passage of the restrictive bill on
geneva and gin imports, the repeal by the CPP government was particularly
galling for it signaled a major political defeat.[74] Young men, whom the chiefs
had worked so hard to deny access to liquor, were now in control of liquor
legislation, and they used their control to open the floodgates to mass popular
consumption.

The Akpeteshie Question

In the election campaigns leading to the CPP victories of 1951 and 1954, some CPP
politicians promised the legalization of *akpeteshie* distillation if the party attained
political power.

> I was in Ashanti when the struggle for independence was on, and I heard
> the CPP politicians on the platform saying the British government is de-
> ceiving us: In those days if they see you with a tot of *akpeteshie*, you were
> in trouble. *Akpeteshie* was banned in the country by the British govern-
> ment, and you would be prosecuted whether you were drinking it or dis-
> tilling it or even holding it. . . . So they [the CPP politicians] said, "the
> British government is bringing their alcoholic beverages from overseas to
> us and is asking us to buy [these], but we make our own [drink] here and
> they say no. If I go to Parliament, I will see to it that it is legalized." And
> they won.[75]

[71]   Gold Coast, *Legislative Assembly Debates*, July 7, 1953.
[72]   Ibid.
[73]   See Chapter 4.
[74]   See Ghana, *Legislative Assembly Debates*, November 4, 1953, for the debate on repealing the Gin and
Geneva (Restriction of Importation) Ordinance, and the opposition of Nene Mate Kole.
[75]   AFN: Interview with Rev. Col. Kofi Asare, Accra, June 30, 1992.

The argument for African self–sufficiency in an independent Ghana was a powerful one when applied to the legalization of *akpeteshie*. Gold Coast newspapers between the 1930s and the 1950s commented on the economic potential of the *akpeteshie*
industry if it was legalized and regulated to ensure good quality.[76]

Akpeteshie distillers and retailers knew the industry was lucrative. In the 1950s,
when Anita was still in her twenties, she was able to put up a sixteen–room storey
building at Efiekuma (Sekondi) through her *akpeteshie* profits.[77] In a reflective mood,
a member of the Western Region Distillers Cooperative concluded:

> Akwasi Broni[78] is a deceiver. He knew if he allowed us to distill our local
> gin, we will not buy his imported drinks. So he cheated us. At present,
> now that *akpeteshie* is legal, some of us have built immense cement houses
> from our *akpeteshie* returns. We have sent our children to secondary school
> on *akpeteshie* money.[79]

Akpeteshie patrons had to convince Nkrumah that legalizing distillation was a desirable end—politically, economically, and socially.

On the streets, highlife songs championed the cause of *akpeteshie* and its legalization represented a popular issue. Songs like Okaija "Coal Boy's" *ka wie nakai*
(Don't say that it [*akpeteshie*] isn't good"), and the Comet's "Akpeteshie" have been
cited.[80] Several *akpeteshie* distillers and retailers had joined the CPP and the party
leadership was sympathetic to their plight.[81] But it appears the dramatic emergence
of the Asante–based National Liberation Movement in September 1954, and the
violence that characterized CPP–NLM confrontations, forced the CPP government
to re–evaluate its position on legalizing *akpeteshie*. In the renewed political struggle,
the connections between alcohol and disorder were very evident. The *akpeteshie*
issue will be shelved by the CPP government until the early years of independ-
dence.

The Unsteady Transfer of Power

All seemed set for the grant of independence after the solid CPP performance in
the 1954 election, when the deceptive calm was disturbed by the formation of the
NLM. Internal conflicts had pervaded the CPP during the 1954 election campaign,
as constituency committees butted heads with the central executive over the selection of candidates for the 1954 election. For the 104 available seats, over 1,000 names

---

[76] See, for examples, *Spectator Daily*, September 14, 1939; *Gold Coast Observer*, March 5, 1943; and *Sunday Mirror*, April 4, 1954.

[77] AFN: Interview with Anita Mensah, August 16, 1994.

[78] Akans refer to a white person as "Akwasi Broni," a person born on Sunday. This may be linked to missionary activity and the Christian sabbath.

[79] AFN: Interview with the Western Region Distillers Cooperative Management Committee, Takoradi, August 16, 1994.

[80] See Chapter 5.

[81] AFN: Interview with Tsotso Alice Akwei; Interview with Albert Prempeh, General Secretary of the Ghana Cooperative Distillers Association Limited, Accra, July 29, 1992.

were submitted by the constituencies to the CPP head office.[82] In the end, Nkrumah chose 104 candidates endorsed by the central executive, but many rejected CPP candidates went ahead and stood as Independents. At a rally in Kumasi on June 6, 1954, Nkrumah expelled 81 "rebels" (mostly Asante), who had insisted on standing as independents.[83]

It was these expelled young men, backed by the traditional power of Asante chiefs and disgruntled cocoa farmers alienated by a government freeze on cocoa prices, who formed the core of the NLM.[84] The movement began a dramatic conquest of Asante, as town after town pulled down the CPP flag and hoisted the NLM flag in its stead. Other opposing parties, sensing a new lease on life for themselves in the dynamism of the NLM, quickly allied themselves to the NLM—even if they did not sincerely subscribe to the NLM's "Federation" slogan.

The golden opportunity for the renaissance of political opposition to the CPP had been presented on August 10, 1954, when K. A. Gbedemah as finance minister presented the Cocoa Duty and Development Funds (Amendment) Bill. The bill pegged the price of a 60 lb bag of cocoa at 72s. for four years. The intention of this bill was to siphon off excess liquidity in the agricultural sector, minimize inflationary tendencies, and redirect the funds towards development projects on behalf of the CPP's urban constituents.[85] The Cocoa Duty and Development Funds (Amendment) Bill was passed on August 13. There was a general outcry by cocoa farmers, and expelled CPP rebels in the Ashanti Youth Association (AYA)—Kusi Ampofo, Osei Assibey Mensah, and E. Y. Baffoe—saw the cocoa issue as a means to organize political opposition against the CPP.[86] The AYA held a meeting on August 25 to discuss the cocoa price issue. The members quickly became divided into two camps—pro–CPP and anti–CPP—and the meeting ended in disorder. As one of the anti–CPP participants, Osei Assibey Mensah, informed Jean Marie Allman:

> we chased them out of the hall! We then went and bought some Schnapps and poured libation, vowing no more support for the CPP. We would form our own party.[87]

The pouring of libation by the anti–CPP AYA members was meant to bond them in their new endeavor. But the young men's ritual use of libation as a binding force, and their appeal to the Asante gods and ancestors for success, foreshadowed their eventual alliance with the chiefs—the earthly representatives of the gods and ancestors.

---

[82]   See *Daily Graphic*, May 4, 1954, and May 12, 1954, on the wave of protests from CPP constituency branches as their chosen candidates were rejected by headquarters.

[83]   *Daily Graphic*, June 7, 1954.

[84]   See Allman, *Quills of the Porcupine*, especially Ch. 2.

[85]   The Cocoa Marketing Board was established in 1947, ostensibly to stabilize producer prices for Gold Coast cocoa farmers. The local producer price was fixed far below the world price and the balance was kept in a reserve fund. Funds were intended to be drawn from the reserve fund to stabilize local producer prices when the world price fell below the local producer price, which was seldom.

[86]   *Daily Graphic*, worried about the politicization of the cocoa price issue in Ashanti, featured a series of commentaries on developments in Ashanti: September 2, 1954; September 6, 1954; and September 16, 1954. Ashanti produced over 50 per cent of the country's cocoa exports in the early 1950s.

[87]   Allman, *Quills of the Porcupine*, 27.

Spearheaded by Baffoe, the young men of the NLM soon adopted the cause of the Asante cocoa farmers, holding meetings with the latter at Asawase, a suburb of Kumasi. After campaign promises by some CPP activists that the party would increase the price of cocoa, the farmers were rightly dismayed at the turn of events, as 72s. represented only 37 percent of the prevailing world market price for cocoa in 1954.[88] But the young men's resurrection of Asante nationalism to counteract the CPP's nationalism had a major deficiency: it lacked the support of the *Asantehene*. As custodian of the Golden Stool—the repository of the "soul" of the Asante nation—there could be no Asante nationalism without the *Asantehene*. The young men approached Baffour Akoto, a favored linguist of the *Asantehene*, and invited him to be the chairman of the new movement.[89] Baffour Akoto accepted the invitation, and the crucial alliance between the young men, the farmers and the chiefs was in place, for it was just a matter of time before Baffour Akoto secured the backing of the Kumasi State Council and the Asanteman Council.

The chiefs of Asante were perturbed by the CPP government's efforts to curtail their power. They remembered, distinctly, Nkrumah's early threat that the chiefs would run and leave their sandals if they did not cooperate with the young men. The 1952 CPP local government reform effectively reduced the powers of chiefs. Many Asante chiefs saw the CPP's antagonism towards them as a continuation of their historic struggle with the young men.[90] But the new movement, launched by the Asante young men, offered Asante chiefs the opportunity to recapture their declining power. So in came the *Asantehene* and his important chiefs with the full backing of ritual power.

The scene of the NLM's inauguration dramatized Asante belief in powerful fluids—alcohol, water, blood—and color symbolism. The venue for the inauguration on September 19, 1954, was the sacred Subin River in Kumasi.

At precisely midday, the leaders of the new movement unfurled its flag. The flag's green symbolized Asante's rich forests, its gold, the rich mineral deposits which lay beneath the earth, and its black, the stools of Asante's cherished ancestors. In the center of the flag stood a large cocoa tree; beneath the tree were a cocoa pod and a porcupine.[91]

The struggle against the CPP was launched with the swearing of oaths by the Golden Stool to persevere in the impending struggle, the pouring of libation to Asante gods and ancestors, and the slaughtering of a sheep. The whole inauguration ceremony enacted the continued spiritual potency of the three historically powerful fluids: alcohol, water, and blood.[92]

Color symbolism and ritual, however, were not the exclusive preserve of the NLM or chiefs. In mass politics, no constituency could be ignored.

Nkrumah gave his CPP a "flag" in colours Ghanaians loved—red, white and green—and Ghanaians had an intuitive traditional understanding of

---

[88] Ibid., 26.

[89] AFN: Interview with K. Attakora Gyimah.

[90] *Daily Graphic*, May 6, 1954.

[91] Allman, "Youngmen and the Porcupine," 263. The porcupine is the age–old symbol of the Asante military.

[92] See Chapters 1 and 2.

the meanings of the colours: Red for blood—danger, determination, military alertness, sacrifice; white for purity, hope and success; and Green for youthfulness (a virgin is called *obaabun*, a green woman), . . . fertility, [and] viability. In physical representation, in some places, Red stands for the Earth (*ntwema*); White for the sea or sun; and Green for the vegetation—the fundamental elements or sources of life.[93]

The CPP party symbol, a cockerel, represented an important sacrificial bird in rituals. Nkrumah participated in rituals involving the blood of sheep.[94] Both nationalist parties, significantly, had chosen party colors that had emotive appeal and ritual importance for most peoples of the Gold Coast. Culture and religion had become contested terrains.

The success of the NLM seemed to be ordained when, soon after its inauguration, the party gained its first martyr. The Akan, Ga–Adangme, and Ewe believe that sometimes blood must be shed for life to be saved.[95] In the precolonial era, circumstances could demand human or animal blood. As an Ewe elder explained:

Blood signifies life in its true form. In order to get the good things of life from the source, the life of another being or animal needs to be sacrificed to pacify whoever it is that controls the keys to good and evil.[96]

Asante's defeat of Denkyira in 1701 and the foundation of the Asante state was achieved through the blood of a martyr. Tweneboah Kodua of Kumawu offered himself for ritual sacrifice to the Asante gods, when the latter demanded royal blood as the price for Asante victory. On October 9, 1954, E. Y. Baffoe, national propaganda secretary of the NLM, was stabbed to death by Twumasi Ankrah (CPP) in Ashanti Newtown, a suburb of Kumasi.[97] Baffoe's "sacrifice" was perceived by Asante NLM to have secured the party's success.

The young men of Ashanti Newtown, like Baffoe and Twumasi Ankrah, had been instrumental in the founding of the CPP in 1949 and the NLM in 1954. In fact, the Ashanti headquarters of the CPP and the NLM were on the same street in Ashanti Newtown. On October 9, 1954, Baffoe was informed that Twumasi Ankrah (regional propaganda secretary for CPP), who had reportedly been drinking all day, had come to remove the NLM flag from the NLM headquarters.[98] Knowing Twumasi's house, Baffoe set off to retrieve the flag and ended up being stabbed to death. Soon Baffoe's sacrifice was being compared to that of Tweneboah Kodua in NLM campaign speeches, Baffoe's death being seen as the basis for the resurrection of Asante glory.

The prominence of drinking bars and drinking in the events of the day Baffoe was murdered, highlighted the central role drinking bars played in the social life of the young men and in political mobilization by both the CPP and the NLM. The day had commenced peacefully, as Twumasi Ankrah and other CPP young men sat drink-

---

93   Hagan, "Nkrumah's Leadership Style," 187.
94   Nkrumah, *Autobiography*, 136.
95   AFN: Interview with Nii Amaakai II, Asere Jaasetse; Interview with Mawere Poku.
96   Personal communication from Togbuivi Kumassah, May 12, 1995.
97   *Daily Graphic*, October 11, 1954. See also, AFN: Interview with Salome Akyeampong (cousin of Baffoe), Kumasi, April 18, 1992; Interview with K. Attakora Gyimah.
98   Allman, *Quills of the Porcupine*, 56.

ing at a popular CPP spot, "Mexico Bar" on Odumasi Road (Ashanti Newtown). In the company of these CPP men was John Kofi Poku, the assistant treasurer of the NLM, who hoped to persuade these Asante young men to join the NLM. Poku's attempts were unsuccessful, and he left for the NLM drinking bar, "Ghana Bar," opposite the NLM office in Ashanti Newtown.[99] Later in the day, Yaw Awuah, assistant propaganda secretary of the NLM, had an argument with Adubofuor Poku, a CPP supporter and close friend of Twumasi Ankrah. Twumasi Ankrah and other CPP stalwarts then came to the NLM office in a show of force, setting off the events that led to Baffoe's death. Leisure was an outdoor activity for young men for they lacked the resources to own or rent houses suitable for home entertainment. Beer bars constituted social institutions where socializing occurred. Bars served as barometers of popular opinion and places of recruitment for party scouts in the 1940s and 1950s.

One of the immediate consequences of Baffoe's murder was the NLM's formation of a paramilitary wing, the "Action Groupers," as a counterforce to the CPP's "Action Troopers." Politics in Kumasi and its environs soon degenerated into bloody violence.[100] NLM membership doubled with Baffoe's death, and the subsequent endorsement of the Kumasi State Council and the Asanteman Council. The option of neutrality was eliminated as the conflict was redefined along the lines of "Asanteness." A true Asante ought to be a supporter of the NLM and anti–CPP.[101] The street fighting after Baffoe's death soon got out of hand.

> On January 5 [1955], the situation reached a critical point. A riot in Kumase Zongo left two NLM members dead and several people wounded. The following day, the home of the regional chairman of the CPP was dynamited. On January 7, the governor decided to intervene and signed the Peace Preservation Ordinance, which forbade "the carrying of dangerous weapons including firearms, cutlasses, daggers . . . in any place or in any vehicle . . . in certain towns."[102]

But as Allman points out, the effect of the peace ordinance was marginal. It was in this atmosphere of everyday violence that both CPP and NLM supporters sought spiritual protection.

Asuman (charms) for physical strength (invincibility) and for disappearing in the midst of danger were eagerly sought in the 1950s. Such charms had a long history in precolonial Ghana. The magical and medicinal functions of Islam exercised great appeal in precolonial Asante. Dupuis referred to "talismatic charms" made by the Muslims as a "source of great emolument as the article is in public demand from the palace to the slave's hut. . . ."[103] Invincibility charms of non–Muslim origin have also enjoyed a long patronage. Brokensha's study of Larteh

---

[99] *Ashanti Pioneer*, December 3, 1954.

[100] Not that violence in the nationalist struggle was limited to Asante or began with the inception of the NLM. See *Daily Graphic*, April 2, 1954, on political violence in Sekondi–Takoradi; and *Daily Graphic*, June 23, 1954, on political violence in Kumasi before the formation of the NLM.

[101] Allman, *Quills of the Porcupine*, 63.

[102] Ibid., 79–80. The violence in Kumasi continued through 1955.

[103] Dupuis, *Journal*, xi. See also, N. Levtzion, "Early Nineteenth Century Arabic Manuscripts from Kumase," *Transactions of the Historical Society of Ghana* 8 (1965): 99–119, on the importance of magical formulae in the early nineteenth–century Muslim literature written in Kumasi; and David Owusu–Ansah, *Islamic Talismanic Tradition in Nineteenth Century Asante* (New York, 1991).

mentioned one charm, *gyuapae*, which gave its possessor the ability to inflict serious injury with just a slight blow.[104] In the CPP/NLM conflict, royal houses with
powerful ancestral stools and gods became strong sources of spiritual protection.
According to an NLM informant:

> There were houses that had *aduru* [medicine] where we bathed. Like the
> *Apagyahemaa* Nana Ama Dapaah's house. That house was versed in *aduru*
> and we bathed there. The house had a *bosom* [god]. This was the time the
> CPP and NLM supporters were killing one another. The CPP supporters
> also bathed in *aduru* at Anwomaso, on the Kumasi–Accra road. The medi-
> cine we bathed had broken bottles in it. We bathed at the *Apagyahemaa's*
> house . . . or at Okyeame Akoto's house at Heman. The medicine had
> pieces of broken bottles, razor blades, knives, and bullets. After we fin-
> ished bathing, we take out knives and try it on one another to see if the
> medicine has been effective. If it cuts you, you go back to bath in the medi-
> cine for you are not ready.[105]

The power of Kofi Banda, a CPP stalwart in Kumasi, was legendary. When
you shot at him, he removed the bullet and gave it back to you. Muslim *alhajis*
provided charms and finger rings that made wearers invincible in battle even when
they were outnumbered.[106] In November 1955, a new wave of violence swept
Kumasi, when the CPP passed a bill reducing the powers of the state councils. On
November 17, Central Market and Odumase Street in Kumasi were rocked by dy-
namite explosions. On November 19, the sister of Krobo Edusei, the CPP's key
man in Asante, was killed when her home was dynamited.[107]

Women were in the thick of the battle, both as victims and as agents. It is
apparent that women, from the inception of the CPP, were determined not to be
ignored in the independence struggle. They had too much to gain. In the 1951
election campaign, a CPP woman, who had adopted the name of "Ama
Nkrumah," ended a fiery speech in Kumasi by slashing her face with a razor
and smearing her blood over her body.[108] Women were prepared to even sacrifice their lives for freedom and the independence movement.[109] The play on the
symbolism of blood—embodying life, danger, sacrifice, and power—is mani-
fest. Both the NLM and the CPP used women as spies.[110] Maame Nyameba, who
led the NLM's women in Kumasi, organized the women to collect bottles and
stones when the Action Groupers clashed with the Action Troopers. And NLM
women now utilized the power of *mmomomme* (female spiritual warfare) against
the CPP.[111]

---

[104]   Brokensha, *Social Change at Larteh*, 185.

[105]   Personal communication, Kumasi, August 19, 1994.

[106]   Ibid.

[107]   Allman, *Quills of the Porcupine*, 129.

[108]   Nkrumah, *Autobiography*, 89.

[109]   Ama Nkrumah, whose original name is Adjoa Naba Nyewe, rose to become CPP Women's Leader of
Sekondi, and a close confidante of Nkrumah. On her life, see AFN: Interview with Ama Nkrumah, Sekondi,
August 15 and August 16, 1994.

[110]   AFN: Interview with Adwoa Abrefi (NLM), Kumasi, August 19, 1994; Interview with Ama Nkrumah,
August 16, 1994; and personal communication from Essie Aluah, Takoradi, August 16, 1994.

[111]   AFN: Interview with Adwoa Abrefi, Kumasi, August 19, 1994; Interview with Obaapanin Afua Pokuah,
Kumasi, August 19, 1994.

Folk explanation of the assassination of the powerful Kofi Banda, illustrates how female spiritual powers had come to be seen as crucial to the nationalist struggle.

We asked a *mate meho* [federation/NLM] woman to go and have an affair with Kofi Banda. . . . Kofi Banda began to confide in the woman because he was not aware that she was *mate meho*. One day the woman asked him about his invincibility to bullets. . . . Kofi Banda confided to her that ordinary bullets could not kill him; what could kill him was a piece from the loin cloth of a menstruating woman, *sasa* [pounded plantain stem], and *atwere tuo* [muzzle–loading rifle]. The woman brought the information to the *mate meho*.[112]

On May 14, 1955, NLM supporters at a rally in Edweso clashed with CPP supporters led by Kofi Banda. Shots rang out from the second floor of the *Edwesohene's* palace and struck Kofi Banda dead. Folk explanation of Banda's death is that *Edwesohene* Nana Kwasi Afranie fired the fatal bullet prepared according to the NLM woman's information. The colonial courts acquitted Kwasi Afranie for insufficient evidence.[113]

Indeed, the perceived spiritual powers immanent in alcohol, blood, and water were summoned to protect Kumasi at the height of the NLM/CPP conflict.

When the NLM/CPP conflict in Kumasi became intense, Osei Assibey [Mensah][114] picked up a sheep, carried it on his shoulders and proceeded with the NLM leaders to the Subin River. The river is not called Subin, it is called *Kukurontim* ["cannot be carried"]. It protected Kumasi, so that no one "could carry Kumasi" (*wo kukuro'a wo ntimi*). The sheep was sacrificed to the river, and the river was asked to aid the NLM so that they could defeat the CPP and exile CPP supporters from Kumasi.[115]

The colonial government was deeply disturbed by the raging battle in Asante. Its model colony, the Gold Coast, was turning into a political nightmare. What had been seen in Britain as a smooth transfer of power was now marked by disorder. In fact, the very legitimacy of the CPP as the dominant party in the Gold Coast had come into question.

In spite of the CPP's opposition to a third general election, the party was compelled to demonstrate its popularity at the polls again. On May 11, 1956, the secretary of state for the colonies announced in the House of Commons that a final election in the Gold Coast appeared to be the only solution to the political impasse.[116] Elections were scheduled for July 17, 1956, and all parties campaigned feverishly. The NLM had developed campaign strategies similar to those of the CPP, the product of the efforts of the NLM young men, and both sides exploited local interests, plied influential elders with drinks, composed special party songs,[117] and promised everything to the electorate. The CPP won 72 seats out of the 104

112 Personal communication, Kumasi, August 19, 1994.
113 Allman, *Quills of the Porcupine*, 104.
114 Osei Assibey Mensah was one of the Asante young men who founded the NLM.
115 Personal communication, Kumasi, August 19, 1994.
116 Nkrumah, *Autobiography*, 252–53.
117 Two popular NLM songs were *Akoko sue sue* ("Cockerel, shoo! shoo!), the CPP's symbol being a red cockerel, and a cocoa highlife song.

constituencies in the Gold Coast. The CPP's image as a "commoner's party" was more appealing than an NLM image that smacked of a rebirth of Asante imperialism. The CPP played on these fears, and its able manipulation of local conflicts as a government in power helped to tilt the scales in its favor. The NLM had played its card and had been defeated, and it grudgingly extended a hand in congratulation to the CPP. Independence was granted on March 7, 1957, and the Gold Coast changed its name to Ghana.

Conclusion

Nationalist politics in the Gold Coast were fought on two fronts: against the European colonial ruler; and amongst African parties once independence was in sight. Nationalist agitation against the colonial ruler included the elimination of colonial control over liquor policy, and the legalization of illicit *akpeteshie*. The internal political struggle was over the crucial question of who would shape the postcolonial society: the chiefs, elders and their educated allies or the young men who had been excluded from sharing power in both precolonial and colonial politics. When a nationalist party of commoners emerged, it was inevitable that it would appeal to the young men and young women for support through their prevailing lifestyle which revolved around dances, beer bars, music, and concerts. Popular culture intertwined with mass politics. To endorse the legalization of *akpeteshie*, so important to urban life, meshed with the image of a "commoner's party."

But it was also a quest for power along very "traditional" lines, for the powerful—male elders in precolonial Gold Coast and the British during colonization—had always controlled access to alcohol. Indigenous culture and religion were vital resources that could not be ignored in the nationalist struggle. The spiritual power of fluids like alcohol, water, and blood were tapped in the struggle for political power. The CPP party won the struggle to form the first government in independent Ghana, and it moved to legalize *akpeteshie* to signify the ascendancy of the new order over the old, to express its political control over access to alcohol, and to elevate the urban popular culture that had aided its rise to power.

But bad times were in store. Urban and rural commoners, in their exuberance over the CPP's political victory, never anticipated that their partnership would soon go sour. Independence had been won, and the CPP leadership, after neutralizing the power of the chiefs and the educated elite through repressive laws, no longer felt bound by its alliance with the commoners. It still retained the image of the "commoners' party," but the party's foot rested heavily on the necks of its rank-and-file, as well as the chiefs and the educated elite. As commoners redefined their lives in the wake of their disillusion, Ghana's economic decline would aggravate their condition, fostering an increase in alcoholism and a worsening of gender relations.

7

A Living Death: Individualism, Alcoholism, and Survival in Independent Ghana

The man could have opened his mouth again, to talk of the irony of it all, of people being given power because they were good at shouting against the enslaving things of Europe, and of the same people using the same power for chasing after the same enslaving things.[1]

Perhaps the greatest tragedy in independent Ghana was the snuffing out of the hopes and expectations ordinary people entertained at independence. That this betrayal would be perpetrated by the supposed "commoner's" government made it more disheartening. The official adoption of a tough stance towards *akpeteshie* distillers and patrons was an early indication of the shift in loyalties among CPP leaders. A gradual disengagement from popular culture ensued among party elite. Democracy was transformed into totalitarian rule, and economic decline—initiated by a long term drop in the world market price for cocoa—intensified the general sense of insecurity. These tensions played themselves out at the family and individual levels. Marriages became fragile. Gender relations were besieged by financial difficulties. Unhappy marriages, divorces, single parenting, and dire financial straits pushed more females into the habit of drinking. For indigent men and women, alcohol provided "comfort" and an avenue for redefining their social identity.

Workers decided to support the CPP because it was the commoners' party and because its leaders, often ridiculed as "verandah boys,"[2] could be expected to iden-

---

[1]   The epigram is culled from Armah's, *The Beautyful Ones Are Not Yet Born*, 149. It captures the process of material accumulation that has characterized postindependent Ghanaian governments, and the disappointment of ordinary workers, for whom independence has brought no significant material benefits.

[2]   Members of the UGCC and Ghana Congress Party tagged their opponents in the CPP as "verandah boys": people who could not even afford roofs over their heads and slept on the open verandahs of houses.

tify with the plight of workers. K. A. Busia in his social survey of Sekondi–Takoradi, in the immediate preindependence period, provided a vivid picture of the squalid social conditions of workers in this predominantly working-class city:

> In some quarters of the town, such as the Zongo, Anaafo, Essikado, Ekuasi, Nkontompo and Essiaman, there were many insanitary houses, and small, dark rooms; people slept on mats spread on the floor; the food of many families was often poor in quality, consisting of little else besides dispro-portionate quantities of cheap, starchy foods. Some, especially at the Zongo, were scantily clothed.[3]

The poor circumstances of workers in the early 1950s were the result of the colonial government's persistence in paying wages that barely met subsistence, and an unwillingness to provide subsidized workers' housing on any substantial scale. For Ghanaian workers caught in this economic vice, the prospect of independence and the promises of the CPP held out very practical potential benefits. Independence meant a visible improvement in their material lives and a more equitable distribution of the country's wealth. Disappointingly, the CPP, and successive Ghanaian governments, proved staunch adherents of the old Akan ideology of accumulating wealth through political power.[4] Social differences widened, authoritarianism became the benchmark of independent regimes in Ghana, and the state became markedly predatory as the economy declined.[5] Disillusioned, ordinary men and women gradually withdrew from participation in public politics to pursue their own private strategies of survival. As the CPP government distanced itself from popular culture, popular culture transformed itself to express its disassociation from the CPP government and the harsh reality of working class existence.

Class distinctions hardened, and the differences between upper class, middle class, and working class were reflected in contrasting drinking patterns. Gender relations underwent further permutations as marriage, family, and kinship adjusted to economic difficulties and moral disillusion. Workers took to drink as one means of regaining control over their lives. Drink also served as an avenue of escape as workers faced wages that failed more than ever to meet the basic needs of their families, paradoxically straining already straitened household budgets. There was a perceptible increase in solitary drinking in urban Ghana and alcohol was singled out as the cause of social ills.[6] But alcoholism

---

[3]   Busia, *Social Survey of Sekondi–Takoradi*, 23.

[4]   McCaskie, "Accumulation, Wealth and Belief," I and II.

[5]   A detailed narrative of political and economic change in independent Ghana is avoided here. For further reading, see Kwame A. Ninsin, *Political Struggles in Ghana 1967–1981* (Accra, 1985); Deborah Pellow and Naomi Chazan, *Ghana. Coping with Uncertainty* (Boulder, 1986); A. Adu Boahen, *The Ghanaian Sphinx: Reflections on the Contemporary History of Ghana, 1972–1987* (Accra, 1989); Douglas Rimmer, *Staying Poor: Ghana's Political Economy 1950–1990* (Oxford, 1992); and Frimpong–Ansah, *Vampire State in Africa*.

[6]   Charges of excessive drinking in Ghana are difficult to substantiate, as alcohol per–capita consumption figures do not exist because of the difficulties in compiling statistics of alcohol imported and produced in the country. Medical records from the Accra Psychiatric Hospital and the AGC hospital at Obuasi, however, show increasing hospital admissions for alcohol–related problems over the past two decades. But this could reflect the growing confidence among the Ghanaian population in Western medicine. Brewery and distillery production figures, particularly since the mid–1980s, reveal a sharp increase in sales, but there has been a parallel decline in the imports of spirits and beer. Evidence of increased consumption of

was more a result of socioeconomic inequity rather than the cause of it. The irony lay in the fact that many workers who became alcoholics took to drinking to gain some sense of control over their precarious existence. At the societal level, growing indices of alcoholism reflected the political, economic, and social decline in independent Ghana. At the personal level, alcoholism presented the grim reality of individual lives, and how belief, knowledge, and circumstances interacted to redefine social identity.

Independence and Popular Expectations: The Success Image

It is relevant to comment on the social aspirations of Ghanaian workers, the continuing pull of cultural and historical definitions of "success," and how eventual disappointment in these expectations led to increased solitary drinking and alcoholism. The first generation of male migrants from the villages had seen their stays in the towns as temporary, hoping to accumulate enough wealth to return prosperously to their villages. The goal of many of these men was to circumvent the control of male elders at home over land, the primary means of rural subsistence, and the concomitant control over women. Their desired social goal was to become elders, and they anticipated that temporary migration to participate in urban wage labor would provide a short cut to this goal.

But the forces of proletarianization—low wages, economic fluctuations, rural economic decline, new aspirations—sometimes conspired to render migration permanent. This process seems to have intensified from the depression of the 1930s. In mining towns, more women joined their husbands and families were established.[7] By the independence era, second generation migrants had begun to reconsider the feasibility of an eventual return to the village. Although they were not original social products of the village, the poverty of urban existence, as depicted in Busia's description of working-class communities in Sekondi–Takoradi, continued to make rural life an important option.

Despite changing historical conditions, successive waves of rural migrants continued to hold the same goal of eventually becoming respected elders of their local communities. From a massive survey of rural and urban households conducted by J. C. Caldwell between 1962 and 1964, he concluded that:

> Over nine–tenths of migrants in the town, recorded in the urban survey, state their intentions of returning and in the rural survey almost four times as many persons over 65 years old were counted, who claimed to have returned to the village after long–term absence in the towns. . . .[8]

---

alcohol is provided in the phenomenal proliferation of drinking outlets, and revenue records for various administrative districts emphasize this trend. On the west wing of the Kumasi Sports Stadium alone, the author counted 23 drinking establishments in 1992. The alcohol industry as a whole has boomed in postindependent Ghana. See Akyeampong, "The State and Alcohol Revenues."

[7]   Crisp, *Story of an African Working Class*, 62.

[8]   J. C. Caldwell, "Determinants of Rural–Urban Migration in Ghana," *Population Studies* 22, 3 (1968): 367.

Even in the late 1960s, Margaret Peil discovered that many factory workers still looked forward to an old age of supporting themselves with rural farming and maintaining their sense of importance as elders.[9]

The ultimate achievement for migrants would be to obtain *obirempon* status; a self–made "big man." The pull of culture and history, to take the example of Asante, has generated a chain of commoners who have sought to become successful through their own efforts. Ordinary Sawua traders formed the core of the *akonkofo* ("new men," i.e. capitalists) at the turn of the twentieth century.[10] In early colonial Asante, the *ahenkwaa* ("stool servants") sought to emulate the *akonkofo* by collaborating with British colonialism. And the *nkwankwaa* (the young men), achieved overnight fame by joining the CPP.[11] On their own level, rural migrants to towns were engaged in an endeavor to acquire the material means to become elders in their villages or hometowns. In their estimation, the only stumbling block was the colonial government—the largest employer of labor and the "collaborator" of expatriate business concerns—and independence would correct that anomaly.[12]

Urban women also held high hopes concerning independence. The initial economic gains women achieved in the interstices of the colonial economy were severely threatened from the 1940s. The colonial state's measures against prostitution and *akpeteshie* sales made these risky occupations. In 1943 a tougher legal definition of prostitution was enacted in the Gold Coast.[13] But the structural causes for the declining conditions of women were long term. To take the example of Ga women, start–up capital for trade grew larger and larger, and expatriate companies pushed Ga women from their intermediary position in trade. Ga women concentrated on the sale of foodstuffs and prepared foods. The growth of Accra as the administrative capital put pressure on land, and land alienation and privatization curtailed women's access to farm land. Women's restricted access to education meant that they did not benefit much from wage and salaried jobs for which literacy was required. Women's position in Ga marriages moved from one of interdependence, or even independence, to that of dependence.[14] With political independence approaching, Ghanaian men and women confidently looked forward to a future of material improvement and political participation.

Independence Gone Sour: The Commoners Abandoned

Independence brought deep divisions within the CPP party. Nkrumah became a ruler, not a leader, and the party was torn by a generation gap (old guard versus new boys), a communication gap (leadership versus rank–and–file), and a means

---

[9]   Margaret Peil, *The Ghanaian Factory Worker: Industrial Man in Africa* (Cambridge, 1972), 181–82.

[10]   See Chapter 3.

[11]   See Chapter 6.

[12]   Ghanaian workers have enthusiastically supported the nationalization of expatriate businesses since the attainment of independence. See Kwesi Jonah, "Imperialism, the State and the Indigenization of the Ghanaian Economy 1957–1984," *Africa Development* 10, 3 (1985): 63–99.

[13]   Department of Social Welfare, "A Social Survey of Obuasi, Ashanti" (Kumasi, 1955), 11.

[14]   Robertson, *Sharing the Same Bowl*; and Leith Mullings, "Religious Change and Social Stratification in Labadi: The Church of the Messiah," in George Bond *et al.*, *African Christianity*, 65–88.

gap (wealthy versus poor).[15] Preindependence legislative assembly debates on legalizing *akpeteshie* heralded these splits. The party leadership seemed divorced from the MP's, who strove to deliver their campaign promise to legalize *akpeteshie*. In the legislative assembly debates of March 25, 1955, Miss Mabel Dove, CPP representative for Ga, inquired:

> whether, in view of the fact that distilling *Akpeteshie* (illicit gin) is a permanent feature of the local industry, despite fines and imprisonments, the Government will consider legalising it so that it can be tested and rendered less dangerous for human consumption.[16]

Other CPP members of the assembly supported Mabel Dove's suggestion that the government should legalize *akpeteshie* distillation.

The CPP government adopted the position the colonial government had taken towards *akpeteshie* distillation, a move which, perhaps, revealed the CPP government's unwillingness to differ from colonial government opinion at such a sensitive time. The NLM threat had turned the colonial government into the CPP government's most valuable ally.

> The question of making the local distillation of spirits legal under proper control and safeguards has been under examination within the last two years. The conclusion now reached is that it would be impossible to guarantee the production of spirits of a quality not injurious to health from the existing illicit industry. . . .[17]

Certain images associated with *akpeteshie*—its connections to political protest and social nonconformism, and its identity as a working class drink—made the CPP government apprehensive about legalizing it. Having patronized popular culture in its election campaigns, the CPP government was very much aware of the mobilizational capacity of popular culture and its potential for political opposition.

Indeed, in the early years of independence, the government actively prosecuted persons dealing in *akpeteshie*. There was widespread political tension in Ghana on the eve of independence as British Togoland (now part of Ghana) threatened to secede and join French Togoland, Asante remained in a state of political unrest, and the Ga Standfast Association raised the banner of opposition in the capital of Accra. The CPP government passed several repressive laws in the early years of independence. The trade union movement was subordinated to the party, the Preventive Detention Act (1958) empowered the state to detain a person without trial for a period of five years, and the Avoidance of Discrimination Act (1957) forced the existing regionalist- and ethnic–based opposition parties to merge into the United Party. Prosecuting *akpeteshie* patrons seemed to be part of the CPP government's endeavor to quell political dissent. This caused unease among CPP rank–and–file. In the parliamentary session of July 23, 1958, the CPP representative for Akwapim South, K. Asiam, queried the minister of interior about arrests and convictions for possessing illicit gin. He was informed by Parliamentary Secretary to the Minister of Interior Mr. E. A. Mahama, that:

15 Hagan, "Nkrumah's Leadership Style," 207.
16 Gold Coast, *Legislative Assembly Debates*, March 25, 1955.
17 Response of the Ministerial Secretary to the Ministry of Trade and Labour, Mr. E. K. Bensah, to Mable Dove's question on legalizing *akpeteshie*. Gold Coast, *Legislative Assembly Debates*, March 25, 1955.

In 1957 there were 712 convictions of persons possessing illicit gin. Between 1st January and 31st March, 1958, there were a further 87 convictions. In addition, in 1957 there were 85 convictions for making gin illic-
itly. Corresponding figures for 1958 are not yet available.[18]

The CPP representative for Agona, W. A. C. Essibrah, demanded to know when the
government intended to legalize the distillation of *akpeteshie* and halt the prosecu-
tions for illicit distillation.[19] It is obvious that the government's activities had become embarrassing for several party members.

The parliamentary opposition capitalized on the government's harassment of
its own "supporters" to criticize liquor policy and to highlight the government's
repudiation of its election promises. J. D. Wireko of the newly formed United Party,
certainly made political capital of the CPP government's dilemma.

> Since the C.P.P. promised the electorate in the 1951 and 1954 elections that
> no arrests of people selling illicit gin would be made, will the minister [of
> interior] instruct the police not to arrest any dealer in illicit gin in order
> that the government might fulfill their promise to the people?[20]

But as a government in power, the CPP government had also come to appreciate
the financial relevance of duties on imported liquor.[21] As the world market price
for cocoa declined sharply from about the time of Ghana's independence, the new
African government desperately searched for other viable sources of revenue. The
government was unwilling to surrender a lucrative alcohol industry into private
Ghanaian hands.[22]

However, the government did legalize *akpeteshie* in 1962, an act attributed to
the political pressure of party members who distilled *akpeteshie*.[23] The Ghana Distillers Cooperative Association was officially recognized, and the state ruled that
all *akpeteshie* distillers should be registered members of this cooperative. The government sought to centralize its control over *akpeteshie* production, and imposed a
tax of 4s. on distillers for every gallon of *akpeteshie* produced.[24] Government revenues continued to decline, leading to budget deficits, deficit financing, huge external debts, general economic decline, loss of jobs, hopes, and homes. In despera-
tion, the government turned to tax the commoners' who had voted it into power.
Amidst rumors of official corruption, the CPP's 1961 budget introduced a compulsory "savings" scheme of 5 percent on wages over 120 Ghanaian pounds per annum and a new purchase tax. Urban workers decided to confront the CPP government.

---

[18] Ghana, *Parliamentary Debates*, July 23, 1958.

[19] Ibid.

[20] Ibid.

[21] See statement by J. Kodzo, parliamentary secretary to the minister of trade and industries. Ghana,
Parliamentary Debates, June 19, 1958.

[22] See the Cabinet Minutes of March 12, 1957 (NAG, Accra, ADM 13/1/26); and May 27, 1958 (NAG,
Accra, ADM 13/1/27).

[23] AFN: Interview with Albert Prempeh, General Secretary of the Ghana Distillers' Cooperative Association, Accra, July 29, 1992.

[24] The "Manufacture and Sale of Spirits Act, 1962" (Act 154) and "The Manufacture and Sale of Spirits
Regulation, 1962" (L.I. 239).

Popular Culture Versus Elite Culture: Articulating Dissent

In the midst of economic austerity, and in spite of the socialist platform adopted in 1961, CPP government officials lived lives of personal ostentation. A new elite culture emerged among CPP officials which emphasized the accumulation of houses, cars, young girlfriends, and the consumption of expensive imported alcohol.[25] Elite culture in the CPP regime was based on the conspicuous display of wealth. This obviously eliminated the participation of the commoners who formed the CPP rank-and-file. Popular culture expressed the social experience of urban workers, constituting, what may be termed, their "social theory."[26] As CPP officials distanced themselves from popular culture, popular culture oriented itself to critique the sociopolitical order.

Elite culture shared much in common with the traditional lifestyles of the *abirempon* (big men) of the precolonial era and the *akonkofo* ("new capitalists") in early colonial Asante.

> Perhaps the most successful among the Asante *nkwankwaa* who joined the CPP was Krobo Edusei, sometime CPP Propaganda Secretary and Minister of the Interior. From his privileged position in a "socialist" government he became the very model of a new model *obirempon*. Ostentatious and generous, the possessor of a large number of houses and (allegedly) a gold bed. . . .[27]

And the CPP elite now spent their leisure hours in geographically secluded spots. In fact, for the urban poor, plush state hotels patronized by politicians represented visible monuments of social inequality. Ayi Kwei Armah's description of the state-owned "Atlantic" Hotel, in his novel on working–class life in Sekondi–Takoradi under the CPP, is very illustrative in this respect.

> On top of the hill, commanding it just as it commanded the scene below, its sheer, flat, multi–storied side an insulting white in the concentrated gleam of the hotel's spotlights, towered the useless structure of the Atlantic–Caprice. Sometimes it seemed as if the huge building had been put there for a purpose, like that of attracting to itself all the massive anger of a people in pain.[28]

The old social clubs of the British colonial servants were now inherited by the new African politicians and bureaucrats, who imitated the speech, clothing, drinking patterns, and other mannerisms of the British.[29]

Even drinking patterns in Ghana were solidifying along class lines. What you drank, with whom you drank, and where you drank had become a social badge.[30]

---

[25] Armah, *The Beautyful Ones*, criticized the conspicuous consumption of these corrupt politicians.

[26] See Karp, "Beer Drinking and Social Experience," 83.

[27] McCaskie, "Accumulation, Wealth and Belief, Part II," 18.

[28] Armah, *The Beautyful Ones*, 10.

[29] Kofi Awoonor, *This Earth My Brother* (London, 1971), documents the social activities of the new African elite in the exclusive male clubs of Accra.

[30] On drinking establishments, types of alcoholic drinks, and the delineation of class distinctions, see also Martin, *Leisure and Society in Colonial Brazzaville*, 137–38; and West, "Equal Rights for All Civilized Men."

A palm–wine bar at the Sekondi Railway Location, Ketan

As Jeffries' interviewees informed him of Pobee Biney, the political and cultural hero of Sekondi–Takoradi railwaymen:

> Biney, everyone knew was a drunkard; but he was a popular drunk, a frequenter of the low bars of Esikado and Ketan, unlike the elite souses in their plush hotels.[31]

Jeffries discerned three distinct drinking patterns in Sekondi–Takoradi clearly expressing social class. The elite kept "closed" houses in the exclusive suburbs, inviting friends over for private dinners and drinks. If they went out to drink, it was to plush hotels like the "Atlantic"—the resort of white expatriates and the new African elite of politicians, government connected businessmen and lawyers. The middle class frequented beer bars, where the music was quiet and the atmosphere "cool."[32]

The working classes were less privileged.

For the urban poor, their house, or more commonly their single room, serves as little more than a bedroom. Life is led almost entirely out of doors, strolling the streets or sitting and talking with friends on street cor-

---

[31] Jeffries, *Class, Ideology and Power in Ghana*, 82. Several railwaymen lived at Essikado (British Sekondi) and Ketan, where the Railway Location workshop had been established.

[32] Photographs 7 and 8 illustrate the contrast in drinking establishments in urban Ghana where different social classes are concerned. Photograph 7 presents a picture of the rather undistinguished "Kae Dabi Da" palm wine bar in Sekondi, with a customer sitting in front. Photograph 8 is a picture of the elegant cocktail bar at "Palmers Palace Hotel" in Obuasi, a resort that caters to the well–to–do. In urban Ghana, drinking patterns have become an accurate indice of class.

Cocktail bar at the Palmers Palace Hotel, Obuasi

ners. They generally drink in the *akpeteshie* bars, which consist of little more than a shack, or occasionally in one of the dancing bars where both beer and local gin are sold.[33]

Poor living spaces partially accounted for the popularity of public bars among urban workers and market places among urban women. Liquor was portable, and a bottle of *akpeteshie* could provide cheap entertainment for a group of friends gathered on a verandah or under a shady tree. Jeffries observed that drinking with friends was a major social activity in Ghana, and saw the different types of drinking establishments as vivid indicators of social class barriers.[34]

With open political dissent rendered dangerous by oppressive laws, disappointed Ghanaian urban workers retreated to their old drinking bars to formulate new strategies of protest and survival. As the CPP government had feared, drinking bars became active places of political resistance to CPP rule. The Sekondi–Takoradi railway workers led a general strike in 1961 against the CPP's compulsory savings scheme. Populist feelings of betrayed trust were whipped up in the bars of Sekondi–Takoradi in the period before the 1961 strike.[35] The strike was brutally suppressed by the CPP government, and several railwaymen were detained. The railwaymen, staunch supporters of the CPP in the 1950 gen-

---

[33]   Jeffries, *Class, Power and Ideology in Ghana*, 181.

[34]   Ibid., 180–81.

[35]   Ibid., 78.

eral strike, had become leaders in the opposition to the CPP. Working–class opposition increasingly took the form of satire in highlife songs.

Highlife songs ridiculed elite culture. A popular highlife song in the 1960s, *Yen nyina ye bow pepeepe* (Twi: "We all booze the same"), sought to ridicule the status connotations attached to expensive imported alcoholic drinks like "White Horse" whiskey. The artiste pointed out to his listeners that workers could get as drunk on *akpeteshie* as on imported whisky.[36] As all formal opposition became illegal with the declaration of a one–party state in 1964, drinking and the use of allegory in highlife music and popular theater became the only means of sociopolitical protest open to the urban poor.[37]

Highlife music expressed the sense of betrayal felt by urban workers and the desolation that pervaded the lives of the poor. In these songs, drinking numbed pain and gave solace.

> Me nom nsa a na m'akae m'asem
> anibere a enso gya koraa
> ampa ara m'akae m'asem
> anibere a enso gya koraa.
>
> Ewiase mu a ye wo yi
> se asem nto wo a, ena wo hu w'adofo
> onipa a one wo ko no na one wo ba no
> onya wo a obe ye wo
> ono ara na onya wo a obe ye wo.
>
> Obiara renom nsa na orefa adwene
> nti me nom nsa a, na m'kae m'asem
> anibere a enso gya koraa.[38]

> When I drink, it is because I have remembered my pain
> but pain cannot be detected in the eyes
>
> In this world, you have friends when you are not in trouble
> the one who goes and comes with you
> is the one who will betray you.
>
> Everyone drinks when they are contemplative
> so when I drink it is because I have remembered my pain
> but pain cannot be detected in the eyes.

Ironically, ordinary workers under attack by the CPP government were seen as having undue influence on the government by the military regime that overthrew the CPP in 1966. The new National Liberation Council (NLC) singled out *akpeteshie* distillers and retailers as a social group that wielded "unhealthy" political influence in the CPP era.[39] In the mid–1960s, the state orchestrated official propaganda to obliterate *akpeteshie*'s popularity. It hoped that *akpeteshie* would "die a natural death."

---

[36]   Collins, "Ghanaian Highlife," 66–67.

[37]   See Sjaak van der Geest and Nimrod Asante–Darko, "The Political Meaning of Highlife Songs in Ghana," *African Studies Review* 25 (March 1982): 27–35.

[38]   Akwaboa's Guitar Band, "Me nom nsa a" (ARF 1021).

[39]   Ghana, *Report of the Committee Appointed to Enquire into the Manner of Operation of the State Distilleries Corporation* (Accra, 1968), 6–7.

Drink and Gender Conflict: The Tenuousness of Adulthood

Akpeteshie was popular among urban workers because it was cheap. The magnetic pull of *akpeteshie* bars is explained not by *akpeteshie*'s harsh taste, but by its assigned function as an elixir for social and economic problems. Through the several changes in government since Ghana attained independence, the declining lot of rural and urban workers have remained constant.[40] Tony Killick noted that the real wage rate of unskilled workers in Accra, taking even the 1939 rate as a base year, had declined to 89 in December 1963.[41] The food retail price index, which stood at 103 in 1931, had soared to 339 in 1964, reaching 10,063 by April 1978. The index of real wages, on the other hand, declined from 154 in 1931 to 105 in 1964 and 83 in 1974.[42] Even under Ghana's acclaimed economic recovery program (1985–1995), workers have fared terribly. The government's pursuit of fiscal discipline have entailed massive layoffs of urban workers.[43] Paltry wages induced a nonchalant attitude among indigent workers towards money matters. Workers often bought food and drink on credit well above their wages. Creditors and wives waylaid urban workers on payday. Indeed, since their wages could buy very little, workers rationalized that they might as well spend it on drink.

This nonchalance is captured in highlife songs like Kwame Ampadu's "ye we nsa wo se shirt" ("when we are drinking you say shirt"), in which the artiste elevates drink over clothing and his wife's feelings, and "Boozing Day" by the Armed Forces Dance Band.[44]

"Boozing Day" (English translation)
Boozing Day!
I long for a drink!
What shall we do?
Well, we can get a kick out of plenty things.
Lets go to that corner.
There, even sixpence will do.
When you are tipsy in the company of friends,
and you have a woman,
you are the best man in the world.
Your finances get worse, and so what?

---

[40] Continued economic decline in independent Ghana generated several coup d'etats with ambitious military officers claiming to have the remedy to Ghana's economic woes. Constitutionally elected civilian governments were toppled in 1966, 1972, and 1981 with other palace coups in between.

[41] Tony Killick, "Labour: A General Survey," in *A Study of Contemporary Ghana* 1, ed. Walter Birmingham, I. Neustadt, and E. N. Omaboe (Evanston, 1966).

[42] Robertson, *Sharing the Same Bowl*, 36.

[43] See the special reports on Ghana's economic recovery program in *West Africa*, July 31–August 6, 1995; and *Financial Times*, August 4, 1995. Once the model for the World Bank's Structural Adjustment Program, serious doubts have been raised about Ghana's economic turn around. Massive demonstrations in mid-1995 against the high cost of living in Accra and Kumasi, dubbed "Kume Preko" ("You might as well kill me") and "Sieme Preko" ("You might as well bury me") respectively, have deepened the sense of gloom.

[44] Armed Forces Dance Band, "Boozing Day" (Philips PF 005), Ghana Broadcasting Corporation Music Archive.

"Boozing Day" on the surface appeared to be a flippant song about drinking, but on a deeper level it reflected the redefinition of social goals as workers scaled down their expectations. Significantly, songs like "ye we nsa wo se shirt" and "Boozing Day" emphasized male individualism, even in marriage. Highlife songs, usually performed by male artists, "form part of a general cultural complex which upholds male superiority over women."[45]

Such male individualism and nonchalance towards financial issues strained marital and conjugal relations. Drinking by urban workers adversely affected already straitened household budgets. Several of the Ga women Claire Robertson interviewed in Accra in 1972 and 1978 were married to men who drank and beat their wives or spent money needed for the upkeep of their wife and children on alcohol. Oblioko, a fish seller, had married a medical dispenser in her second marriage. He gave good "chop money" but beat her every time he drank, which was often. She was thus forced to divorce him.[46] Kate Mensah's husband even failed to provide enough chop money.

> I was with my husband for three years. He was a goldsmith and already had one wife. Your joy after marriage depends on how your husband treats you. You may not be happy. This man did not provide enough chop money. He was a drunkard and we had no children. For these reasons my parents said I should leave him.[47]

Concert parties (comic opera), composed of working–class men and women, always worked around themes of current social concern. The issue of drinking, irresponsible husbands was taken up as a popular theme.[48]

Highlife songs blamed estranged marriages and drinking husbands on financial difficulties. A. B. Crentsil's "I go pay you tomorrow" highlights the painful embarrassment of an indigent husband and father.

> *Akpeteshie* seller give me quarter [size]
> I go pay you tomorrow
> Akpeteshie seller give me half
> I go pay you moon die [on pay day]
> My wife dey shout for money
> My children de cry for chop [food]
> So so wahala [trouble] in my house
> I go pay you tomorrow.
> I want to forget my troubles
> I want to forget my sorrows.
> Life hard for me
> I go pay you tomorrow.[49]

---

[45] Nimrod Asante–Darko and Sjaak van der Geest, "Male Chauvinism: Men and Women in Ghanaian Highlife Songs," in Oppong, ed., *Female and Male in West Africa*, 254.

[46] Robertson, *Sharing the Same Bowl*, 206.

[47] Portrait of Kate Mensah (1891–1976), in Robertson, *Sharing the Same Bowl*, 226–37.

[48] See, for example, "The Taxi Driver and the Wicked Friend," by Onyinah's Band. Kwame N. Bame, *Come to Laugh: African Traditional Theatre in Ghana* (New York, 1985), 87–88.

[49] A. B. Crentsil, "I Go Pay You Tomorrow," Wazuri Productions, WAZ 101 (1985).

Ghanaian culture encourages a man to endure pain or grief quietly over a drink. Poverty has driven many husbands and fathers to alcohol. The consequences on families have been disastrous.

In 1992, the author made several visits to *akpeteshie* bars in Accra, Sekondi– Takoradi, and Kumasi. Several urban workers stopped by the *akpeteshie* bar as early as 6:00 am to fortify themselves before they sallied off to work. At the "Green Partition," a popular *akpeteshie* bar on the border of Nima and Newtown in Accra, workers streamed in around 6:00 am to take their "APC" before leaving for work.[50] On another occasion in Kumasi, the author went to interview workers at a popular *akpeteshie* bar, "Back Yard VC 10 Bar" as they stopped by from work.[51] He returned at 6:00 am the next morning and encountered, again, most of the workers he had interviewed the evening before, stopping by for their "APC" before heading off to work. Workers had become dependent on *akpeteshie* as a fortifier before going to jobs they often detested. Another dose of *akpeteshie* in the evenings served as a relaxer after work, and for some as a fortifier before they went back home to unhappy marriages.

Drunken husbands often assaulted their wives. A young woman showed the author a scar on her forehead and related how she acquired it. Her husband, who had gone drinking as usual, returned home to find her at home. The husband strangely asked her where *she* had been, and she retorted that she should rather pose that question to the husband. The husband got angry, gave the wife such a beating that she had to jump from the window of their second floor room to safety. Rescuers found her bleeding profusely from the forehead and rushed her to the hospital. The husband materialized at the hospital some hours later—sober. He could not even recall what had started his assault on his wife.[52] At the core of these gender conflicts were money problems, and men vented their frustrations on their wives and children.

Women responded by adopting their own strategies of survival. For bad marriages, divorce was readily resorted to. Some women postponed marriage and/or childbirth until they were financially prepared, and others even dismissed marriage as a viable option.[53] Carmel Dinan concluded, after her interviews with several single women in Accra in the 1970s, that:

> As marriage was understood by their menfolk, it did not meet any of the women's emotional, sexual, social, or economic desires. In their minds marriage as an institution in Ghana was a totally inequitable arrangement: the constraints from their point of view were numerous and the rewards minimal.[54]

Female quest for self-sufficiency sometimes had contradictory effects. Single mothers, stuck with the responsibility of raising their kids, resorted to retailing liquor—

---

[50] In 1992, *akpeteshie* was sold in "standard" measures in Ghana. The bottle of APC analgesic tablets was used for a 50 cedi–measure, the bottle of TCP disinfectant was used for the 100–cedi measure ("quarter"), "half" was a full bottle of coca cola, and "full" (a bottle of beer) sold for 400 cedis.

[51] These interviews were on June 8, 1992.

[52] Personal communication, Kumasi, June 9, 1992.

[53] See Eugenia Date–Bah, "Female and Male Factory Workers in Accra," in Oppong, ed., *Female and Male*, 266–74; and Dinan, "Sugar Daddies and Gold Diggers," 344–66.

[54] Dinan, "Sugar Daddies and Gold Diggers," 352.

the very commodity which tore several families apart. The repercussions divided women themselves.[55]

In a country without a social security system, women in their seventies still struggled to peri-urban villages to purchase palm wine for sale in big cities like Sekondi–Takoradi and Obuasi. Kae Dabi Da has maintained a palm wine bar in Ketan (Sekondi) since 1971, making the journey to Fijai each morning to buy her palm wine.[56] Several of the female *akpeteshie* sellers the author interviewed in Accra, Sekondi–Takoradi, Obuasi, and Kumasi were single and with children. Philippina Baidoo in 1992 was forty–two years old, divorced with two children. She was anxious about the proliferation of *akpeteshie* bars in Fijai, which were cutting into the trade at her bar, "Sailors' Inn."[57] On a larger scale, women had become concerned about their continued financial dependence on unreliable men. Their solution was to work.

In the 1970s and 1980s, women became very visible in their acquisition of wealth. Ghanaian men, firm believers in the principle of accumulation through political appointment, argued that these women were "clients" of politicians and powerful soldiers. The National Redemption Council Regime (1972–1978) in the 1970s earned the epithet, *fa woto begye Golf* ("bring your backside for a VW Golf"), due to the liberal manner in which VW Golf cars were dispensed to mistresses. Indeed, Adu Boahen has remarked that: "Never in the history of this country have we seen so many businesswomen and women contractors whose usual qualifications were simply their attractive figures."[58]

Increasingly, businesswomen became targets of resentment for male urban workers, and highlife songs even advocated that men and women should keep separate budgets. A. B. Crentsil's "Mbesia fo ntonsa" ("Women should also buy drinks") urged men not to buy drinks for women anymore, describing women as parasites.[59] Urban workers who could neither attack the corrupt Ghanaian governments nor their protected mistresses, blamed ordinary market women for the high cost of living and all Ghana's social ills. It was not surprising then that the lower ranks of the army, when they overthrew the Supreme Military Council in 1979, bulldozed the largest market in Accra, Makola No. 1. As one soldier put it: "That will teach Ghanaian women to stop being wicked."[60] Soldiers publicly caned women in a state of nudity without any display of disapproval from the new Armed Forces Revolutionary Council.[61]

Beneath these gender conflicts and hostility was the reality of the tenuousness of adulthood. The economic realities of proletarianization do not mesh with the cultural definitions of success. Urban workers are frustrated by the elusive quest for "big man" status. A significant change in gender struggles in the twentieth century has been the shift from intergenerational conflict (male elders ver-

---

[55] See also, Ilsa Schuster, "Beer, Gender and Class in Lusaka" (paper presented at the African Studies Association, 1988).

[56] AFN : Interview with Madam Kae Dabi Da, Ketan, March 7, 1992.

[57] AFN : Interview with Philippina Baidoo, Fijai, March 7, 1992.

[58] Boahen, *Ghanaian Sphinx*, 13.

[59] A. B. Crentsil, "Mbesia fo ntonsa" (Women should also buy drinks"), PERSCO PR. 001.

[60] Robertson, *Sharing the Same Bowl*, 244. See also, Robertson, "Death of Makola."

[61] Boahen, *Ghanaian Sphinx*, 23.

sus young women) to intragenerational conflict (young men versus young women). Traditional conceptions of production and reproduction among the Akan, Ga–Adangme, and Ewe perceived women as the bearers of children and the custodians of homes. Adulthood for women was achieved in marriage and childbirth. Men were assigned the role of material providers and protectors of families. The socialized role of the man as provider is reflected in a Twi proverb: *obaa yen guan a, obarima na oton* ("when a woman rears a sheep, it is a man that sells it"). The man must be seen visibly as the provider—even if that is far from the truth. In traditional society, nothing is more crushing for a woman than barrenness, or more emasculating for a man than impotency or the inability to provide for his family. Ghana's political and economic decline since independence had drastically revised these expectations. The towns lacked the structured, assured assumption of male adulthood that existed in agrarian society. Land was communally owned in the village, and at the appropriate age, a young man was allotted a piece of land and was assisted by his older kinsmen in the acquisition of a wife. Social failures—in terms of a man's economic inability to sustain himself and his family—were rare. With adulthood threatened, tensions pervaded relations between urban young men and young women. Urban men and women turned to drink. And with general socioeconomic decline, these changes are extending to the villages.

Alcoholism and the Redefinition of Social Identity

It was in this context that alcohol's spiritual connections, indigenous interpretations of the causes of alcoholism, and Ghanaian concepts of health and illness, converged with contemporary socioeconomic conditions to redefine social identity. Popular Ghanaian perspectives on the causes of frequent drunkenness and alcoholism can be captured through popular literature and highlife songs. The loss of loved ones, unemployment, and other sudden turns in fortune were often seen as the immediate factors precipitating habitual drinking.[62] In *When the Heart Decides*[63] and its sequel *Who Killed Lucy?*[64], drink plays a central role in assuaging wounded hearts in disastrous love relationships. That one drinks when one is in pain is a cultural fact in Ghana. This reality is underscored in Cameron Duodu's *The Gab Boys*. The hero, Asamoa, received a visit from his supervisor, who informed him of the death of Asamoa's close friend. Apprehending the stunned look on Asamoa's face, the supervisor, Mr. Akporley, inquired: "You get drink?" Asamoa replied in the negative. He received a lecture from Akporley:

---

[62] Others turn to the independent African churches that have flourished during Ghana's socioeconomic decline. By one count, there were 300 African churches in Ghana by 1970. In The Church of the Messiah at Labadi (Accra), salvation was associated "with divine assistance in solving everyday problems of "unbeez" ("unbusiness" or unemployment), family relations, and health." Mullings, "Religious Change in Labadi," 66 and 75. "Spiritual" churches, emphasizing speaking in tongues, healing, etc., have proliferated in Ghana. Religion has gained a new saliency in everyday life. See Margaret Peil with K. A. Opoku, "The Development and Practice of Religion in an Accra Suburb," *Journal of Religion in Africa*, 24, 3 (1994): 198–227.

[63] E. K. Mickson, *When the Heart Decides* (Accra: Graphic Press, 1966).

[64] E. K. Mickson, *Who Killed Lucy?* (Accra, 1967).

Man always mohst get drink for house. You no know what time trouble dey come. Like you get drink johst now, you go feel alright at once.[65]
A man must always have drink in his house. No one knows when trouble will come. If you had drink in the house just now, you would feel alright at once.

However, the ultimate explanation for alcoholism was placed in the spiritual realm. The envy of family members was often cited as an explanation of why alcoholism was *inflicted* on progressive individuals.[66] This perception is aptly captured by K. Gyasi and his Noble Kings in a highlife song, *Nsa me nnim nom* ("I did not know how to drink").

Me gye me ho a engye (x2)
efie nipa pe ade'a aye me
ama me aye mmobo.

Nsa yi me nnim nom
afei me de aye m'adwuma
me sore na mantwa bi a, na me wu
me sore na mannom bi a, na me wu.[67]

I cannot free myself (x2)
I have been bewitched by a member of my family
It has made me pathetic

I did not know how to drink
now it has become my preoccupation
If I get up and I don't cut a drink I feel faint
If I get up and I don't drink I feel faint.

Margaret Field observed in her ethno–psychiatric study of rural Ghana, "that the *face–saving* role of witchcraft is perhaps its [alcoholism's] most welcome `social function.'"[68]

Ironically, psychiatric practice in colonial and independent Ghana confirmed the view that alcoholism was a spiritual illness. From the colonial times, alcoholics have been treated at mental institutions. Mental disorders were viewed by Ghanaians as spiritual ailments, and the treatment of alcoholics in mental asylums reinforced the association of alcoholism with spiritual causes.[69] It is instructive that the herbs some African healers used in treating "madness" were the same herbs used in treating alcoholism.[70] Mental illness, in the Ghanaian mind, was inflicted on stubborn and disobedient persons by the ancestors or gods. The sudden, terrifying ap-

---

[65] Cameron Duodu, *The Gab Boys* (Suffolk, 1967), 179–80.

[66] The strategy was similar in many documented cases: the confessed witches claimed that they had placed a big empty pot in the stomachs of men, creating an insatiable thirst for drink and, consequently, alcoholism. The Akan believe that only blood relatives can bewitch a person. See, for example, Hans Debrunner, *Witchcraft in Ghana* (Kumasi, 1959), 40.

[67] K. Gyasi and his Noble Kings, "Nsa me nnim nom" ("I did not know how to drink"), Dix EB. 224.

[68] M. J. Field, *Search for Security: An Ethno-Psychiatric Study of Rural Ghana* (Evanston, 1960), 109.

[69] E. B. Forster, "A Historical Survey of Psychiatric Practice in Ghana," *Ghana Medical Journal*, (September 1962): 25–29.

[70] AFN : Interview with George Koranteng, Managing Herbalist of APAAK Herbal Clinic, Accra, July 24, 1992.

pearance of an ancestor or god before an individual was enough to send the person insane. Thus, people often made the comment concerning the insane: *ohuu bibi* (Twi: "he saw something"). A healer, versed in spirituality, was needed to initiate healing through pacifying the offended spirits.[71]

The belief in the spiritual causation of alcoholism reflects Ghanaian concepts of health and illness. The cognitive differences between Western societies and African societies leads to different emphasis in their definitions of health and illness. In the Ghanaian context, health implies well–being of mind, body, and spirit; and this is expressed in a person's ability to perform his social roles or responsibilities to the optimum. A barren woman is not physically unwell, but has failed in her crucial social role as a mother. In the Ghanaian mind, she is ill: *ontumi nwo* (Twi: "she cannot give birth"). Western societies may define health as the absence of disease.[72] Charles Leslie distinguishes "between disease as a biological reality and illness as an experience and social role."[73] Akan society, for example, perceives a man free from disease as ill if he is unable to perform expected socioeconomic roles.

In Ghana's political and economic decline since independence, the inability of an adult to discharge his/her social responsibilities encouraged the inducement of a forced state of "illness" through habitual drinking. Alcoholism then redefines the social identity of the unemployed father or single mother who is incapable of looking after his/her family. The unemployed husband moves from a state of being physically healthy and a social failure to being considered "ill," and his inability to maintain his family excused by his alcoholism, the cause of which is ascribed to witchcraft. The crisis of individual culpability has been resolved.

Not only is "alcoholism" subject to potential manipulation by individuals, the individual may sincerely believe that his misfortune and drinking are the result of witchcraft. Coincidence rarely features in the intentional world of the Akan, Ga–Adangme, and Ewe. Witchcraft explains *why* things happen to individuals at the time it does.[74] A man, whose wife is expecting a baby, loses his job. The man and his community see this development as more than coincidence—the timing is uncanny. The man gravitates to drink in his worries; both he and his community view this further development as firm evidence of spiritual maleficence. Either the man or his family would consult a healer. The man subsequently gains a new job, becomes financially solvent and resumes his social responsibilities. With his worries resolved, he quits drinking. But the man and his community believe that the healer discovered and neutralized the spiritual cause of the man's misfortune and drinking.[75]

---

[71]   AFN : Interview with Kofi Akyerem, Sekondi, August 16, 1994.

[72]   See G. K. Nukunya, P. A. Twumasi, and N. O. Addo, "Attitudes Towards Health and Disease in Ghanaian Society," in Max Assimeng, ed., *Traditional Life, Culture and Literature in Ghana* (London, 1976), 113–36; Kofi Appiah–Kubi, *Man Cures, God Heals: Religion and Medicine among the Akans of Ghana* (Totowa, 1981); and Megan Vaughan, *Curing their Ills: Colonial Power and African Illness* (Stanford, 1991).

[73]   Charles Leslie, "Medical Pluralism in World Perspective," *Social Science and Medicine*, 14B (1980), 193.

[74]   Appiah–Kubi, *Man Cures, God Heals*, 13.

[75]   The author's interview with Okyeame Asonade, interpreter for the god Nyano, underscored this popular belief in spiritual etiology. Okyeame Asonade informed the author that no set cure for alcoholism existed, but the god directs the priest–healer—during divination—to the specific herbs necessary to the cure. AFN: Interview with Okyeame Asonade, Ayigya, June 7, 1992. Evidence points to the possible existence of specific herbs generally used to wean alcoholics off drink, although herbal treatment is accompanied by combating the "evil powers through divination." Appiah–Kubi, *Man Cures, God Heals*, 65.

An increasingly new phenomenon is the visibility of female alcoholism. Commenting on her clientele, Akosua Anorbah, proprietor of an *akpeteshie* bar at Roman Hill (Kumasi), remarked that: "Some of the women also just can't stay away from *akpeteshie*."[76] Medical statistics at the Accra Psychiatric Hospital and the Ashanti Goldfields Corporation Hospital in Obuasi from the mid–1980s underscore this trend.[77] What is striking from the Accra Psychiatric Hospital's statistics is that the majority of these female alcoholics were married traders between the ages of twenty and forty. It could not be ascertained from the statistics whether this drive towards alcohol was a result of marriage problems, financial stress, or both. A second occupational category with a relatively high number of alcoholic cases were nurses. One was found unconscious in a nurses' room in 1990 reeking of alcohol.

The case history of a forty–one year old female nurse illustrates the social pressures of single parenting and migrant life on urban women. In 1990 this nurse was admitted at the Okomfo Anokye Hospital (Kumasi) for "alcohol dependence syndrome" and "grandmal seizures." The nurse's drinking habit developed at Bolgatanga in the 1980s, when she was stationed there as a nurse. It was a habit spawned through socializing activities like parties and dances. She was later transferred to Kumasi. She had had twins in 1975 by a former boyfriend who denied paternity. Her medical problem with alcohol was detected in 1990, when the father of the twins decided to claim the children and take them away. The patient lived under constant fear that her children would be taken away from her. It did not help her situation that she lived in the same house with Krobo migrants who sold *akpeteshie*. In her distress she turned to drink, sometimes buying on credit. She improved remarkably under medical attention.

The social circumstances of two medical cases of alcoholism, including one "remarkable recovery," provide valuable insights into alcoholism and the fluidity of social identity. In case one, a man attempted to jump a freight train and slipped, having his left arm and left foot amputated by the train in the process.[78] He was brought to the Okomfo Anokye Teaching Hospital in Kumasi, reeking of drink. Even while hospitalized, this man would sneak out of the ward and go and drink. On inquiry, the welfare officers found out that this man used to work at the Customs and Excise Preventive Service, and was dismissed for embezzlement. He subsequently embarked on private business and became bankrupt. Married with three children, this man seemed unable to reconcile himself to his reversal of fortune. His family lived in Tema, but he had long disconnected himself from them. He was unwilling to quit drinking or to return to his family. Social failure was too powerful an indictment for this patient. He chose to be a homeless drifter and an alco-

[76] AFN: Interview with Akosua Anorbah, Kumasi, June 8, 1992.

[77] I am grateful to Dr. J. B. Asare of the Accra Psychiatric Hospital and Dr. J. A. Ansah of the AGC Hospital for allowing me to consult their medical records. I also acknowledge my gratitude to the records officers of both hospitals, Messrs Donkor and Andoh at the AGC Hospital and Mr. Daniels at the Accra Psychiatric Hospital. Confidentiality dictates that I do not disclose the identities of patients.

[78] AFN: Interview with Gladys Adjetey Adjei and Rosemond Appiah–Owusu, Social Welfare Officers, Okomfo Anokye Teaching Hospital, Kumasi, June 12, 1992. The author is grateful to these officers for their assistance, and we all agreed to delete names of patients in the interview process in our mutual understanding of the need for anonymity.

holic, rather than remain in the same community with his family as a visibly incapable head of household.

In case two, a man lost his job, took to habitual drinking and ended up at the Okomfo Anokye Teaching Hospital. Under Dr. Yaw Osei, the man began rehabilitation, attending weekly counselling sessions.[79] The man regained his job, decided to work full–time, and informed Dr. Osei of his intention to come for counselling only once a month because of the requirements of his job. He swore he was determined never to drink again. When Dr. Osei followed up six months later, the man had truly stayed away from drink, even gaining a promotion at work. A lucky break at work produced a sober man, emphasizing the importance of social factors and inner strength in explaining alcoholism and recovery from alcoholism. More important, probably, is the cultural absence of a medical explanation of alcoholism as a disease. Many Ghanaians remain ignorant about the health complications associated with chronic drinking and the medical belief that alcoholics cannot cure themselves. Many, "when told firmly about the causal links, are able to stop drinking immediately without further treatment."[80]

Conclusion

Ghanaian elders often complain that the "youth" of today drink too much. Aside from the elders' sentimental attachment to the "good old days," their observation of rising alcoholism is historically accurate. From the 1970s, medical statistics in Ghanaian hospitals have documented this increase. The lack of similar statistics from the colonial era prevent the establishment of long–term patterns. This chapter has attempted to situate rising alcoholism within the declining political, economic, and social conditions of independent Ghana. Alcoholism was often the result of social disruption rather than its cause. In a country where the status of elderhood is the desired social goal of all, indigence and the inability to meet social obligations is an acute embarrassment. Within southern Ghanaian cultures where drinking and pain are associated and alcoholism assigned a supernatural cause, drink facilitated the redefinition of social identity. The paradox is that those who turned to drink for solace and strength sometimes lost their control over it. Alcohol's symbolic and substantive importance continues to influence the struggle for power and autonomy. For the winners, alcohol has been a prized commodity; ironically, it has also been a consolation prize for the losers.

---

[79] AFN: Interview with Dr. Yaw Osei, Head of Psychiatric Unit, Okomfo Anokye Teaching Hospital, Kumasi, June 10, 1992.

[80] Adomako, "Alcoholism: The African Scene," 44.

Epilogue:
Alcohol, Spirituality, and Power in Ghanaian History

Wo te se ye ton tumi na wo ni sika a, ton wo maame na ko to bi, na wo nya tumi a, wo begye wo maame kwa (Twi).[1]

If you hear that *tumi* ("the ability to produce change") is being sold and you have no money, sell your mother and purchase *tumi* for with your newly acquired *tumi* you shall easily redeem your mother.

Okyeame Owusu Banahene, spokesperson to the Asantehene.

Alcohol provides an important prism for reviewing the social history of Ghana for it expresses perceptions of empowerment and disempowerment. The ritual use of alcohol, and its ability to bridge the gap between the physical and spiritual worlds, is crucial to understanding alcohol's appeal. The belief systems of the peoples of southern Ghana affirmed that success in this physical world could be achieved only through the assiduous cultivation of supernatural forces in the spiritual realm.[2] But alcohol was not the only fluid with the ability to traverse worlds. It shared this fascinating quality with blood and water. The different, and sometimes competing, uses of alcohol, water, and blood were reflected in intergenerational, gender, and class struggles. What was being contested was the very definition of power, a contest accentuated with the introduction of Christianity. Power has been coveted and jealously guarded in the history of southern Ghana. It brought wealth and security.

Control over alcohol meshed with the male ideology that supported gerontocracy, patriarchy, and the state. The ideology of power submerged the equalitarian notions associated with water. Colonial rule redefined the ritual uses of blood through the ban on human sacrifices. In precolonial Ghana, male elders excluded

---

[1]   AFN: Interview with Okyeame Banahene, Kumasi, August 18, 1994.

[2]   Greene, *Gender, Ethnicity, and Social Change*, documents the close connection between spiritual power and secular authority among the Anlo from the seventeenth century on.

women and young men from participating in the ritual and social use of alcohol. The ritual use of alcohol necessitated that its social use be regulated to avoid profanation. But alcohol held multiple meanings because it was simultaneously a cultural artifact, a ritual fluid, a social good, and an economic commodity. European presence, expanding commerce, colonial rule, and missionary activity would liberate alcohol from the rigid parameters of the precolonial era.

In the towns and villages in the late–nineteenth and twentieth centuries, people utilized alcohol in constructing new social identities and in opposing imposed ones. For young men and women, social drinking was an expression of their new independence and their earning power. Drinking places became important social institutions in urban Ghana, and drinking, highlife music, dances, comic opera, film, and sports formed the pillars of an emerging popular culture. Popular culture served not only to interpret the social experience of urban migrants, it also provided much needed jobs for men and women in the colonial economy. When the colonial government opted for indirect rule and support for the chiefs and elders in the ongoing struggle over alcohol, it intensified the intergenerational and gender contests over the uses and meanings of alcohol.

The Convention People's Party became the major beneficiary of the contest over alcohol and popular culture. The nationalist struggle lent a new legitimacy to popular culture as the mirror of the "Ghanaian experience," not just the social experience of the poor. But elite acceptance of popular culture proved to be a brief flirtation. Independence won, the CPP settled down to autocratic rule. The economy declined, precipitated by a sharp drop in the price of cocoa on the world market. Unemployment soared, real wages dropped. Workers became bitter and angry as their earnings fell behind the cost of living. Tension pervaded marriages with straitened finances being the major cause. Fragile marriages broke up, and women were often saddled with the responsibility for the children. The tranquilizing effect of alcohol beckoned to powerless men and women, and clothed them in the illusion of empowerment.

Alcohol, Wealth, Knowledge, and Power

Alcohol's versatility and ubiquitousness in the history of southern Ghana lies in its crucial position at the nexus of principles that influenced social organization: "wealth in people," "wealth in things," and "wealth in knowledge."[3] The concept of wealth in people or rights in persons has been utilized effectively in the anthropological and historical literature for precolonial Africa.[4] As Jane Guyer cogently summarizes:

> It offers a useful descriptive term for the well–appreciated fact that interpersonal dependents of all kinds—wives, children, clients and slaves—

---

[3]   The argument here owes its coherence to a recent article by Jane I. Guyer and Samuel M. Eno Belinga, "Wealth in People as Wealth in Knowledge: Accumulation and Composition in Equatorial Africa," *JAH* 36:1 (1995): 91–120. The parallels between the Equatorial African examples and southern Ghana were instructive.

[4]   See, for examples, S. Miers and I. Kopytoff, eds., *Slavery in Africa: Historical and Anthropological Perspectives* (Madison, 1977); and Joseph C. Miller, *Way of Death: Merchant Capitalism and the Angolan Slave Trade, 1730–1830* (Madison, 1988).

were valued and paid for at considerable expense in material terms in some places they were the pinnacle, and even the unit of measurement of ultimate value.[5]

Scholars of Africa have debated whether this feature of wealth in people is explained by a labor shortage in the face of vast land resources[6] or by cultural peculiarities in African property law.[7] Perhaps, it needs to be noted as a universal fact that the perception that a person's labor could be dissociated from his person is relatively recent.[8]

Wealth in people was also wealth in knowledge, for African cosmologies privilege knowledge about the universe as crucial in the process of accumulation.[9] By increasing his followers, a big man or chief expanded his network of resources, his access to knowledge crucial to the ritual transformations necessary for social existence and success. Herbert concluded, after her examination of rituals and processes of transformation in African societies, that:

> Whether power is conceptualized as *nyama*, its Yoruba component *ase*, or the Rwandan variant of *imaana* [or the Twi equivalent *tumi*], any person who makes exceptional claims on the earth or the forest [mining, farming, hunting] must have great quantities of it to succeed and to survive. . . .[10]

Wealth in people as wealth in knowledge overlapped with wealth in things. People assiduously acquired old forms of wealth like gold and land and incorporated new forms of wealth—Western clothes, furniture, imported liquor—into what Appadurai described as "tournaments of value."[11] Wealth in things could be converted into wealth in people as goods could be redistributed to attract clients. Alcohol was thus tied to accumulation and redistribution.

Alcohol was indispensable in these social processes because it was a ritual fluid, an economic commodity, and a social lubricant. The art of libation, the knowledge of which gods liked what types of liquor, provided access to the deities and the ancestors. The most elevated drink in present day Ghana is schnapps, which is used in ritual but not preferred for social drinking. One cannot pay a courtesy call on a chief or elder without a wrapped bottle of schnapps as a gift. For those who conduct scholarly research in Ghana, the transfer of schnapps in exchange for knowledge from elders is key to the success of their work. Alcohol, as demonstrated in the structure of libation, is a mnemonic device for the storage and cataloguing of information. The elders pour libation to solicit the permission of the ancestors to reveal privileged information to researchers. The act of libation serves as a retrieval system. When it comes to unlocking "traditional" knowledge about the Akan, Ga–Adangme, and Ewe cosmos, billboards all over southern Ghana testify that Schnapps

5   Guyer and Belinga, "Wealth in People," 92.
6   See Joseph Inikori's Introduction in *Forced Migration: The Impact of the Export Slave Trade on African Societies*, ed. Joseph Inikori (London, 1981), 13–60.
7   John Thornton, *Africa and Africans in the Making of the Atlantic World 1400–1680* (Cambridge, 1992), 72–97.
8   Moses I. Finley, "Slavery," in *International Encyclopaedia of the Social Sciences* 14 (1968): 308.
9   Guyer and Belinga, "Wealth in People," 103.
10 Herbert, *Iron, Gender, and Power*, 186–87.
11 Appadurai, "Introduction: Commodities and the Politics of Value," 21.

J. H. Henkes Schnapps billboard at Cape Coast

is indeed the "king of drinks." (See photo above.) Alcohol was thus linked to the acquisition and transmission of knowledge which unlocked potent spiritual power. As a coveted good, alcohol quickly gained economic value and became a store of wealth easily convertible into cash, other goods or people.

Reflections on the Culture of Power in Contemporary Ghana

Perhaps alcohol's enduring legacy in the history of Ghana is due to its connections with spiritual power. Politicians in independent Ghana have not neglected the spiritual dimension of power, and they have nurtured public belief in their unusual powers through their idiosyncrasies. Part of Nkrumah's mystique was associated with his being an Nzema, and the reputation of Nzema people for being versed in powerful witchcraft.

> No one was prepared to say Nkrumah walked on his head at night. But quite a few people were prepared to believe that he had power to make himself invisible, power to disappear when he found himself in danger, and power to be in several places at once.[12]

Indeed, there was a popular belief that Nkrumah communed "periodically with *Mame Wata*, a sea goddess, which gave him privy information about the 'machina-

---

[12]   Hagan, "Nkrumah's Leadership Style," 192.

tions of imperialism.'"[13] A leader has to be spiritually strong in Ghana, and a failed coup attempt is attributed not only to the loyalty of defending soldiers, but also to the spiritual power of the head of state: *wa bin ne ho* (Twi: "he is versed in medicine").

Politicians sought spiritual protection at shrines all over Ghana. Cabinet ministers in the Nkrumah government, and Nkrumah himself, visited the famous Akonedi shrine in Larteh.

> In the course of his trial for treason in October 1963, Mr Tawia Adamafio (former Minister of Information) admitted that he had "sought protection from the Akonedi priest at Larti, after he had received threatening letters . . . there are many mysterious phenomena in Africa which have not yet been discovered."[14]

Knowledge to tap this "mysterious phenomena" was acquired, stored, and transmitted through, among other things, the ritual use of alcohol. Wealth in knowledge has been an important factor in Ghanaian history, for knowledge spelled power. In the epigram at the beginning of this chapter, knowledge and power are synonymous in the concept of *tumi*. The cultural value of knowledge among the Asante justified selling one's mother to acquire it. The loss was temporary, for knowledge was easily transferable into power which would redeem one's mother.[15]

Recent allegations of "occultism" leveled by the vice president of Ghana, K. N. Arkaah, against President Rawlings give food for thought. Concerns about "occultism" in Ghana have been prominent since the summer of 1994, when human blood and skulls were discovered in the hospital premises of Dr. Ram Beckley in Accra. Several Hindu gods and other religious paraphernalia were also found on the premises.[16] General opinion in Ghana has credited Rawlings's political longevity to his supernatural protection. Indeed, the president is believed to have "swallowed a whole live frog on a mountain as part of his spiritual fortification. . . ."[17] The vice president's allegations reportedly followed his refusal to accompany the president to a shrine.[18] Arkaah claimed his Christian faith as his reason for rejecting the appeal to "occultism." Disagreements between the president and his vice president degenerated into fisticuffs at a cabinet meeting on December 28, 1995.

To trace the general impact of Christianity on Ghanaian society is beyond the scope of this book. But certain observations on the parallels between Christianity and indigenous religions in southern Ghana, where alcohol, blood, and water are concerned, are relevant to the culture of power. It was an important coincidence that alcohol, blood, and water had ritual significance in Christianity and the religions of southern Ghana. Wine was used in the sacrament of the holy communion, where it represented the blood of Jesus Christ. Although the use of alcoholic wine

---

[13]   Kwame Arhin, *A View of Kwame Nkrumah 1909–1972* (Accra, 1990), 19.

[14]   *West Africa*, October 19, 1963, as cited in Brokensha, *Social Change in Larteh*, 174.

[15]   The connections between knowledge and power are especially dramatized in chieftaincy or succession disputes. See Michelle Gilbert, "The Cimmerian Darkness of Intrigue: Queen Mothers, Christianity and Truth in Akuapem History," *Journal of Religion in Africa* 23, 1 (1993): 2–43.

[16]   See, for example, *People and Places*, July 28–August 4, 1994.

[17]   See the *Ghanaian Chronicle*, May 8–10, 1995. What is relevant here is not whether Rawlings indeed swallowed a live frog, but the very existence of these rumors.

[18]   *Ghanaian Chronicle*, March 2–5, 1995.

has been devalued in several Christian churches today, wine (as a sacred fluid) and winegrowers were crucial to the definition of community in sixteenth–century Burgundy.[19] Some Ghanaian Christians are quick to point out that Christ's first miracle was to transform water into wine at the wedding at Cana,[20] and note Paul's advise to Timothy to take a little wine to aid his digestion.[21] The symbolic connection between wine and Christ's blood underscores the life–giving qualities of wine and the bonding experience of communicants with Christ through the rite of communion. Cultus and ritual feature prominently in the Akan expression of religion. In his examination of indigenous beliefs and practices that facilitated Akan conversion to Christianity, Williamson commented on the parallels between the devotees of an *obosom* acknowledging allegiance by chewing or drinking the appropriate "medicine" and the rite of communion.[22] Alcohol's spiritual ties were thus not dismissed by Christianity.

The temperance onslaught of the 1920s and, significantly, the advent of "water carrying" prophets elevated the theology of water and subdued the ritual relevance of alcohol in Gold Coast Christianity. Prophetic movements such as the Musama Disco Christo Church and the *Memeneda Gyidifo* (the "Saturday Believers," also known as The Saviour Church) preached a strict teetotalism.[23] Indeed, the *Memeneda Gyidifo* used water instead of wine in the holy communion.[24] Water baptism became the sacred rite of admission to these prophetic churches, and spiritual healing through "holy water" their distinctive badge. But devaluing the use of alcohol in Christian ritual did not minimize its relevance in the culture of accumulation. In 1903, a German missionary noted:

> There are people who earn £10–£60 from their cocoa. This stirs up even the most confirmed lazy bones to plant cocoa—everybody wants money. He who has money is respected and can afford all his heart desires—women, beautiful things, alcoholic drinks.[25]

What the missionary considered to be signs of spiritual decadence were the traditional objects of conspicuous consumption for the powerful. Today, education and high income jobs have multiplied claimants to *abirempon* status.

The ritual use of blood in the Gold Coast was redefined with the colonial imposition as human blood, arguably the most potent type of blood, was abolished through the ban on human sacrifice. Ironically, menstrual blood retained its defiling image in Gold Coast Christianity. As with the old shrines of the gods and ancestors, menstruating women were often forbidden from entering independent African churches.[26] Although the orthodox churches did not officially impose such restrictions, women were discouraged or chose to abstain from holy communion

---

[19]   Mack P. Holt, "Wine, Community and Reformation in Sixteenth–Century Burgundy," *Past and Present* 138 (1993): 58–93.

[20]   John 2:1–11.

[21]   1 Timothy 5:23.

[22]   Williamson, *Akan Religion*, 74.

[23]   Baeta, *Prophetism in Ghana*, Chs. 3 and 4.

[24]   Ibid., 72.

[25]   Debrunner, *History of Christianity in Ghana*, 254.

[26]   Baeta, *Prophetism in Ghana*, 99 and 124.

during menstruation.[27] But the image of blood as a redemptive fluid, especially in its association with the lamb of God (Jesus Christ), remained key in Christian doctrine.[28] In Christian theology, the supreme sacrifice is the crucifixion of Christ. One could actually argue that Christianity is a religion based on sacrifice; the sacrifice of a human life. In Akan culture, the lamb or sheep was the quintessential sacrificial animal. The Musama Disco Christo Church retained the use of the sheep as a sacrificial animal in its rituals.[29] Hence, the ritual significance of the blood of sheep and humans in indigenous religions received confirmation in the Old Testament and in Christ's sacrifice in the New Testament.

The parallel importance of alcohol, water, and blood in Christianity and indigenous African religions reinforced their value as fluids that facilitated communion between the physical and spiritual worlds. Not only has the culture of power remained intact in southern Ghana, it seemed to have influenced the activities of Christian churches, especially the prophetic ones. Power was exhibited in unusual feats: the "fearful" and the "wonderful" in Michelle Gilbert's terminology.[30] An area of tension between the orthodox churches and the prophetic churches revolves around the role of "spiritual healing." Although the orthodox churches prioritize teaching over healing, some orthodox Christians, such as the Methodist catechist Samuel Yankson, achieved fame in Gomoa Dunkwa in the early–twentieth century as a spiritually gifted person.

> He was a divine healer who, apart from curing many illnesses by supernatural means, also performed other miracles. On one occasion, when a heavy forest tree was about to fall on some huts in a village, Nyankson stopped it from coming down completely by merely placing his walking-stick under it. The villagers were thereby enabled to clear the huts; but even when the tree finally came to the ground, it did not fall on the huts, but in an open space nearby, although this had not been in the original direction of the fall of the tree. Also Prophet Yankson, by prayer, caused the body of a youth who had been drowned in the Offin River to come up after the bereaved family had searched for it five days but in vain.[31]

The reluctance of Orthodox churches to indulge in or approve of spiritual healing has raised questions over the source of this power that enables Christian "prophets" to perform wonderful feats. Nigerian Christians were traumatized by the apparent inability of the Christian churches to provide healing during the 1918 influenza pandemic. "Are these churches" queried Ade Aina, one of the founders of the Aladura Church?[32]

But the source and nature of the power used in Christian miracles in Ghana is itself, sometimes, disputed. A prophetic church in Tesano (Accra), called "Power," has enjoyed immense popularity in the 1990s. Its leader publicly promised spiritual assistance for people with marriage problems, cases of infertility, and those

---

27   Williamson, *Akan Religion*, 74.

28   See, for examples, Matthew 26:28; Mark 14:24; and Hebrews 9:12–14.

29   Baeta, *Prophetism in Ghana*, 52.

30   Michelle Gilbert, "Sources of Power in Akuropon–Akuapem: Ambiguity in Classification," in Arens and Karp, eds., *Creativity of Power*, 60.

31   Baeta, *Prophetism in Ghana*, 29.

32   "A Theology of Water," in Turner, *Religious Innovation*, 229.

who needed visas to travel abroad. Apparently, the founder of "Power" was originally an *odunsini* (herbalist and healer), who founded the church as an investment with a loan from a manager of the Social Security Bank. The proceeds from the church were supposed to be split between the founder and the bank manager. This arrangement became public in Tesano when the bank manager lost his job through an internal audit, and the pastor of "Power" refused to honor the financial arrangement.[33] Such incidents have created the impression that spiritual churches are really small businesses, and their founders establish these churches as potentially lucrative investments.[34]

Perhaps such incidents help to explain the cynicism (and professional interest?) of *odunsini* Kofi Akyerem of Sekondi, where wonder–working Christian prophets are concerned. Kofi Akyerem's argument was simple but insightful. Though not phrased in Christian theology, it touched on the nexus of grace, works, faith, and healing. He used Mami Wata (a sea goddess) as an example.[35]

> Mami Wata has no power to help humans. God created her to live in the sea; God created humans to live on land [*asase*]. There should be no interaction. Before you call Mami Wata, you use white calico, incense, candle, then you need the Sixth and Seventh books of Moses, for the Europeans have noticed that that is her special prayer. That attracts the attention of Mami Wata, and she proceeds to find out who is calling her. She comes surrounded by a ball of fire. She comes to stand on the white calico that you put out on the beach. If you flee, she will strike you with madness. After you deliberate with her, you use the Sixth and Seventh Books of Moses to return her to the sea. . . . Her requirements are purity. Since humans are not pure, Mami Wata's power is rendered ineffective.[36]

Kofi Akyerem believed most Christian prophets had tapped into non–Christian powers.[37] In his opinion, healing is based not only on faith but also on personal purity. It is not in the nature of humans to aspire to or to achieve purity. This remark echoes the absence of a concept of original sin in indigenous religions in Ghana and the dismissal of spiritual perfection as an attainable human goal.

Financial difficulties, fragile marriages, infertility, and other health problems, have intensified the search for spiritual succor and relief in Ghana. Miracle working prophets attract needy people and prophetic movements have boomed in the past two decades. This trend has heightened the disbelief in coincidence, and spiritual causes are sought in all developments. In Ghanaian society, things seldom happen by coincidence.

The implications for the culture and exercise of power are profound. Political quiescence has become a feature of Ghanaian politics, especially in the last two

---

[33]   Personal communication from Ruth Osebre, February 16, 1996.

[34]   Mullings, "Religious Change," 80–81.

[35]   On *Mami Wata* in African spirituality, see John Henry Drewal, "Performing the Other: Mami Wata Worship in West Africa," *Drama Review* 118 (1988): 38–45; John Henry Drewal, "Interpretation, Invention, and Representation in the Worship of Mami Water," *Journal of Folklore Research* 25, 1–2 (1988): 101–39; and Kathleen O'Brien Wicker, "*Mami Water* in African Religion and Spirituality," in *African Spirituality*, ed. Jacob K. Olupona and Charles H. Long (forthcoming).

[36]   AFN: Interview with Kofi Akyerem, Kweikuma (Sekondi), August 16, 1994.

[37]   In the Akuapem town of Akropong, even Christians retained their belief in the efficacy of *abosom* (deities) and *suman* (charms and talismans). Gilbert, "Sources of Power in Akuropon–Akuapem," 61.

decades. The reality of military rule is only a partial explanation, and deeper questions need to be raised about the general retreat from political participation. The abuse of power is tolerated in contemporary Ghana, as people wait passively for someone more knowledgeable and more powerful to redeem them. This belief is underscored in popular highlife songs like Nana Kwame Ampadu's "Obiara wo dee etumi no" ("every power is subject to a superior force").[38] The culture and politics of power are aptly summed up in Ampadu's words: *dee obebowo mmaye a, wo se obi ntumi wo* ("you consider yourself invincible until a superior force arrives"). In Ghanaian cultures, claimants to power have always been numerous. The epicenter of power thus shifts continuously. The reality, as Arens and Karp point out, is that "power does not emanate from a single source and social formations are composed of centers and epicenters of power in dynamic relationship with one another."[39] The centers and epicenters of power in Ghana are rooted in the fusion of the secular and sacred worlds. This fusion has also meant that the material world has been incapable of explaining the totality of human experience. It followed that humans, even powerful politicians, could not monopolize power. The dynamics of power have always spawned challengers. Political quiescence and political hope are thus two sides of the same cultural coin.

---

[38] Released in 1978.

[39] Arens and Karp, "Introduction," *Creativity of Power*, xvi.

Bibliography

I. ARCHIVES

Ghana

Accra Psychiatric Hospital
Admission Records
Ashanti Goldfields Corporation (Obuasi)
Medical Records of the Mine's Hospital
Bokoor Music Archives (Accra)
Collection on Ghanaian Highlife Music
Ghana Broadcasting Corporation (Accra)
Music and Film Archives
National Archives of Ghana
Accra, Cape Coast, Sekondi and Kumasi depositories
Okomfo Anokye Teaching Hospital (Kumasi)
Medical Records.

England

Institute of Commonwealth Studies Library (London)
Collection on Alcohol in Africa
National Sound Archives (Kensington)
Collection on Ghanaian Highlife Music
Public Records Office (Kew)
CO 554 and CO 96 Series
Rhodes House Library (Oxford University)
J. B. Kirk Private Papers
A. F. L. Wilkinson Private Papers
Charles Harper Private Papers
C. H. Imray Memoirs
University of London (SOAS)
Wesleyan Methodist Missionary Archives

United States

Moorland-Spingarn Research Library, Howard University (Washington, D.C.)
Dabu Gizenga Collection on Kwame Nkrumah
Kwame Nkrumah Private Papers

II. SERIALS

African Times
Asantesem: The Asante Collective Bibliography Project Bulletin
Ashanti Pioneer
Ashanti Times
Co-op Distillers News
Daily Graphic
Evening News
Financial Times
Gold Coast Chronicle
Gold Coast Independent
Gold Coast Leader
Gold Coast Observer
Gold Coast Times
Mirror
People and Places
Spectator Daily
West Africa

III. PUBLISHED PRIMARY AND SECONDARY WORKS

Acquah, I. *Accra Survey*. London: University of London Press, 1958.

Adomako, C. C. "Alcoholism: The African Scene." *Annals of the New York Academy of Sciences* 273 (1976): 39–46.

Afrifah, Kofi. "The Impact of Christianity on Akyem Abuakwa Society, 1852–1887." *Transactions of the Historical Society of Ghana* 16, 1 (1975): 67–86.

Agovi, Kofi E. "The Political Relevance of Ghanaian Highlife Songs since 1957." *Research in African Literatures* 20, 2 (1989): 194–201.

Aidoo, Agnes A. "The Asante Succession Crisis 1883–1888." *Transactions of the Historical Society of Ghana* 13, 2 (1972): 163–80.

Akrofi, C. A. *Twi Mmebusem: Twi Proverbs*. Accra: Waterville Publishing House, n.d.

Akyeampong, Emmanuel K. "The State and Alcohol Rvenues: Promoting `Economic Development' in Gold Coast/Ghana." *Histoire Sociale/Social History* 27, 3 (1994): 393–411.

———. "Alcoholism in Ghana: A Socio-Cultural Exploration." *Culture, Medicine and Psychiatry* 19, 2 (1995): 261–80.

Akyeampong, Emmanuel, and Pashington Obeng. "Spirituality, Gender and Power in Asante History." *International Journal of African Historical Studies* 28, 3 (1995), 481–508.

Akyeampong, Emmanuel. "What's in a Drink? Class Struggle, Popular Culture and the Politics of *Akpeteshie* (Local Gin) in Ghana, 1930–1967." *Journal of African History* 37, 2 (1996).

Allen, Marcus. *The Gold Coast*. London: Hodder and Stoughton, 1874.

Allman, Jean M. "The Youngmen and the Porcupine: Class, Nationalism and Asante's Struggle for Self-Determination, 1954-1957." *Journal of African History* 31 (1990): 263–79.

———. "Of `Spinsters,' `Concubines' and 'Wicked Women': Reflections on Gender and Social Change in Asante." *Gender and History* 3, 2 (1991): 176–89.

———. *The Quills of the Porcupine: Asante Nationalism in an Emergent Ghana*. Madison: University of Wisconsin Press, 1993.

———. "Making Mothers: Missionaries, Medical Officers and Women's Work in Colonial Asante, 1924–1945." *History Workshop* 38 (Autumn 1994), 23–47.

Ambler, Charles H. "Alcohol and Disorder in Precolonial Africa." Boston: Boston University African Studies Center, Working Paper No. 126, 1987.

———."Alcohol, Racial Segregation and Popular Politics in Northern Rhodesia." *Journal of African History* 31, 2 (1990): 295–313.

————. "Drunks, Brewers and Chiefs: Alcohol Regulation in Colonial Kenya, 1900–1939." In *Drinking: Behavior and Belief in Modern History*, ed. Robin Room and Susanna Barrows. Berkeley: University of California Press, 1991.

Amenumey, D. E. K. *The Ewe in Pre-Colonial Times*. Accra: Sedco Publishing Limited, 1986.

Appadurai, Arjun. "Introduction: Commodities and the Politics of Value." In *The Social Life of Things: Commodities in Cultural Perspective*, ed. A. Appadurai. New York: Cambridge University Press, 1986.

Appadurai, Arjun, ed. *The Social Life of Things: Commodities in Cultural Perspective*. New York: Cambridge University Press, 1986.

Appiah-Kubi, Kofi. *Man Cures, God Heals: Religion and Medicine among the Akans of Ghana*. Totowa: Allanheld, 1981.

Apter, David E. *Ghana In Transition*. Princeton: Princeton University Press, 1972.

Arden-Clarke, Charles. "Eight Years of Transition in Ghana." *African Affairs* 57 (1958): 29–37

Arens, W., and Ivan Karp. *Creativity of Power: Cosmology and Action in African Societies*. Washington, D.C.: Smithsonian Institution Press, 1989.

Arhin, Kwame. "Rank and Class among the Asante and Fante in the Nineteenth Century." *Africa* 53:1 (1983): 2–22.

————. "Peasants in 19th-Century Asante." *Current Anthropology* 24, 4 (1983): 471–79.

————. "A Note on the Asante Akonkofo: A Non-Literate Sub-Elite, 1900-1930." *Africa* 56, 1 (1986): 25–31.

————. ed. *The Life and Work of Kwame Nkrumah*. Accra: Sedco Publishing Limited, 1991.

————. *A View of Kwame Nkrumah 1909–1972*. Accra: Sedco Publishing Limited, 1990.

————. "Monetization and the Asante State." In *Money Matters: Instability, Values and Social Payments in the Modern History of West African Communities.*, ed. Jane I. Guyer. Portsmouth, NH: Heinemann, 1995.

————. "The Political Economy of a Princely City: The Economy of Kumasi in the Nineteenth Century." *Research* Review Supplement 5 (1993): 16–36.

Arhin, Kwame, and K. Afari-Gyan, eds. *The City of Kumasi*. Legon: Institute of African Studies, 1992.

Armah, Ayi Kwei. *The Beautyful Ones Are Not Yet Born*. London: Heinemann, 1969.

Arnstein, Walter L. *Britain Yesterday and Today*. Lexington: D. C. Heath, 1988.

Asante–Darko, Nimrod, and Sjaak van der Geest, "Male Chauvinism: Men and Women in Ghanaian Highlife Songs." In *Female and Male in West Africa*, ed. Christine Oppong, 254. London: Allen and Unwin, 1983.

Assimeng, Max, ed. *Traditional Life, Culture and Literature in Ghana*. London: Conch, 1976.

Atkins, Keletso E. *The Moon is Dead! Give Us Our Money! The Cultural Origins of an African Work Ethic, Natal, South Africa, 1843–1900*. Portsmouth, NH: Heinemann, 1993.

Austin, Dennis. *Politics in Ghana 1946-1960*. London: Oxford University Press, 1964.

Austin, Gareth. "Capitalists and Chiefs in the Cocoa Hold-Ups in South Asante, 1927–1938." *International Journal of African Historical Studies* 21, 1 (1988): 63–95.

————. "Human Pawning in Asante, 1800–1950: Markets and Coercion, Gender and Cocoa." In *Pawnship in Africa: Debt Bondage in Historical Perspective*, ed. Toyin Falola and Paul Lovejoy. Boulder: Westview Press, 1994.

Awoonor, Kofi. *This Earth My Brother*. London: Heinemann, 1971.

Baeta, C. G. *Prophetism in Ghana: A Study of Some 'Spiritual' Churches*. London: SCM Press Ltd., 1962.

Bame, Kwame N. *Come to Laugh: African Traditional Theatre in Ghana*. New York: Barber Press, 1985.

Barrows, Susanna, and Robin Room, eds. *Drinking: Behavior and Belief in Modern History*. Berkeley: University of California Press, 1991.

Birmingham, David. "Carnival at Luanda." *Journal of African History* 29, 3 (1988): 93–103.

Birmingham, Walter, I. Neustadt, and E. N. Omaboe. *A Study of Contemporary Ghana.* Vol 1. Evanston: Northwestern University Press, 1966.

Bleek, Wolf. "Did the Akan Resort to Abortion in Pre-Colonial Ghana?" *Africa* 60, 1 (1990): 121–31.

Boahen, Adu A. *Ghana: Evolution and Change in the Nineteenth and Twentieth Centuries.* London: Longman, 1975.

———. *The Ghanaian Sphinx: Reflections on the Contemporary History of Ghana 1972–1987.* Accra: Ghana Academy of Arts and Sciences, 1989.

———. "Politics and Nationalism in West Africa, 1919–1935." In *General History of Africa* Vol. 7, ed. A. Adu Boahen. Berkeley: University of California Press, 1990.

———. "The State and Cultures of the Lower Guinean Coast." In *General History of Africa* Vol. 5, ed. B. A. Ogot. Berkeley: University of California Press, 1992.

———, ed. *General History of Africa: VII Africa Under Colonial Domination 1880–1935*, abridged ed. Berkeley: University of California Press, 1990.

Bond, George, Walton Johnson, and Sheila S. Walkers, eds. *African Christianity: Patterns of Religious Continuity.* London and New York: Academic Press, 1979.

Bosman, W. *A New and Accurate Description of the Coast of Guinea, Divided into the Gold, the Slave, and the Ivory Coasts.* London: J. Knapton, 1705.

Bowdich, Thomas Edward. *Mission from Cape Coast Castle to Ashantee*, 3rd ed. London: Frank Cass, 1966.

Bradford, Helen. "'We Are Now Men': Women's Beer Protests in the Natal Countryside, 1929." In *Class, Community and Conflict: South African Perspectives*, ed. by Belinda Bozzoli. Johannesburg: Ravan Press, 1987.

Bradford, Helen. "'We Women Will Show Them': Beer Protests in the Natal Countryside, 1929." In *Liquor and Labor in Southern Africa*, ed. Jonathan Crush and Charles Ambler. Athens: Ohio University Press, 1992.

Breidenbach, S. "Colour Symbolism and Ideology in a Ghanaian Healing Movement." *Africa* 46, 2 (1976): 137–45.

Brokensha, David. *Social Change at Larteh, Ghana.* Oxford: Clarendon Press, 1966.

Brooks, George E. "The *Signares* of Saint-Louis and Goree: Women Entrepreneurs in Eighteenth-Century Senegal." In *Women in Africa: Studies in Social and Economic Change*, ed. Nancy J. Hafkin and Edna G. Bay. Stanford: Stanford University Press, 1976.

Brooks, George E. *Landlords and Strangers: Ecology, Society, and Trade in Western Africa, 1000–1630.* Boulder: Westview Press, 1993.

Buckley, Thomas and Alma Gottlieb, eds. *Blood Magic: The Anthropology of Menstruation.* Berkeley: University of California Press, 1988.

Buell, Raymond Leslie. *The Native Problem in Africa.* Vol 2. New York: Macmillan, 1928.

Busia, K. A. "Ashanti." In *African Worlds*, ed. Daryll Forde. London: Oxford University Press, 1954.

———. *The Position of the Chief in the Modern Political System of Ashanti: A Study of the Influence of Contemporary Social Changes on Ashanti Political Institutions.* London: Frank Cass, 1968.

———. *Report on the Social Survey of Sekondi-Takoradi.* London: Crown Agents, 1950.

Caetano, Raul. "Hispanic Drinking in the U.S.: Thinking in New Directions." *British Journal of Addiction* 85 (1990): 1231–36.

Caldwell, J. C. "Determinants of Rural-Urban Migration in Ghana." *Population Studies* 21 (1968): 361–77.

Cardinall, A. W. *The Gold Coast, 1931.* Accra: Government Printer, 1931.

Casely-Hayford, Augustus, and Richard Rathbone. "Politics, Families and Freemasonry in Colonial Gold Coast." In *People and Empires in African History: Essays in Memory of Michael Crowder*, ed. J. F. Ade Ajayi and J. D. Y. Peel. London: Longman, 1992.

Casely Hayford, J. E. *Ethiopia Unbound.* London: C. M. Phillips, 1911.

———. *Gold Coast Native Institutions.* London: Sweet and Maxwell, 1903.

Chazan, Naomi, and Deborah Pellow. *Ghana: Coping With Uncertainty.* Colorado: Westview Press, 1986.

Chernela, Janet M. "Rethinking History in the Northwest Amazon: Myth, Narrative, Structure, and History in an Arapaco Narrative." In *Rethinking History and Myth: Indigenous South American Perspectives on the Past,* ed. Jonathan D. Hill. Chicago: University of Chicago Press, 1989.

Chukwukere, I. "Perspectives on the *Asafo* Institution in Southern Ghana." *Journal of African Studies* 7, 1 (1980): 39–47.

Clark, Gracia. *Onions Are My Husband: Survival and Accumulation by West African Market Women.* Chicago: University of Chicago Press, 1994.

Clayton, Anthony, and David Killingray. *Khaki and Blue: Military and Police in British Colonial Africa.* Athens: Ohio University Center for International Studies, 1989.

Collins, E. J. "Comic Opera in Ghana." *African Arts* 9, 2 (1976): 50–57.

———. "Ghanaian Highlife." *African Arts* 10, 1 (1976): 62–68.

———. *West African Pop Roots.* Philadelphia: Temple University Press, 1992.

Colson, Elizabeth, and Thayer Scudder. *For Prayer and Profit: The Ritual, Economic, and Social Importance of Beer in the Gwembe District, Zambia, 1950–1982.* Stanford: Stanford University Press, 1988.

Cooper, Frederick, ed. *Struggle for the City: Migrant Labor, Capital and the State in Urban Africa.* Beverly Hills: Sage Publications, 1983.

Coplan, David. "Go to My Town, Cape Coast! The Social History of Ghanaian Highlife." In *Eight Urban Musical Cultures,* ed. Brunno Nettl. Urbana: University of Illinois Press, 1978.

Crisp, Jeff. *The Story of an African Working Class: Ghanaian Miners Struggles, 1870-1980.* London: Zed, 1984.

Cruickshank, Brodie. *Eighteen Years on the Gold Coast of Africa.* 2 vols. London: Hurst and Blackett, 1853.

Crush, Jonathan, and Charles H. Ambler, eds. *Liquor and Labor in Southern Africa.* Athens: Ohio University Press, 1992.

Curto, Jose C. "Alcohol in Africa: A Preliminary Compilation of the Post-1875 Literature." *A Current Bibliography on African Affairs* 21, 1 (1989): 3–31.

Daaku, K. Y. *Trade and Politics on the Gold Coast, 1600–1720.* Oxford: Oxford University Press, 1970.

Dakubu Kropp, M. E. "Creating Unity: The Context of Speaking Prose and Poetry in Ga." *Anthropos* 82 (1987).

Danquah, F. Introduction to *Gold Coast Men of Affairs,* by Magnus J. Sampson. London: Dawsons, 1969.

Date–Bah, Eugenia. "Female and Male Factory Workers in Accra." In *Female and Male in West Africa,* ed. Christine Oppong, 266–74. London: Allen and Unwin, 1983.

Datta, Ansu. "The Fante Asafo: A Re-Examination." *Africa* 42, 4 (1972): 305–15.

de Heusch, Luc. *The Drunken King or the Origin of the State.* Trans. Roy Willis. Bloomington: Indiana University Press, 1982.

de Marees, Pieter. *Description and Historical Account of the Gold Kingdom of Guinea.* Trans. and ed. Albert van Dantzig and Adam Jones. Oxford: Oxford University Press, 1987.

Debrunner, Hans. *Witchcraft in Ghana.* Kumasi: Presbyterian Book Depot, 1959.

———. *A History of Christianity in Ghana.* Accra: Waterville, 1967.

———. *The Story of Sampson Opong.* Accra: Waterville, 1965.

Diduk, Susan. "European Alcohol, History, and the State in Cameroon." *African Studies Review* 36, 1 (1993): 1–42.

Dinan, Carmel. "Sugar Daddies and Gold-Diggers: The White Collar Single Women in Accra." In *Female and Male in West Africa,* ed. Christine Oppong. London: Allen and Unwin, 1983.

Dingle, A. E. *The Campaign for Prohibition in Victorian England, the United Kingdom Alliance, 1872–1895.* London: Croom Helm, 1980.

Douglas, Mary, ed. *Constructive Drinking: Perspectives on Drink from Anthropology.* Cambridge: Cambridge University Press, 1987.

Douglas, Mary. *Purity and Danger: An Analysis of the Concepts of Pollution and Taboo.* London: Routledge, 1966.

Douglas, Mary, and Baron Isherwood. *The World of Goods.* New York: Basic Books, 1981.

Drewal, John Henry. "Performing the Other: Mami Wata Worship in West Africa." *Drama Review* 118 (1988): 38–45.

———. "Interpretation, Invention, and Representation in the Worship of Mami Water." *Journal of Folklore Research* 25, 1–2 (1988): 101–39.

Dummett, Raymond. "The Social Impact of the European Liquor Trade on the Akan of Ghana (Gold Coast and Asante), 1875–1910." *Journal of Interdisciplinary History* 5 (1974): 69–101.

Duodu, Cameron. *The Gab Boys.* Suffolk: Chaucer Press, 1967.

Dupuis, Joseph. *Journal of a Residence in Ashantee.* 2nd ed. London: Frank Cass, 1966.

Eisenstadt, S. N., ed. *Max Weber on Charisma and Institution Building.* Chicago: University of Chicago Press, 1968.

Ellis, A. B. *The Tshi-Speaking Peoples of the Gold Coast of West Africa.* Oosterhout: Anthopological Publications, 1887.

Fabian, Johannes. "Popular Culture in Africa: Findings and Conjectures." *Africa* 48, 4 (1978): 315–34.

Fashole-Luke, Edward, *et al.*, eds. *Christianity in Independent Africa.* Bloomington: Indiana University Press, 1978.

Feinberg, H. M. "Who are the Elmina?" *Ghana Notes and Queries* 11 (June 1970): 20–26.

Field, M. J. *Religion and Medicine of the Ga People.* London: Oxford University Press, 1937.

———. *Search for Security: An Ethno-Psychiatric Study of Rural Ghana.* Evanston; Northwestern University Press, 1960.

———. *Social Organization of the Ga People.* London: Crown Agents, 1940.

———. *Akim-Kotoku.* Westport: Negro Universities Press, 1970.

Field, Peter B. "A New Cross-Cultural Study of Drunkenness." In *Society, Culture and Drinking Patterns*, ed. D. Pitman and C. Snyder. New York: John Wiley and Sons, 1962.

Finley, Moses I. "Slavery." In *International Encyclopaedia of the Social Sciences* 14 (1968): 307–13.

Fitch, Bob and Mary Oppenheimer. *Ghana: End of an Illusion.* New York: Monthly Review Press, 1966.

Forster, E. B. "A Historical Survey of Psychiatric Practice in Ghana." *Ghana Medical Journal* (September 1962): 25–29.

Fortes, Meyer. "Ritual and Office." In *Essays in the Ritual of Social Relations*, ed. Max Gluckman. Manchester: Manchester University Press, 1962.

Freeman, Thomas Birch. *Journal of Various Visits to the Kingdoms of Ashanti, Aku and Dahomi in Western Africa* [1844]. London: Frank Cass, 1968.

Frick, John W. "'He Drank from the Poisoned Cup': Theatre, Culture, and Temperance in Antebellum America." *Journal of American Drama and Theatre* 2, 2 (1992): 21–41.

Frimpong-Ansah, Jonathan H. *The Vampire State in Africa: The Political Economy of Decline in Ghana.* London: James Currey, 1992.

Gerritsen, Rolf. "The Evolution of the Ghana Trades Union Congress under the Convention People's Party: Towards a Reinterpretation." *Transactions of the Historical Society of Ghana* 13, 2 (1972): 229-44.

Gilbert, Michelle. "The Sudden Death of a Millionaire: Conversion and Consensus in a Ghanaian Kingdom." *Africa* 58, 3 (1988): 291–313.

———. "Sources of Power in Akuropon–Akuapem: Ambiguity in Classification." In *Creativity of Power: Cosmology and Action in African Societies*, ed. W. Arens and Ivan Karp, 60. Washington: Smithsonian Institution Press, 1989.

————. "The Cimmerian Darkness of Intrigue: Queen Mothers, Christianity and Truth in Akuapem History." *Journal of Religion in Africa* 23, 1 (1993): 2–43.

Ghana Notes and Queries 9 (1966). Special issue on the Akan of Ghana.

Glassman, Jonathon. *Feasts and Riots: Revelry, Rebellion and Popular Consciousness on the Swahili Coast, 1856–1888.* Portsmouth, NH: Heinemann, 1995.

Gocking, Roger. "British Justice and the Native Tribunals of the Southern Gold Coast Colony." *Journal of African History* 34, 1 (1993): 93–113.

————. "Competing Systems of Inheritance before the British Courts of the Gold Coast." *International Journal of African Historical Studies* 23, 4 (1990): 601–18.

————. "Indirect Rule in the Gold Coast: Competition for Office and the Invention of Tradition." *Canadian Journal of African Studies* 28, 3 (1994): 421–45.

Greene, Sandra E. *Gender, Ethnicity, and Social Change on the Upper Slave Coast: A History of the Anlo-Ewe.* Portsmouth, NH: Heinemann, 1996.

Grier, Beverly. "Pawns, Porters, and Petty Traders: Women in the Transition to Cash Crop Agriculture in Colonial Ghana." *Signs* 17, 2 (1992): 304–28.

Gusfield, Joseph R. *Symbolic Crusade: Status Politics and the American Temperance Movement.* Urbana: University of Illinois Press, 1972.

Guyer, Jane I., ed. *Money Matters: Instability, Values and Social Payments in the Modern History of West African Communities.* Portsmouth, NH: Heinemann, 1995.

Guyer, Jane I., and Samuel M. Eno Belinga. "Wealth In People as Wealth in Knowledge: Accumulation and Composition in Equatorial Africa." *Journal of African History* 36, 1 (1995): 91–120.

Gyekye, Kwame. *An Essay on African Philosophical Thought: The Akan Conceptual Scheme.* New York: Cambridge University Press, 1987.

Hafkin, Nancy J., and Edna G. Bay, eds. *Women in Africa: Studies in Social and Economic Change.* Stanford: Stanford University Press, 1976.

Hagan, George P. "Nkrumah's Leadership Style—An Assessment from a Cultural Perspective." In *The Life and Work of Kwame Nkrumah*, ed. Kwame Arhin. Accra: Sedco Publishing Limited, 1991.

Hair, P. E. H., Adam Jones, and Robin Law, eds., *Barbot on Guinea: The Writings of Jean Barbot on West Africa 1678–1712 II.* London: The Hakluyt Society, 1992.

Harries, Patrick. *Work, Culture, and Identity: Migrant Laborers in Mozambique and South Africa, c.1860–1910.* Portsmouth, NH: Heinemann, 1994.

Harrison, Brian. *Drink and the Victorians: The Temperance Question in England, 1815–1872.* Pittsburgh: University of Pittsburgh Press, 1971.

Herbert, Eugenia W. *Iron, Gender, and Power: Rituals of Transformations in African Societies.* Bloomington: Indiana University Press, 1993.

Hill, Polly. *The Migrant Cocoa Farmers of Southern Ghana.* Cambridge: Cambridge University Press, 1963.

Holt, Mack P. "Wine, Community and Reformation in Sixteenth-Century Burgundy." *Past and Present* 138 (1993): 58–93.

Horton, Donald. "The Functions of Alcohol in Primitive Societies: A Cross-Cultural Study." *Quarterly Journal of Studies on Alcohol* 4, 2 (1943): 199–320.

Huber, Hugo. *The Krobo: Traditional Social and Religious Life of a West African People.* St. Augustin: The Anthropos Institute, 1963.

Inikori, Joseph. "Introduction." In *Forced Migration: The Impact of the Export Slave Trade on African Societies*, ed. Joseph Inikori, 13–60. London: Hutchison, 1981.

James, C. L. R. *Nkrumah and the Ghana Revolution.* Westport: Lawrence Hill and Co., 1977.

Jeffries, Richard. *Class, Power and Ideology in Ghana: The Railwaymen of Sekondi.* Cambridge: Cambridge University Press, 1978.

Jonah, Kwesi. "Imperialism, the State and the Indigenization of the Ghanaian Economy 1957-1984." *Africa Development* 10 (1985): 63–99.

Jones, Adam, ed. *Aussereuropäische Frauengeschichte: Probeleme der Forschung*. Pfaffenweiler: Centaurus-Verl.-Ges., 1990.

——. "'My Arse for Akou': A Wartime Ritual of Women on the Nineteenth-Century Gold Coast." *Cahiers d'Etudes Africaines*. 132, 33-4 (1993): 545–66.

Karp, Ivan. "Beer Drinking and Social Experience in an African Society: An Essay in Formal Sociology." In *Explorations in African Systems of Thought.*, ed. Ivan Karp and Charles S. Bird. Bloomington: Indiana University Press, 1980.

Karp, Ivan, and Charles S. Bird, eds. *Explorations in African Systems of Thought*. Bloomington: Indiana University Press, 1980.

Kay, G. B. *The Political Economy of Colonialism in Ghana: A Collection of Documents and Statistics 1900-1960*. Cambridge: Cambridge University Press, 1972.

Kea, Ray. *Settlements, Trade and Polities in the Seventeenth-Century Gold Coast*. Baltimore: Johns Hopkins University Press, 1982.

Killick, Tony. "Labour: A General Survey." In *A Study of Contemporary Ghana*, 1, ed. Walter Birmingham, I. Neustadt, and E. N. Omaboe. Evanston: Northwestern University Press, 1966.

Kilson, Marion. "Libation in Ga Ritual." *Journal of Religion in Africa* 2, 3 (1969): 161–78.

Kimble, D. *Political History of Ghana*. Oxford: Clarendon Press, 1963.

Klausner, Samuel Z. "Sacred and Profane Meanings of Blood and Alcohol." *Journal of Social Psychology* 64 (1964): 27–43.

Konadu, Asare. *The Wizard of Asamang*. Accra: Anowuo, 1988.

Kraus, Jon. "On the Politics of Nationalism and the Social Change in Ghana." *Journal of Modern African Studies* 7 (1969): 107–30.

Kuklick, Henrika. *The Savage Within: The Social History of British Anthropology*. Cambridge: Cambridge University Press, 1991.

La Hausse, Paul. *Brewers, Beerhalls and Boycotts: A History of Liquor in South Africa*. Johannesburg: Ravan Press, 1988.

Ladurie, Emmanuel Le Roy. *Carnival in Romans*. Trans. by Mary Feeney. New York: George Braziller, Inc., 1979.

Lenski, Gerhard. "Power and Privilege." In *Power*, ed. Steven Lukes. New York: New York University Press, 1986.

Leslie, Charles. "Medical Pluralism in World Perspective." *Social Science and Medicine* 14B (1980): 191–95.

Levtzion, N. "Early Nineteenth Century Arabic Manuscripts from Kumase." *Transactions of the Historical Society of Ghana* 8 (1965): 99–119.

Lin, T. Y., and David T. C. Lin. "Alcoholism among the Chinese: Further Observations of a Low-Risk Population." *Culture, Medicine and Psychiatry* 6 (1982): 109–16.

Little, Kenneth. *Women in African Towns*. Cambridge: Cambridge University Press, 1973.

Lorimer, Douglas A. *Colour, Class and the Victorians*. Leicester: Leicester University Press, 1978.

Lovejoy, Paul E. *Caravans of Kola: The Hausa Kola Trade 1700–1900*. Zaria: Ahmadu Bello University Press, 1980.

Lovett, Margot. "Gender Relations, Class Formation, and the Colonial State in Africa." In *Women and the State in Africa*, ed. Jane L. Parpart and Kathleen A. Staudt. Boulder, Colo.: Lynne Rienner, 1989.

Lukes, Steven, ed. *Power*. New York: New York University Press, 1986.

MacAndrew, Craig and Robert Edgerton. *Drunken Comportment: A Social Explanation*. Chicago: Aldine Press, 1969.

Maier, D. J. E. *Priests and Power: The Case of the Dente Shrine in Nineteenth Century Ghana*. Bloomington: Indiana University Press, 1983.

Mancall, Peter C. *Deadly Medicine: Indians and Alcohol in Early Africa*. Ithaca: Cornell University Press, 1995.

Mandelbaum, D. G. "Alcohol and Culture." *Current Anthropology* 6 (1965): 281–93.

Mann, Michael. *The Sources of Social Power. Volume 1: A History of Power from the Beginning to A. D. 1760.* Cambridge: Cambridge University Press, 1986.

Manoukian, Madeline. *Akan and Ga-Adangme Peoples.* London: International African Institute, 1950.

———. *The Ewe-Speaking People of Togoland and the Gold Coast.* London: International African Institute, 1952.

Manuh, Takyiwah. "Women and Their Organization During the Convention Peoples' Party Period." In *Life and Work of Kwame Nkrumah,* ed. Kwame Arhin. Accra: Sedco Publishing Limited, 1991.

———. "Changes in Marriage and Funeral Exchanges among the Asante: A Case Study from Kona, Afigya-Kwabre." In *Money Matters: Instability, Values and Social Payments in the Modern History of West African Communities,* ed. Jane I. Guyer. Portsmouth, NH: Heinemann, 1995.

Martin, Phyllis M. "Contesting Clothes in Colonial Brazzaville." *Journal of African History* 35, 3 (1994): 401–26.

———. *Leisure and Society in Colonial Brazzaville.* Cambridge: Cambridge University Press, 1995.

Mauss, Marcel. *The Gift.* Trans. by Ian Cunnison. New York: W. W. Norton, 1967.

McCaskie, T. C. "Office, Land and Subjects in the History of the Manwere Fekuo of Kumase: An Essay in the Political Economy of the Asante State." *Journal of African History* 21, 2 (1980): 189–208.

———. "State and Society, Marriage and Adultery: Some Considerations Towards a Social History of Pre-Colonial Asante." *Journal of African History* 22, 3 (1981): 477–94.

———. "Anti-Witchcraft Cults in Asante: An Essay in the Social History of an African People." *History in Africa* 8 (1981): 125–54.

———. "People and Animals: Constru(ct)ing the Asante Experience." *Africa.* 6, 2 (1992): 221–44.

———. "Accumulation, Wealth and Belief in Asante History: I To the Close of the Nineteenth Century." *Africa* 53, 1 (1983): 23–43.

———. "Accumulation, Wealth and Belief in Asante History: II The Twentieth Century." *Africa* 56, 1 (1986): 3–23.

———. *State and Society in Pre-Colonial Asante.* Cambridge: Cambridge University Press, 1995.

———. "Konnurokusem: Kinship and Family in the History of the Oyoko Kokoo Dynasty of Kumase." *Journal of African History* 36, 3 (1995).

McFarland, Daniel Miles. *Historical Dictionary of Ghana.* Metuchen: Scarecrow Press, 1985.

McLeod, Malcolm D. *Asante.* London: British Museum Publications, 1981.

———. "The Golden Ax of Asante." *Natural History* 93 (October 1984).

Mickson, E. K. *When the Heart Decides.* Accra: Graphic Press, 1966.

———. *Who Killed Lucy?* Accra: [Graphic Press ?], 1967.

Miers, S., and I. Kopytoff. *Slavery in Africa: Historical and Anthropological Perspectives.* Madison: University of Wisconsin Press, 1977.

Mikell, Gwendolyn. *Cocoa and Chaos in Ghana.* New York: Paragon House, 1989.

———. "The State, the Courts, and `Value': Caught between Matrilineages in Ghana." In *Money Matters: Instability, Values and Social Payments in the Modern History of West African Communities,* ed. Jane I. Guyer. Portsmouth, NH: Heinemann, 1995.

Miller, Joseph C. *Way of Death: Merchant Capitalism and the Angolan Slave Trade, 1730–1830.* Madison: University of Wisconsin Press, 1988.

Mills, Wallace G. "The Roots of African Nationalism in the Cape Colony: Temperance, 1866–1898." *International Journal of African Historical Studies* 13, 2 (1980): 197–213.

Mullings, Leith. "Religious Change and Social Stratification in Labadi: The Church of the Messiah." In *African Christianity: Patterns of Religious Continuity,* ed. George Bond, Walton Johnson, and Sheila S. Walker, 65–88. London: Academic Press, 1979.

Netting, Robert. "Beer as a Locus of Value among the West African Kofyar." *American Anthropologist* 66 (1964): 375–84.

Ninsin, Kwame A. *Political Struggles in Ghana 1967–1981.* Accra: Tornado Publishers, 1985.

Nkrumah, Kwame. *Ghana: An Autobiography.* New York: Thomas Nelson and Sons, 1957.

Nörregård, Georg. *Danish Settlements in West Africa 1658–1850.* Trans. Sigurd Mammen. Boston: Boston University Press, 1966.

Nukunya, G. K. *Kinship and Marriage among the Anlo Ewe.* London: Athlone Press, 1969.

Nukunya, G. K., P. A. Twumasi, and N. O. Addo. "Attitudes Towards Health and Disease in Ghanaian Society." In *Traditional Life, Culture and Literature in Ghana,* ed. Max Assimeng, 113–36. London: Conch, 1976.

Obeng, Ernest. *Ancient Ashanti Chieftaincy.* Tema: Ghana Publishing Corporation, 1968.

Okali, Christine. "Kinship and Cocoa Farming in Ghana." In *Female and Male in West Africa,* ed. Christine Oppong, 169–78. London: Allen and Unwin, 1983.

Okali, Christine. *Cocoa and Kinship in Ghana: The Matrilineal Akan of Ghana.* London: Kegan Paul, 1983.

Okali, Christine, ed. *Female and Male in West Africa.* London: Allen and Unwin, 1983.

Olorunfemi, A. "The Liquor Traffic in British West Africa: The Southern Nigerian Example, 1895-1918." *International Journal of African Historical Studies* 17:2 (1984): 220–42.

Olukoju, Ayodeji. "Prohibition and Paternalism: The State and the Clandestine Liquor Traffic in Northern Nigeria, c. 1889-1918." *International Journal of African Historical Studies* 24, 2 (1991): 349–68.

Olupona, Jacob K., and Charles H. Long, eds. *African Spirituality.* Forthcoming.

Opoku, Kofi A. "Changes within Christianity: The Case of the Musama Disco Christo Church." In *Christanity in Independent Africa,* ed. Edward Fashole-Luke *et al.* Bloomington: Indiana University Press, 1978.

Oppong, Christine, ed. *Female and Male in West Africa.* London: Allen and Unwin, 1983.

Owusu, Maxwell. *Uses and Abuses of Political Power: A Case Study of Continuity and Change in the Politics of Ghana.* Chicago: University of Chicago Press, 1970.

Owusu-Ansah, David. *Islamic Talismanic Tradition in Nineteenth Century Asante.* New York: Edwin Mellen Press, 1991.

Pan, Lynn. *Alcohol in Colonial Africa.* Uppsala: Scandinavian Institute of African Studies, 1975.

Parkin, David J. *Palms, Wine, and Witnesses: Public Spirit and Private Gain in an African Community* [1972]. Prospect Heights: Waveland Press, 1994.

Parpart, Jane L. "'Where Is Your Mother?': Gender, Urban Marriage, and Colonial Discourse on the Zambian Copperbelt, 1925–1945." *International Journal of African Historical Studies* 27, 2 (1994).

Parpart, Jane L., and Kathleen A. Staudt, eds. *Women and the State in Africa.* Boulder: Lynne Rienner, 1989.

Partanen, Juha. *Sociability and Intoxication: Alcohol and Drinking in Kenya, Africa, and the Modern World.* Helsinki: Finnish Foundation for Alcohol Studies, 1991.

Peil, Margaret. *The Ghanaian Factory Worker: Industrial Man in Africa.* Cambridge: Cambridge University Press, 1972.

Peil, Margaret, with K. A. Opoku. "The Development and Practice of Religion in an Accra Suburb." *Journal of Religion in Africa* 24, 3 (1994), 198–227.

Pellow, Deborah, and Naomi Chazan. *Ghana. Coping with Uncertainty.* Boulder: Westview Press, 1986.

Pitman, D., and C. Snyder, eds. *Society, Culture and Drinking Patterns.* New York: John Wiley and Sons, 1962.

Platvoet, J. G. "Cool Shade, Peace and Power." *Journal of Religion in Africa* 15, 3 (1985): 174–99.

Priebe, Richard K., ed., *Ghanaian Literatures.* New York: Greenwood Press, 1988.

Priestley Margaret. *West African Trade and Coastal Society*. London: Oxford University Press, 1969.

Ramseyer, F. A., and J. Kühne. *Four Years in Ashantee*. London: James Nisbet and Co., 1875.

Ranger, Terrence. *Dance and Society in Eastern Africa, 1890–1970: The Beni Ngoma*. London: Heinemann, 1975.

Rathbone, Richard. "Businessmen in Politics: Party Struggle in Ghana, 1949–57." *Journal of Development Studies* 9, 3 (1973): 391–402.

———. *Murder and Politics in Colonial Ghana*. New Haven: Yale University Press, 1993.

Rathbone, Richard, and Jean Marie Allman. "Discussion: The Youngmen and the Porcupine." *Journal of African History* 32, 3 (1991): 333–38.

Rattray, R. S. *Ashanti Proverbs*. Oxford: Clarendon Press, 1916.

———. *Ashanti*. Oxford: Clarendon Press, 1923.

———. *Religion and Art in Ashanti*. Oxford: Clarendon Press, 1927.

———. *Ashanti Law and Constitution*. Oxford: Clarendon Press, 1929.

Reindorf, C. C. *History of Gold Coast and Asante*. Basel: Basel Mission, 1895.

Rhodie, Sam. "The Gold Coast Cocoa Hold-Up of 1930–31." *Transactions of the Historical Society of Ghana* 9 (1968): 105–18.

Ricard, Alain. "The Concert Party as a Genre: The Happy Stars of Lome." *Research in African Literatures* 5, 2 (1974): 165–79.

Rimmer, Douglas. *Staying Poor: Ghana's Political Economy, 1950-1990*. Oxford: Pergamon Press, 1992.

Roberts, Andrew. "The Imperial Mind." In *The Colonial Moment in Africa*, ed. Andrew Roberts. Cambridge: Cambridge University Press, 1990.

Roberts, A. R., ed. *The Colonial Moment in Africa*. Cambridge: Cambridge University Press, 1990.

Roberts, Penelope. "The State and the Regulation of Marriage: Sefwi Wiawso (Ghana), 1900–1940." In *Women, State and Ideology: Studies from Africa and Asia*, ed. Haleh Afshah. London: Macmillan, 1987.

Robertson, Claire. "The Death of Makola and Other Tragedies." *Canadian Journal of African Studies* 17, 3 (1983): 469–95.

———. "Ga Women and Socioeconomic Change in Accra, Ghana." In *Women in Africa*, ed. Nancy J. Hafkin and Edna G. Bay. Stanford: Stanford University Press, 1976.

———. *Sharing the Same Bowl: A Socioeconomic History of Women and Class in Accra, Ghana* [1984]. Ann Arbor: University of Michigan Press, 1990.

Robertson, Claire and Martin A. Klein. *Women and Slavery in Africa*. Madison: University Wisconsin Press, 1983.

Rodney, Walter. "Gold and Slaves on the Gold Coast." *Transactions of the Historical Society of Ghana* 10 (1969): 13–28.

Room, Robin. "Alcohol Problems and the City." *British Journal of Addiction* 85 (1990): 1395–1402.

Sampson, Magnus J. *Gold Coast Men of Affairs*. London: Dawsons, 1969.

Sangree, Walter. "The Social Functions of Beer Drinking in Bantu Tiriki." In *Society, Culture and Drinking Patterns*, ed. by D. Pitman and C. Snyder. New York, 1962.

Sarbah, Mensah John. *Fanti Customary Laws*. London: William Clowes and Sons, 1897.

———. *Fanti National Constitution*, 3rd ed. London: Frank Cass, 1968.

Sarpei, Annorbah James. "A Note on Coastal Elite Contact with Rural Discontent Before the First World War: The 'Good Templars' in Akyem Abuakwa," In *Akyem Abuakwa and the Politics of the Inter-War Period in Ghana*. Basel: Basel African Bibliography, 1975.

Sarpong, Peter. *Girls' Nubility Rites in Ashanti*. Tema: Ghana Publishing Corporation, 1977.

Schleh, P. A. "The Post-War Careers of Ex-Servicemen in Ghana and Uganda." *Journal of Modern African Studies* 6, 2 (1968): 203–20.

Scott, James. *Weapons of the Weak: Everyday Forms of Peasant Resistance*. New Haven: Yale University Press, 1985.

Sekyi, Kobina. *The Blinkards*. London: Heinemann, 1974.

Serebro, Boris. "Total Alcohol Consumption as an Index of Anxiety among Urbanised Africans." *British Journal of Psychiatry* 67 (1972): 251–54.

Simensen, Jarle. "Nationalism from Below. The Akyem Abuakwa Example." In Communications from the Basel African Society. *Akyem Abuakwa and the Politics of the Inter-War Period in Ghana*. Basel: Basel African Bibliography, 1975.

———. "Rural Mass Action in the Context of Anti-Colonial Protest: The Asafo Movement of Akyem Abuakwa, Ghana." *Canadian Journal of African Studies* 8, 1 (1974): 25–41.

Sournia, Jean-Charles. *A History of Alcoholism*. Trans. by Nick Handley and Gareth Stanton. Oxford: Basil Blackwell, 1990.

Southall, Roger J. "Polarisation and Dependence in the Gold Coast Cocoa Trade, 1897–1938." *Transactions of the Historical Society of Ghana* 16, 1 (1975): 93–115.

Spitzer, Leo, and La Ray Denzer. "I. T. A. Wallace Johnson and the West African Youth League." *International Journal of African Historical Studies* 6, 3 (1973): 413–52.

Stone, Robert. "Rural Politics and the States of the Central Province." In Communications from the Basel African Society. *Akyem Abuakwa and the Politics of the Inter-War Period*. Basel: Basel African Bibliography, 1975.

Sutherland, Efua. *The Original Bob*. Ho: E.P. Church Press, 1970.

Swaniker, G. R. E. "Beer—The National Drink." *Ghana Medical Journal* (December 1975): 332-42.

Taylor, Christopher C. *Milk, Honey and Money: Changing Concepts in Rwandan Healing*. Washington, D. C.: Smithsonian Institution Press, 1992.

Tenkorang, S. "The Importance of Firearms in the Struggle between Ashanti and the Coastal States." *Transactions of the Historical Society of Ghana* 9 (1968): 1–16.

Thompson, E. P. "Eighteenth-Century English Society: Class Struggle Without Class." *Social History* 3, 2 (1978): 133–65.

———. *The Making of the English Working Class*. New York: Pantheon Books, 1964.

Thornton, John. *Africa and Africans in the Making of the Atlantic World 1400–1680*. Cambridge: Cambridge University Press, 1992.

Turner, Harold W. *Religious Innovation in Africa: Collected Essays on New Religious Movements*. Boston: G. K. Hall and Co., 1979.

van Dantzig, Albert. *The Dutch and the Guinea Coast 1674-1742: A Collection of Documents from the General State Archives at the Hague*. Accra: Ghana Academy of Arts and Sciences, 1978.

———. *Forts and Castles of Ghana*. Accra: Sedco Publishing Limited, 1980.

van der Geest, Sjaak, and Nimrod Asante-Darko. "The Political Meaning of Highlife Songs in Ghana." *African Studies Review* 25 (1982): 27–35.

van der Walle, Etienne. "Marriage Drinks and Kola Nuts." In *Nuptiality in Sub-Saharan Africa: Contemporary Anthropological and Demographic Perspectives*, ed. Caroline Bledsoe and Gilles Pison. Oxford: Clarendon Press, 1994.

van Onselen, Charles. "Randlords and Rotgut, 1886–1903." *History Workshop* 2 (1976): 32–89.

———. *Chibaro: African Mine Labour in Southern Rhodesia*. London: Pluto Press, 1976.

Vaughan, Megan. *Curing Their Ills: Colonial Power and African Illness*. Stanford: Stanford University Press, 1991.

Walker, Sheila S. "The Message as the Medium: The Harrist Churches of the Ivory Coast and Ghana." In *African Christianity: Patterns of Religious Continuity*, ed., George Bond, Walton Johnson, and Sheila S. Walker. London: Academic Press, 1979.

Washburne, Chandler. *Primitive Drinking: A Study of the Uses and Functions of Alcohol in Preliterate Societies*. New York: New York University Press, 1961.

Weber, Max. *The Protestant Ethic and the Spirit of Capitalism*, Trans. Talcott Parsons. New York: Charles Scribner's Sons, 1958.

180 Bibliography

Weaver, R. H., ed. *The Dictionary of National Biography.* London: Oxford University Press, 1922–30.

West, Michael O. "'Equal Rights for All Civilized Men': Elite Africans and the Quest for 'European' Liquor in Colonial Zimbabwe, 1924–1961." *International Review of Social History* 37, 3 (1992): 376–97.

White, Luise. *The Comforts of Home: Prostitution in Colonial Nairobi.* Chicago: University of Chicago Press, 1990.

Wicker, Kathleen O'Brien. "*Mami Water* in African Religion and Spirituality." In *African Spirituality,* ed. Jacob K. Olupona and Charles H. Long. Forthcoming.

Wilks, Ivor. *Asante in the Nineteenth Century.* Cambridge: Cambridge University Press, 1975.

————. "Asante: Human Sacrifice or Capital Punishment? A Rejoinder." *International Journal of African Historical Studies* 21, 3 (1988): 443–52.

————. "Aspects of Bureaucratization in Ashanti in the Nineteenth Century." *Journal of African History* 7, 2 (1966): 215–33.

————. "Dissidence in Asante Politics: Two Tracts from the Late Nineteenth Century." In *African Themes,* ed. Ibrahim Abu-Lughod. Evanston: Northwestern University Press, 1975.

————. *Forests of Gold: Essay on the Akan and the Kingdom of Asante.* Athens: Ohio University Press, 1993.

————. "The Golden Stool and the Elephant Tail: An Essay on Wealth in Asante." *Research in Economic Anthropology* 2 (1979): 1–36.

————. "The Mossi and Akan States 1500–1800." In *History of West Africa* Vol. 1, ed. J. F. Ade Ajayi and Michael Crowder. London: Longman, 1976.

Williams, Clifford. "Asante: Human Sacrifice or Capital Punishment? An Assessment of the Period 1807–1874." *International Journal of African Historical Studies* 21, 2 (1988): 433–41.

Williamson, S. G. *Akan Religion and the Christian Faith.* Ed. Kwesi Dickson. Accra: Ghana Universities Press, 1974.

Wilson, Louis E. *The Krobo People of Ghana to 1892: A Political and Social History.* Athens: Ohio University Center for International Studies, 1991.

Wolf, Eric. *Europe and the People without History.* Berkeley: University of California Press, 1982.

Yarak, Larry. *Asante and the Dutch, 1744–1873.* Oxford: Clarendon Press, 1990.

IV. UNPUBLISHED WORKS

Akyeampong, Emmanuel K. "Alcohol, Social Conflict and the Struggle for Power in Ghana." Ph.D. diss., University of Virginia, 1993.

————. "Constructing and Contesting Sexuality: 'Prostitution' in the Gold Coast, c. 1650 to 1950." Paper presented at the annual meeting of the African Studies Association, 1995.

————. "Powerful Fluids: Alcohol and Water in the Struggle for Social Power in Urban Gold Coast." Paper presented at Northwestern University, Evanston, 1994.

Allman, Jean M. "Rounding up Spinsters: Unmarried Women, Moral Crisis and Gender Chaos in Colonial Asante." Paper presented at the African Studies Association meeting, Boston, 1993.

Ambler, Charles. "Alcohol and the Imperial Discourse: The 1909 Southern Nigerian Liquor Commission." Paper presented at the Social History of Alcohol Conference, Ontario, 1993.

Bayor, B. K. "The Social Relevance of Pito Drinking among the Dagaaba." B. A. thesis, University of Ghana, 1978.

Beniako, Agyemang Yaw. "The Social Significance of Palm Wine Drinking—A Case Study at Bechem." B. A. thesis, University of Ghana, 1979.

Brown, Wilson James. "Kumasi, 1896-1923: Urban Africa During the Early Colonial Period." Ph.D. diss., University of Wisconsin, 1972.

Casely-Hayford, Augustus. "The Cape Coast Stool Dispute of 1916." School of Oriental and African Studies, African History Seminar, 1991.

Cole, Catherine M. "Reading Blackface in West Africa: Signs Taken for Wonders." Paper presented at the annual meeting of the African Studies Association, Orlando, 1995.

Davison, R. B. "African Labour: Studies of Migrancy and Industrial Relations in a Factory in the Gold Coast." Ph.D. diss., University of London, 1955.

Djoleto, Ofeibia. "A Historical Study of Changes in Traditional Funeral Rites in Ghana." B.A. thesis, University of Ghana, 1986.

Hagaman, Barbara. "Beer and Matriliny: The Power of Women in a West African Society." Ph.D. diss., Northeastern University, 1977.

Jenkins, Paul. "Abstracts Concerning Gold Coast History from the Basel Mission Archives." [n.p., n.d.]

Maison, K. B. "The History of Sekondi." B.A. thesis, University of Ghana, 1979.

Miescher, Stephan F. "Boakye Yiadom—The Life History of a *Krakye*: Gender, Identities and the Construction of Manhood in Colonial Ghana." Paper presented at the University of Michigan, 1995.

Robertson, Joyce. "The Beer Drinking Phenomena: A Study of Beer Drinkers in Legon." B. A. thesis, University of Ghana, 1978.

Schuster, Ilsa. "Beer, Gender and Class in Lusaka." Paper presented at the African Studies Annual Association, Chicago, 1988.

Tashjian, Victoria B. "'You Marry to Beget': Menopause and Non-Marriage in Asante." Paper presented at the African Studies Association annual meeting, 1993.

Turner, Eaton G. W. "A Short History of the Ashanti Goldfields Corporation Ltd., 1897–1947." [London, 1947]. Issued to the members to commemorate the Corporation's Jubilee.

Yarak, Larry W. "'A Man with Whom We Can Do as We Please': Inventing Kingship (and the State) in Elmina." Paper presented at the African Studies Association meeting, 1994.

INDEX

182

As a status symbol, 72, 74
Missionaries and, 17, 71, 74, 86–88, 164
Temperance societies, 72–79, 87
Women and, 15, 64, 74–75
Thomas, Shenton, 109–10
Tiger Society, 44, 73
Tobacco, 92
Togo, 22, 83, 93, 127
Togoland Congress, 127
Trade Union Congress, 18–19
Two Bobs, The, 103
Uganda, 4
Union Trading Company, 122
United African Company, 119–20, 122
United Gold Coast Convention, 18, 117–19, 123–27
United Party, 143–44
Urbanization, xv, 2, 16, 48–49, 60–62, 101, 103, 114; *See also* Migration
Volta River District, 68, 71–72, 100, 105, 110
Walker, Sheila, 12
Walker, W. F., 66
Ware I, Opoku, 107
Water, 5, 8–9, 11–12, 14, 19, 23, 28–30, 33, 35, 38, 54, 70, 133, 159, 166
As a symbol, 9, 12, 28–30
Communion and, 12, 164
Ritual uses of, xvi, xxi, 5, 8–9, 11–12, 19, 22, 28–29, 32–33, 35, 38, 71, 87–88, 118, 163, 164
Waterworks Ordinance (1934), 96
Watson Commission of Inquiry, 117, 122–123, 125
Webb, Sidney, 94
Weber, Max, 13
Wenkyi, 77, 79
West African Youth League, 123
West, W., 52
When the Heart Decides, 153
Whisky, 19, 54, 94, 97, 129, 148
Who Killed Lucy?, 153
Wilkinson, A. F. L., 53
Williamson, S. G., 30
Wine, 12, 32, 34, 37–39, 54, 81, 163–64
Communion wine, 12, 86–88, 163–64

Corn wine, 33
French wine, xix
Palm wine, *See* Palm wine
Winnebah, 16, 44, 73, 75–78
Winnebah Tiger Club, 53–55, 73
Wireko, J. D., 144
Women,
Akpeteshie and, 100–101, 104-105, 114–15, 142, 156
Alcohol and, xv–xvii, xxi, 3–6, 15, 25, 34–35, 49–53, 71–75, 128, 149–53, 156
As mistresses of Europeans, xviii, xix
As sellers of alcohol, xvi, xix, 48, 62–64, 101, 104–105, 108–109, 114, 130, 142, 151–52
Childbirth and, 11, 31–33
Economic autonomy of, xvii–xx, 16, 48, 62, 65, 142, 151–52
Fertility and, 24, 35–36
Infertility and, xx, 14, 40, 153, 155
Inheritance and, 23, 65
Menstruation and, 10–11, 23–24, 34, 137, 164–65
Physical abuse of, xx, 3, 10–11, 35, 150–52
Prostitution of, xvii–xix, 48, 62–64, 103, 114, 125–26, 142
Sexuality and, 16, 48, 65–67
Social clubs and, 75
Spinsters, xix, 9, 48, 65–67
Subordination to males, xvii, xix, 6, 21, 30–31, 35–37, 49–50, 62–67, 150, 152–53, 160
World War II, 18, 48, 111
Yalley, Teacher, 102–3
Yankson, Samuel, 165
Yewuh, Abba, 64
Young men, 15–18, 21, 23, 25, 30, 44–46, Ch. 3 *passim*, 71–79, 118–20, 132–33, 149–52, 159–67
Alcohol and, 15-16, 25, 44–46, Ch. 3 *passim*, 71–79, 83, 94, 97, 130, 160
Zambia, 20
Zimbabwe, 114